™

References for the Rest of Us!®

BESTSELLING BOOK SERIES

Do you find that traditional reference books are overloaded with technical details and advice you'll never use? Do you postpone important life decisions because you just don't want to deal with them? Then our *For Dummies*® business and general reference book series is for you.

For Dummies business and general reference books are written for those frustrated and hard-working souls who know they aren't dumb, but find that the myriad of personal and business issues and the accompanying horror stories make them feel helpless. *For Dummies* books use a lighthearted approach, a down-to-earth style, and even cartoons and humorous icons to dispel fears and build confidence. Lighthearted but not lightweight, these books are perfect survival guides to solve your everyday personal and business problems.

"More than a publishing phenomenon, 'Dummies' is a sign of the times."

— The New York Times

"A world of detailed and authoritative information is packed into them..."

— U.S. News and World Report

"...you won't go wrong buying them."

— Walter Mossberg, Wall Street Journal, on For Dummies books

Already, millions of satisfied readers agree. They have made For Dummies the #1 introductory level computer book series and a best-selling business book series. They have written asking for more. So, if you're looking for the best and easiest way to learn about business and other general reference topics, look to For Dummies to give you a helping hand.

Wiley Publishing, Inc.

5/09

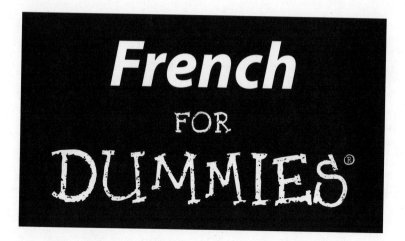

by **Dodi-Katrin Schmidt**
Michelle M. Williams
Dominique Wenzel

Berlitz® Series Editor: Juergen Lorenz

Wiley Publishing, Inc.

French For Dummies®

Published by
Wiley Publishing, Inc.
909 Third Avenue
New York, NY 10022
www.wiley.com

Copyright © 2000 by Wiley Publishing, Inc., Indianapolis, Indiana

Published by Wiley Publishing, Inc., Indianapolis, Indiana

Published simultaneously in Canada

For general information on our other products and services or to obtain technical support, please contact our Customer Care Department within the U.S. at 800-762-2974, outside the U.S. at 317-572-3993, or fax 317-572-4002.

Wiley also publishes its books in a variety of electronic formats. Some content that appears in print may not be available in electronic books.

Library of Congress Cataloging-in-Publication Data:

Library of Congress Control Number: 99-67160

ISBN: 0-7645-5193-0

Manufactured in the United States of America

10 9

About the Authors

Dodi-Katrin Schmidt has been a writer, a translator, and an editor for almost ten years. Aside from translating German, French, and English texts of various kinds, including linguistic handbooks, film reviews, travel guides, and children's books, she has also been involved in developing language textbooks, language courses, teachers' handbooks, and grammar companions for video language courses. Dodi has been teaching for more than two decades at high school, adult education, and college levels in Europe as well as the United States. She also writes test items for various national language tests and recorded textbook and test material. Together with her husband, she travels a great deal, and they continually house and entertain foreign students and former students in their home in Princeton, NJ.

Michelle Williams is an editor at a major educational publisher. A former French teacher, she has taught students ranging form 2 years old to adults, in both the public and private sectors. She is currently a private French tutor to a young Olympic-hopeful figure skater. She is a firm believer in making the language fun and accessible to all who want to learn. Her most rewarding experience, however, is in watching and listening to her 3-year-old son, Nathaniel, learn to speak and sing in French.

Dominique Wenzel has been a freelance teacher of French and translator for 15 years. Born and raised in France, she received a Master's degree from the University of Paris-Sorbonne and studied at the University of Chicago on a postgraduate Fulbright scholarship. Her students include business professionals, children, and adults of all levels and interests. She travels regularly to France. Dominique raised two bicultural, bilingual children who are both active in the international field.

About Berlitz

The name "Berlitz" has meant excellence in language services for more than 120 years. At more than 400 locations and in 50 countries worldwide, Berlitz offers a full range of language and language-related services, including instruction, cross-cultural training, document translation, software localization, and interpretation services. Berlitz also offers a wide array of publishing products, such as self-study language courses, phrase books, travel guides, and dictionaries.

The world-famous Berlitz Method is the core of all Berlitz language instruction. From the time of its introduction in 1878, millions have used this method to learn new languages. For more information about Berlitz classes and products, please consult your local telephone directory for the Language Center nearest you or visit the Berlitz Web site at www.berlitz.com, where you can enroll in classes or shop directly for products online.

Authors' Acknowledgments

Dodi-Katrin Schmidt: A great many thanks go to all the people at Wiley for making this book possible and for editing it according to *Dummies* guidelines. I also want to give special recognition and much appreciation to Juergen Lorenz at Berlitz Publishing for his invaluable help and for coordinating the three authors writing this book. It must have been a nightmare.

In addition, special thanks go to my French friend and resource Sylvie Debrosse, who researched and verified much of the information in this book. She also reviewed and proofread my part of the book (Chapters 11-21) and was relentlessly available for quick feedback. Furthermore, I owe much gratitude to my eternal French contact Fabienne Cywinski, who helped brainstorm and verify many details, and to her husband Edward for never minding those late help calls. Last but not least, a big hug to my husband Frank: fellow brainstormer, happy critic and forever patient troubleshooter for the computer.

Michelle Williams: Heartfelt appreciation and gratitude goes out to the people at Berlitz and Wiley, including Tim Gallan, Juergen Lorenz, and especially, Sheryl Olinsky Borg, for their support and professional encouragement. Thanks also to the copy editors for their insight and tactfulness, and to the production staff at Wiley for making this book a success.

I am forever grateful to my parents, Tom & Marie Zanavich, and my sister, Kristin Zanavich, for their unending support and belief in me. They never doubted, even when I did.

Dominique Wenzel: First, I want to thank our Berlitz coordinators, Juergen Lorenz and Sheryl Olinsky Borg, who saw us through each step of the writing in smooth and hectic times, while dealing at the same time with the Spanish, Italian, and German *For Dummies* books. I would also like to acknowledge the work of my coauthor Dodi Schmidt, who is, in fact, the main contributor to this book and whose expertise helped me write my own chapters (3 through 6). Special loving thanks to my children, Nikolai and Sophie, for their continuous support from far and close.

Berlitz would like to thank the following:

Dodi-Katrin Schmidt, Dominique Wenzel, and Michelle M. Williams, an out-standing team of writers, for their tireless dedication to creating this book.

Professor Jean Antoin Billard for helping to get this project started.

Our NY audio producer, Paul Ruben, who developed the audio CD, bringing the written French language to life!

Our editors, Juergen Lorenz and Sheryl Olinsky Borg, for their professional-ism and commitment to putting this challenging and exciting project together.

And our deep appreciation goes to the staff at Wiley, especially Holly McGuire, Pam Mourouzis, and Tim Gallan, who guided *French For Dummies* from start to finish!

Publisher's Acknowledgments

We're proud of this book; please send us your comments through our online registration form located at www.dummies.com/register.

Some of the people who helped bring this book to market include the following:

Acquisitions and Editorial

Editors: Tamara Castleman, Donna Frederick, Tim Gallan, Tina Sims, Janet Withers

Acquisitions Editor: Holly McGuire

Acquisitions Coordinator: Karen Young

Media Development Coordinator: Megan Roney

Editorial Manager: Pamela Mourouzis

Media Development Manager: Heather Heath Dismore

Editorial Assistant: Carol Strickland

Reprint Editor: Michelle Hacker

Production

Project Coordinator: Regina Snyder

Layout and Graphics: Amy M. Adrian, Angela Chaney-Granger, Jill Piscitelli, Brent Savage, Janet Seib, Michael A. Sullivan, Maggie Ubertini, Erin Zeltner

Proofreaders: Laura Albert, Rebecca Senninger, Charles Spencer

Indexer: Mary Mortensen

Special Help
Seta K. Frantz, Sherry Gomoll

Publishing and Editorial for Consumer Dummies
Diane Graves Steele, Vice President and Publisher, Consumer Dummies
Joyce Pepple, Acquisitions Director, Consumer Dummies
Kristin A. Cocks, Product Development Director, Consumer Dummies
Michael Spring, Vice President and Publisher, Travel
Brice Gosnell, Associate Publisher, Travel
Suzanne Jannetta, Editorial Director, Travel

Publishing for Technology Dummies
Richard Swadley, Vice President and Executive Group Publisher
Andy Cummings, Vice President and Publisher

Composition Services
Gerry Fahey, Vice President of Production Services
Debbie Stailey, Director of Composition Services

Contents at a Glance

Cartoons at a Glance

By Rich Tennant

page 311

page 7

page 183

page 291

page 53

Fax: 978-546-7747
E-mail: richtennant@the5thwave.com
World Wide Web: www.the5thwave.com

Table of Contents

Introduction

As society becomes more and more international in nature, knowing how to say at least a few words in other languages becomes more and more useful. Inexpensive airfares make travel abroad a more realistic option. Global business environments necessitate overseas travel. Or you may just have friends and neighbors who speak other languages, or you may want to get in touch with your heritage by learning a little bit of the language that your ancestors spoke.

Whatever your reason for wanting to learn some French, *French For Dummies* can help. Two experts at helping readers develop knowledge — Berlitz, experts in teaching foreign languages; and Wiley Publishing, Inc., publishers of the bestselling *For Dummies* series — have teamed up to produce a book that gives you the skills you need for basic communication in French. We're not promising fluency here, but if you need to greet someone, purchase a ticket, or order off a menu in French, you need look no further than *French For Dummies*.

This book is designed to give you pleasure and lead you with a friendly hand towards an almost effortless success. Of course, you will have to be attentive to certain parts of each chapter where tricky grammatical rules are stressed. But these difficulties will be tackled gradually, in small doses.

Remember that everyday French is like everyday English and makes use of simplified lingual forms which, although perfectly correct, avoid and ignore certain complicated verb tenses and moods such as, say, the past definite or the subjunctive. In everyday French, like in English, you can express yourself adequately with a minimum number of words. So you should find the lessons in this book to be fun and not the least bit overwhelming.

Now is playtime : C'est la récréation.

About This Book

This is not a class that you have to drag yourself to twice a week for a specified period of time. You can use *French For Dummies* however you want to, whether your goal is to learn some words and phrases to help you get around when you visit France, or you just want to be able to say "Hello, how are you?" to your French-speaking neighbor. Go through this book at your own pace, reading as much or as little at a time as you like. You don't have to trudge through the chapters in order, either; just read the sections that interest you.

Note: If you've never taken French before, you may want to read the chapters in Part I before tackling the later chapters. Part I gives you some of the basics that you need to know about the language, such as how to pronounce the various sounds.

Conventions Used in This Book

To make this book easy to navigate, we've set up some of conventions:

- ✓ French terms are set in **boldface** to make them stand out.
- ✓ Pronunciations set in *italics* follow the French terms.
- ✓ The nasal sound (see Chapter 1) is indicated by a capital N.

Language learning is a peculiar beast, so this book includes a few elements that other *For Dummies* books do not. Following are the new elements that you'll find:

- ✓ **Talkin' the Talk dialogues:** The best way to learn a language is to see and hear how it's used in conversation, so we include dialogues throughout the book. The dialogues come under the heading "Talkin' the Talk" and show you the French words, the pronunciation, and the English translation.

- ✓ **Words to Know blackboards:** Memorizing key words and phrases is also important in language learning, so we collect the important words in a chapter (or section within a chapter) in a chalkboard, with the heading "Words to Know."

- ✓ **Fun & Games activities:** If you don't have actual French speakers to practice your new language skills on, you can use the Fun & Games activities to reinforce what you learn. These word games are fun ways to gauge your progress.

Also note that, because each language has its own ways of expressing ideas, the English translations that we provide for the French terms may not be exactly literal. We want you to know the gist of what's being said, not just the words that are being said. For example, the phrase **C'est normal** *(say nohr-mal)* can be translated literally as "It's normal," but the phrase really means "It's no big deal." This book gives the "It's no big deal" translation.

Foolish Assumptions

To write this book, we had to make some assumptions about who you are and what you want from a book called *French For Dummies.* Here are the assumptions that we've made about you:

- ✔ You know no French — or if you took French back in school, you don't remember a word of it.
- ✔ You're not looking for a book that will make you fluent in French; you just want to know some words, phrases, and sentence constructions so that you can communicate basic information in French.
- ✔ You don't want to have to memorize long lists of vocabulary words or a bunch of boring grammar rules.
- ✔ You want to have fun and learn a little bit of French at the same time.

If these statements apply to you, you've found the right book!

How This Book Is Organized

This book is divided by topic into parts, and then into chapters. The following sections tell you what types of information you can find in each part.

Part I: Getting Started

This part lets you get your feet wet by giving you some French basics: how to pronounce words, what the accents mean, and so on. We even boost your confidence by reintroducing you to some French words that you probably already know. Finally, we outline the basics of French grammar that you may need to know when you work through later chapters in the book.

Part II: French in Action

In this part, you begin learning and using French. Instead of focusing on grammar points as many language textbooks do, this part focuses on everyday situations, such as shopping, dining, and making small talk.

Part III: French on the Go

This part gives you the tools you need to take your French on the road, whether it's to a local French restaurant or to a museum in France. This part covers all aspects of travel in French-speaking parts of the world, and it even has a chapter on how to handle emergencies.

Part IV: The Part of Tens

If you're looking for small, easily digestible pieces of information about French, this part is for you. Here, you can find ten ways to learn French quickly, ten useful French expressions to know, ten things never to say in French, and more.

Part V: Appendixes

This part of the book includes important information that you can use for reference. We include verb tables, which show you how to conjugate a regular verb and then how to conjugate those verbs that stubbornly don't fit the pattern. We also give you a mini-dictionary in both French-to-English and English-to-French formats. If you encounter a French word that you don't understand, or you need to say something in French that you can't find in the book, you can look it up here. Finally, we provide a listing of the tracks that appear on the audio CD that comes with this book so that you can find out where in the book those dialogues are and follow along.

Icons Used in This Book

You may be looking for particular information while reading this book. To make certain types of information easier for you to find, we've placed the following icons in the left-hand margins throughout the book:

This icon highlights tips that can make learning French easier.

This icon point out interesting information that you ought not forget.

To help you avoid linguistic, grammatical, and cultural faux pas, we use this icon.

Languages are full of quirks that may trip you up if you're not prepared for them. This icon points to discussions of these weird grammar rules.

If you're looking for information and advice about culture and travel, look for these icons. They draw your attention to interesting tidbits about the countries in which French is spoken.

The audio CD that comes with this book gives you the opportunity to listen to real French speakers so that you can get a better understanding of what French sounds like. This icon marks the Talkin' the Talk dialogues that you can find on the CD.

Where to Go from Here

Learning a language is all about jumping in and giving it a try (no matter how bad your pronunciation is at first). So make the leap! Start at the beginning, pick a chapter that interests you, or pop the CD into your stereo or computer and listen to a few dialogues. Before long, you'll be able to respond, "Oui!" when people ask, "Parlez-vous français?"

Part I
Getting Started

The 5th Wave — By Rich Tennant

©RICHTENNANT

"Here's something. It's a language school that will teach you to speak French for $500, or for $200 they'll just give you an accent."

In this part . . .

You have to start somewhere, but we bet that you know a lot more French than you think. Don't think so? Then check out Chapter 1. *C'est magnifique.* (And we know you know what that means.) Chapters 2 and 3 cover some nuts-and-bolts grammar info that, well, you need to absorb. But don't worry: We make it fun.

Chapter 1

You Already Know a Little French

This chapter lets you get your feet wet. Well, actually, we kind of throw you right into the pond. We start by showing you how French and English are similar; then we present some French expressions that you probably already know and understand; then we talk about pronunciation.

The French You Know

People tend to forget that French was the English court language for a very long time. Today, about 45 percent of English vocabulary is of French origin. That being the case, you already know an impressive amount of French, whether you realize it or not. That's what you are going to find out in this chapter. The only pitfall you have to watch for is that sometimes these English words have a different meaning from their French counterparts, and they almost certainly have a different pronunciation.

Friendly allies — bons alliés (bohN-zah-lyay)

The following list shows words that are spelled the same — and have the same meaning — in French and English. The only thing that may be different is the pronunciation.

art *(ahr)*

brave *(brahv)*

bureau *(bew-ro)*

client *(klee-yahN)*

concert *(kohN-sehr)*

condition *(kohN-dee-syohN)*

content *(cohN-tahN)*

courage *(koo-razh)*

cousin *(koo-zaN)*

culture *(kewl-tewr)*

différent *(dee-fay-rahN)*

excellent *(ayk-say-lahN)*

garage *(gah-razh)*

guide *(geed)*

important *(aN-pohr-tahN)*

journal *(zhoor-nahl)*

machine *(mah-sheen)*

moment *(moh-mahN)*

nation *(nah-syohN)*

orange *(oh-rahNzh)*

parent *(pah-rahN)*

possible *(poh-seebl)*

principal *(praN-see-pahl)*

probable *(pro-bahbl)*

question *(kehs-tyohN)*

radio *(rah-dyo)*

répétition *(ray-pay-tee-syohN)*

restaurant *(rehs-to-rahN)*

rose *(roz)*

rouge *(roozh)*

route *(root)*

science *(syahNs)*

secret *(suh-kreh)*

service *(sehr-vees)*

signal *(see-nyahl)*

silence *(see-lahNs)*

solitude *(soh-lee-tewd)*

sport *(spohr)*

station *(stah-syohN)*

statue *(stah-tew)*

suggestion *(sewg-zhehs-syohN)*

surprise *(sewr-preez)*

table *(tahbl)*

taxi *(tahk-see)*

tennis *(tay-nees)*

train *(traN)*

urgent *(ewr-zhahN)*

violet *(vyo-leh)*

voyage *(vwah-yahzh)*

Kissing cousins

Table 1-1 shows words that are spelled almost the same in French and English and have similar meanings.

Table 1-1 Words Similar in Meaning, Slightly Different in Spelling

French	English
acteur *(ahk-tuhr)*	actor
adresse *(ah-drehs)*	address
allée *(ah-lay)*	alley
américain *(ah-may-ree-kaN)*	American
âge *(ahzh)*	age
artiste *(ahr-teest)*	artist
auteur *(o-tuhr)*	author
banque *(bahNk)*	bank
chèque *(shehk)*	check
classe *(klahs)*	class
chambre *(shaNbr)*	chamber (or bedroom)
comédie *(koh-may-dee)*	comedy
congrès *(kohN-greh)*	congress
démocratie *(day-moh-krah-see)*	democracy
développement *(day-vlohp-mahN)*	development
gouvernement *(goo-vehr-nuh-mahN)*	government
hôtel *(o-tehl)*	hotel
leçon *(luh-sohN)*	lesson
lettre *(lehtr)*	letter
musique *(mew-zeek)*	music
mémoire *(may-mwahr)*	memory
nationalité *(nah-syo-nah-lee-tay)*	nationality

(continued)

Table 1-1 *(continued)*

French	English
nécessaire *(nay-say-sehr)*	necessary
ordinaire *(ohr-dee-nehr)*	ordinary
papier *(pah-pyay)*	paper
potentiel *(po-tahN-syehl)*	potential
problème *(proh-blehm)*	problem
poème *(poh-ehm)*	poem
saison *(seh-zohN)*	season
sénateur *(say-nah-tuhr)*	senator
tragédie *(trah-zhay-dee)*	tragedy
visite *(vee-zeet)*	visit

False friends — faux amis

The words that follow look similar to English words, but they don't have the same meaning:

- **actuellement** *(ak-tew-ehl-mahN)*: This word means "now" not "actually." The French word for "actually" is **en fait** *(ahN feht)*.

- **assister** *(ah-sees-tay)*: This word means "to attend" not "to assist." The French word for "to assist" is **aider** *(ay-day)*.

- **attendre** *(ah-tahNdr)*: This word means "to wait for" not "to attend." The French word for "to attend" is **assister à** *(ah-sees-tay ah)*.

- **bague** *(bahg)*: This word means "ring" not "bag." The French word for "bag" is **sac** *(sahk)*.

- **librairie** *(lee-breh-ree)*: This word means "bookstore" not "library." The French word for "library" is **bibliothèque** *(bee-blee-oh-tehk)*.

- **place** *(plahs)*: This word means "square or seat at the theater or on the bus" not "place." The French word for "place" is **lieu** or **endroit.**

- **rester** *(rehs-tay)*: This word means "to stay or remain" not "to rest." The French word for "to rest" is **se reposer** *(suh-ruh-po-zay)*.

Lenders and borrowers

Quite a few English words have been borrowed from French, thus retaining their French meaning with a different pronunciation.

However, French has also borrowed many words from English and continues to do so in spite of the loud protest by purists who condemn this trend as a sign of cultural contamination and name it **franglais** *(frahN-gleh):*

- ✔ le week-end
- ✔ le parking
- ✔ le steak
- ✔ le shopping

- ✔ le jet set
- ✔ cool
- ✔ le business
- ✔ le tunnel
- ✔ le manager
- ✔ le marketing
- ✔ le budget
- ✔ le rock
- ✔ le job (la job in Québec)
- ✔ le fast food

Talkin' the Talk

Take a look at this conversation between two young French people making plans for their weekend:

Thomas: **Sylvie, qu'est-ce que tu fais ce week-end?**
seel-vee kes-kuh tew feh suh wee-kehnd
Sylvie, what are you doing this weekend?

Sylvie: **Oh, du shopping probablement. Tu veux venir avec moi?**
o dew shoh-peeng pro-bah-bluh-mahN tew vuh vuh-nee-rah-vehk mwa
Oh, I'll probably go shopping. Do you want to come with me?

Thomas: **OK, cool, et après, on va aller manger dans un fast food.**
o-keh koo-lay-apreh ohN vah ah-lay mahN-zhay dahN-zaN fahst-food
OK, cool, and afterwards, we'll go eat in a fast food restaurant.

Sylvie: **J'espère qu'on va trouver un parking!**
zhehs-pehr kohN vah troo-vay aN pahr-keeng!
I hope we'll be able to find a parking space.

Quebec is pure French

The rules of good and pure French speech are especially enforced in Quebec. People in Quebec will easily understand your **franglais** *(frahN-gleh),* but you may be taken aback when you hear Quebeckers talk about the following, where the French use the English word:

✔ **la fin de semaine** *(lah faN duh suh-mehn)* (weekend)

✔ **le magasinage** *(luh mah-gah-zee-nazh)* (shopping)

✔ **le stationnement** *(luh stah-syoh-nuh-mahN)* (parking)

✔ **la mise en marché** *(lah mee-zahN mahr-shay)* (marketing)

✔ **un hambourgeois** *(aN ahN-boor-zhwah)* (hamburger)

✔ **un emploi** *(aN-nahN-plwah)* (a job)

Quebec's purism is easily explained:

✔ The proximity of the United States south of its border, plus the English-speaking majority in Canada threatens the French cultural identity of the Quebec's 7 million inhabitants. For Quebeckers, their language constitutes a rampart against the all powerful presence of the English — spoken by 300 million people — surrounding them.

✔ People who lived mostly in rural isolation for 300 years are now living in modern cities like Montreal, Quebec, Sherbrooke, and a few others where cable TV is constantly bombarding them with American commercials, movies, and variety shows.

Although protective of their language, French-Canadians are an extremely gentle people who welcome their southern neighbors.

Sounds outrageous? It is not. Many English words have creeped into French conversation especially among the young. But this is typically French.

Idioms and Popular Expressions

French, like English, has many *idioms* (unusual ways of expressing feelings and ideas). You may find the meaning of these expressions puzzling if you try to translate them word for word.

These fixed forms of expression — you should recognize and use them as such — belong specifically to the language in question. If you walked up to a French man and said, **"Il pleut des chats et des chiens"** *(eel plew day shah ay day shy-aN)* (It's raining cats and dogs), he'd question your sanity. You may find yourself wondering what a French man means when using one of his language's idioms, such as **"Il tombe des cordes"** *(eel tohNb day kohrd)*, literally, "ropes are falling," the corresponding French expression to "it's raining cats and dogs."

Apart from those idioms, which take a long time to apprehend and belong specifically to a culture, there are many expressions and phrases which cannot be translated word for word but can easily be learned and used.

Here are a few of these useful expressions you frequently hear in French:

- **Allez! Un petit effort!** *(ah-lay uhn puh-tee-teh-for)* (Come on! Try a little!)
- **à mon avis** *(ah mohN-nah-vee)* (in my opinion)
- **bien sûr** *(byaN sewr)* (of course)
- **de rien** *(duh ryaN)* (don't mention it)
- **d'accord** *(dah-kohr)* (okay)
- **jamais de la vie!** *(zhah-meh dlah vee)* or **pas question !** *(pah kes-tyohN)* (no way)
- **tant mieux** *(tahN my-uh)* (so much the better)
- **tant pis** *(tahN pee)* (too bad)
- **tout à fait** *(too-tah feh)* (quite)

Here are other miscellaneous expressions with **faire** *(fehr)* (to do; to make):

- **faire une promenade** *(feh-rewn pro-muh-nahd)* (to take a walk)
- **faire le plein** *(fehr luh plaN)* (to fill up)
- **faire attention** *(feh-rah-tahN-syohN)* (to pay attention)
- **faire partie de** *(fehr pahr-tee duh)* (to be part of)
- **faire ses valises** *(fehr say vah-leez)* (to pack)

GRAMMATICALLY SPEAKING

Weather or not, here I come

The French way of expressing weather differs from English. If you say, **"Il est froid"** *(ee-leh frwah)* (It's cold or he is cold) in French, you would be understood as saying that someone is cold to the touch or even dead. In Quebec, **Il est chaud** *(ee-leh sho)* (it's warm or he is warm) means "he is hot to the touch; he's drunk."

Use the French verb **faire** *(fehr)* to talk about the weather: **Alors, quel temps fait-il?** *(ah-lohr kehl tahN feh-teel)* (So what's the weather like?)

Here are some other expressions with **avoir** *(ah-vwahr)* (to have):

- **avoir besoin de** *(ah-vwahr buh-zwaN duh)* (to need something)
- **avoir peur de** *(ah-vwahr puhr duh)* (to fear)
- **avoir envie de** *(ah-vwah-rahN-vee duh)* (to feel like)
- **avoir mal à la tête** *(ah-vwahr-mah-lah-lah teht)* (to have a headache)
- **avoir chaud** *(ah-vwahr sho)* (to be hot)
- **avoir froid** *(ah-vwahr frwah)* (to be cold)
- **avoir faim** *(ah-vwahr faN)* (to be hungry)
- **avoir soif** *(ah-vwahr swahf)* (to be thirsty)
- **avoir raison** *(ah-vwahr reh-zohN)* (to be right)
- **avoir tort** *(ah-vwahr tohr)* (to be wrong)
- **en avoir assez** *(ahN-nah-vwah-rah-say)* literally to have enough; in Quebec: **être tanné** *(eh-truh tah-nay)* (to be fed up)

Mouthing Off: Basic Pronunciation

The hardest part of pronunciation is overcoming your fear of not sounding French when you speak the language. You're probably afraid that you'll never be able to reproduce the sounds that you hear in French songs or movies. Remember, though, that any time any one hears any foreign language spoken or sung at a normal speed, the words — which don't make sense to begin with — create a muddle of sounds impossible to reproduce. Once you overcome your fear of sounding "funny," everything else is fun and easy. Hopefully, our reassurance helps reduce your fear.

Before you can enjoy watching or playing a game, you have to understand its basic rules. Acquiring another language is no different. Once you master these pronunciation rules, you need to practice whenever you have a moment to do so, just as you had to practice the piano as a child. (Aim for short but frequent practice sessions.) Your best bet is simply to listen and repeat over and over again, no matter how boring that sounds.

The French alphabet

The French alphabet has the same number of letters as the English alphabet — 26. As you already know, many of the letters are pronounced differently. Table 1-2 lists the letters and their pronunciation, which you may find useful to refer to, if, for instance, you have to spell your name on the phone or write down an address. Whenever possible, there is a reference to an English word in this table so you can have a pretty good idea of the way the letter is pronounced. It is not always possible, of course, because, even though many sounds are roughly the same in French and in English, some French sounds do not exist in the English language, which does not mean you cannot pronounce them. Just read the next few sections for some help and tips.

Table 1-2	The French Alphabet	
Letter	*Sound*	*As in English*
a	*ah*	card
b	*bay*	baby
c	*say*	say
d	*day*	date
e	*uh*	but
f	*ehf*	effort
g	*zhay*	
h	*ahsh*	ash
i	*ee*	igloo
j	*zhee*	
k	*kah*	car
l	*ehl*	elegant
m	*ehm*	employee
n	*ehn*	end
o	*o*	rose
p	*pay*	paper
q	*kew*	
r	*ehr*	ersatz
s	*ehs*	estimate
t	*tay*	take
u	*ew*	

(continued)

Table 1-2 (continued)

Letter	Sound	As in English
v	*vay*	vague
w	*doobluhvay*	
x	*eeks*	
y	*eegrehk*	
z	*zehd*	

 The first track on the CD gives you all of the sounds of the French alphabet.

Vowel sounds

Vowel sounds are the most difficult to pronounce in French. They are shorter than in English and usually end a syllable. Almost all of them have an equivalent in English. Take a look at Table 1-3.

Table 1-3		French Vowel Sounds	
Sound	**Spelled**	**As In English**	**French Word**
ah	a, â	card	**la tasse** *(lah tahs)* (the cup)
uh	e, eu	but	**le petit** *(luh puh-tee)* (the little one)
ay	é, ez, er,et	take	**les cafés** *(lay kah-fay)* (coffee houses)
eh	è, ê, ai	day	**la mère** *(lah mehr)* (the mother)
ee	i, y	igloo	**vite** *(veet)* (quickly)
o	o, ô, au, eau	boat	**l'eau** *(lo)* (water)
oh	o	love	**la pomme** *(lah pohm)* (the apple)
oo	ou	you	**l'amour** *(lah-moor)* (love)
wah	oi, oy	watch	**la soie** *(lah swah)* (silk)
*ew**	u		**salut** *(sah-lew)* (hello)

The ew sound, represented in French by the letter u does not exist in English, but it is not difficult to pronounce. Here is a little trick to help you: Say ee; the tip of your tongue is against your front bottom teeth. Keeping this position, you then round your lips and the sound coming out of your mouth is . . . the French ew (u).

The accent

The accent over a vowel in French does not indicate that a syllable is stressed. It only affects the letter on which it stands and does not even change the pronunciation of that letter unless it is an e (see Table 1-3).

The mute e

At the end of a word or between two consonants, the *e* is usually not pronounced; it is called mute. For example, you do not pronounce the *e* at the end of **grande** *(grahNd)* (tall) or in the middle of **samedi** *(sahm-dee)* (Saturday). (See also the section "The elision" for more about final *e*.)

The nasal sounds

The nasal sound is very common in French and does not exist in English. It is also fairly easy to pronounce. Imagine you have a cold and pronounce the sounds *ah, ee, oh,* through your nose. They will come out nasalized. Be sure not to pronounce the consonant **n** afterwards.

Table 1-4 lists the nasal sounds.

Table 1-4	Nasal Sounds	
Sound	*Spelled*	*French Word*
ah -> ahN	an, en	**grand** *(grahN)* (large)
ee -> aN	ain, in, un, aim, im	**pain** *(paN)* (bread)
oh -> ohN	on	**bon** *(bohN)* (good)

Consonants

French consonants are pronounced almost like in English, except that you don't linger on them; let them explode and move on to the vowel which follows. French cannot be pronounced with a lazy mouth. Remember to articulate.

Another few words of caution: In French, the consonants at the end of a word are not usually pronounced, except for **c, f, r** and **l** (the consonants in the word careful) which are usually pronounced.

Table 1-5 lists French consonant sounds that may puzzle you either because they come in different spellings or because you think they don't exist in English.

Table 1-5		Tricky French Consonants	
Sound	*Spelled*	*In English*	*French Word*
s	ss (between two vowels), c (in front of e and i), ç (in front of a, o, u)	sole	**poisson** *(pwah-sohN)* (fish), **ciel** *(see-ehl)* (sky) **garçon** *(gar-sohn)* (boy)
g	g (in front of a, o, u), gu (in front of e and i)	greed	**gâteau** *(gah-to)* (cake), **guerre** *(gehr)* (war)
zh	j, g (in front of e and i)	azure	**jour** *(zhoor)* (day), **genou** *(zhuh-noo)* (knee)
sh	ch	ship	**chapeau** *(shah-po)* (hat)
ny	gn	canyon	**montagne** *(mohN-tany)* (mountain)

Two extra consonants to mention:

- ✔ The letter **h** is always silent in French. Just ignore it.
- ✔ The French **r** often scares foreigners. No need to be scared. You have to pronounce it with your throat, but make it as soft and gentle as you can and you are in business.

The liaison

Have you ever thought, when listening to a French conversation, that it sounded like a great big long word? Probably. That is because of a French phenomenon called the liaison. **Faire la liaison** *(fehr lah lyay-zohN)* (to make a liaison) means that the last consonant of a word is linked with the vowel which begins the following word. Check out these examples:

> **C'est_un petit_appartement.** *(seh-tahN puh-tee-tah-pahr-tuh-mahN)* (It's a small apartment.)

> **Vous_êtes mon_ami depuis six_ans.** *(voo-zeht-moh-nah-mee duh-pwee see-zahN)* (You have been my friend for six years.)

Getting romantic

French is a romance language, which may be why the "French lover" has such a reputation. Actually, the French have some competition because Spanish, Italian, Romanian, and Portuguese are romance languages, too.

Romance languages — also known as the Latin of Rome — share the same origin and thus, the same characteristics. One of the most important characteristics of the romance languages is that

their sound is based on vowels, unlike the Anglo-Saxon languages — English and German — which are based on consonants. The emphasis on vowels gives French its soft, smooth, even, and musical character. French words certainly contain consonants, but compared to the consonants in English, French consonants are much softer.

But the French language being full of exceptions, you have to be careful each time you learn a new grouping of words: The liaison is not systematic. One important exception is for words following the word **et** *(ay)*, which means and.

> **un livre et // un crayon** *(aN leev-ray // aN kray-yohN)* (a book and a pencil.)

The elision

When a word ending with an **e** or an **a** (usually an article or a pronoun) is followed by a word starting with a vowel, the first **e** or **a** disappears and is replaced by an apostrophe. This rule, like the liaison, contributes to the easy flowing of the French language. Here are some examples:

> la + école => **l'école** *(lay-kohl)* (the school)
>
> je + aime => **j'aime** *(jehm)* (I like)
>
> le + enfant => **l'enfant** *(lahN-fahN)* (the child)

Stress

Don't stress! In French, every syllable is of equal importance in volume and stress. The emphasis in French words of two or more syllables is on the last one — but that stress is moderate. For instance, the stress — very slight — in the French word **photographie** *(fo-to-grah-fee)* (photography) is on the last syllable of the word.

Remembering to "unstress" the syllable you're used to pronouncing in those words that have similar spellings in French and in English may take quite a bit of practice. It's like ironing the pleat out of a pair of trousers over and over again.

Using Gestures

French people express themselves with hand and body gestures to a greater extent than English speakers, who generally tend to be more reserved. The actual expression or word doesn't have to accompany these gestures, although it often does.

Following are some examples of some common French gestures:

- ✔ Pulling on your eye as if to open it with your finger and saying, **"Mon oeil!"** *(mo-nuhy)* means "No way! You're pulling my leg!" (*Literally:* my eye).

- ✔ Raising your thumb, demonstratively shaking it in front of someone means "Perfect!"

- ✔ Scratching your cheek with the back of your hand and saying **"Ah! la barbe!"** (*ah-lah bahrb*) (*Literally:* the beard) means "What a pain!"

- ✔ Using the same scratching gesture and saying, **"Une vraie barbe!"** *(ewn vreh bahrb)* about something or someone means "A real bore!" (*Literally:* a real beard)

- ✔ Extending both arms on each side of your hips and shrugging your shoulders, means "There's nothing I can do about it!" Actually, this gesture is so commonly associated with the French, that it is often referred to in this country as the Gallic shrug.

You'll no doubt come across other gestures — many of which are not appropriate for a family book. We trust that you can use your own, ample wits to make sense out of them.

Chapter 2

The Nitty Gritty: Basic French Grammar

In This Chapter

▶ Constructing simple sentences

▶ Forming questions the easy way

▶ Introducing regular and irregular verbs

▶ Conjugating verbs in the simple tenses: past, present, and future

▶ Solving the gender debate: pronouns, articles, adjectives

▶ Getting to know "you": the tu/vous issue

▶ Counting your fingers and toes (1–20)

Although the word "grammar" may make you as nervous now as it did when you were in grammar school, you can relax your grip on that number 2 pencil: Grammar is merely the school glue that holds your French sentences together. In fact, grammar is simply a word for ways of combining nouns (to name things), adjectives (to qualify these nouns), verbs (to show action or a state of being), and adverbs (to describe verbs, adjectives, or other adverbs). This combination of words makes possible the expression of our needs, desires, likes, and dislikes; our present, past, and future actions; and the ways and means of these actions.

In our daily life, **bien sûr et heureusement** *(byaN sew-ray uh-ruhz-mahN)* (of course and fortunately), we speak without thinking of the grammar rules that structure our speech. Obviously, you don't carry and consult a grammar book for all life's occasions, yet you are still able to say more or less everything you want. Actually, **en réalité** *(ahN ray-ah-lee-tay)*, you did not even know the word grammar until you went to school. So instead of taking a schoolbook approach, this chapter makes following French grammar rules as natural as putting one foot in front of the other when you walk.

The key to success is to remain cool and patient. Throughout this book you will find dialogs dealing with basic sentences that you will also be able to hear on the accompanying CD. Tricky problems will be marked with a Grammatically speaking icon, which will explain how to overcome them. And little by little, you will simply speak French.

Simple Sentence Construction

A simple sentence construction (in French or in English) consists of a noun, an adjective, a verb, and, possibly an adverb.

Nouns

All French nouns have a sex instead of being just neutral like nouns in English: They are either masculine or feminine. But, instead of calling it sex, grammarian-types talk about the gender of a noun (perhaps to avoid giggling too much).

Also in French, as in English, nouns are either singular or plural. The French say they have a number.

French nouns are almost always preceded by articles — small words like "the" or "a/an" in English — which mark the gender and the number of nouns. The best way to get used to knowing the right gender of a noun in French is to try to remember the article with the noun. In other words, never memorize a noun without its marker. Instead of **table** *(tahbl)* (table), say to yourself **la table** *(lah tahbl)* (the table) or **une table** *(ewn tahbl)* (a table). Instead of **livre** *(leevr)* (book), think **le livre** *(luh leevr)* (the book) or **un livre** *(aN leevr)* (a book). Chapter 5 looks at this gender issue in more detail.

Whereas in English the plural of nouns is not always marked by an article, for example, "a table" becomes plural "tables," in French, the masculine article for "the," **le** *(luh)* and the feminine **la** *(lah)* both become **les** *(lay)* in the plural. The masculine article for "a," **un** *(aN)*, and the feminine **une** *(ewn)* both become **des** *(day)*. Le livre *(luh leevr)* (the book) becomes **les livres** *(lay leevr)* (the books), and **une table** *(ewn tahbl)* (a table) becomes **des tables** *(day tahbl)* (tables).

Adjectives

Adjectives describe nouns. Because French nouns have both gender and number, any adjectives have to match the nouns they qualify in gender and number. Remember, too, that in French, some adjectives are placed before the noun while others follow the noun (more on that in Chapter 12). For example:

✔ **le papier blanc** *(luh pah-pyay blahN)* (the white paper)

✔ **la grande maison** *(lah grahNd meh-zohN)* (the big house)

✔ **les feuilles vertes** *(lay fewy vehrt)* (the green leaves)

✔ **les petits oiseaux** *(lay puh-tee-zwah-zo)* (the little birds)

Verbs

A verb expresses an action or a state of being. This action has a subject (such as the person who acts or the thing or idea that exists). This subject may be a noun (as in, "The leaf falls") or a pronoun (as in, "They sing").

Just as in English, you make the verb match the subject (you don't say, of course, "the leaf fall"), so, in French, the verb has a special ending for each subject (I, you, we, she, and so on).

Here's what a simple sentence looks like:

Les petits oiseaux chantent.

lay puh-tee zwah-zo shahNt

The little birds sing (or are singing).

Part II covers more details about how to conjugate verbs — that is, make the verb match the subject.

Adverbs

An adverb is a word which modifies (describes) a verb, an adjective, or another adverb. In English, most adverbs end with *–ly*, as in, "Please, speak slowly." In French, the adverbs end in *-ment.* So the same sentence would be: **"Parlez lentement, s'il vous plaît"** *(pahr-lay lahNt-mahN seel-voo-pleh).*

The sample sentence is now complete and reads like this:

Les petits oiseaux chantent joyeusement.

lay puh-tee-zwah-zo shahNt zhwah-yewz-mahN

The little birds sing happily.

Things That Are Easier in French

Believe it or not, some grammar issues in French are easier than in English. A good example of this is the way you can form questions.

- ✔ The easiest way, of course, is to use intonation by raising your voice at the end of your statement.

   Vous avez un ticket? *(voo-zah-vay-zaN tee-keh)* (Do you have a ticket?)

- ✔ Another easy way is to add **est-ce que** *(ehs-kuh)* at the beginning of your phrase.

   Est-ce que vous avez un ticket? *(ehs-kuh voo-zah-vay-zaN tee-keh)* (Do you have a ticket?)

Note that these easy forms of questioning are valid no matter what the tense of the verb is: present, past, or future.

But take note of the fact that if a word beginning with a vowel follow **est-ce que** *(ehs-kuh)*, it becomes: **est-ce qu'** *(ehs-k)*. For example:

- ✔ **Est-ce qu'elle a un ticket?** *(ehs-keh-lah aN tee-keh)* Does she have a ticket?
- ✔ **Est-ce qu'il fait chaud?** *(ehs-keel feh sho)* Is it warm?

Regular and Irregular verbs

In French as in English, the verb form that has no marking to indicate a subject or a tense (past, present, future) for the action is called the infinitive form. For example, English infinitives begin with *to,* as in "to go" or "to speak." In French, infinitives have special endings, such as *-er,-ir* or *-re*: **aller** *(ah-lay)* (to go), **parler** *(pahr-lay)* (to speak), **finir** *(fee-neer)* (to finish), **être ou ne pas être** *(eht-roo nuh pah-zehtr)* (to be or not to be).

The conjugation (adding the markers for subject and tense) of verbs is based on the infinitive form. In English and in French, verbs are either regular or irregular in their conjugations.

Regular verbs follow a common pattern. For example, in English, the verb *to love* is spelled the same way whoever the subject is except for the third person (he, she or it):

I love, you love, he/she love**s**, we love, you love, they love.

To love is a regular English verb because many English verbs follow this same conjugation.

But *to be* is irregular. The form of the verb depends on the subject:

I **am**, you **are**, he/she **is**, we **are**, you **are**, they **are**.

Regular verbs

In French, regular verbs belong to three large groups which are determined by the ending of their infinitive:

✔ The largest group, whose infinitive ends with **–er**: ache**ter** *(ah-shuh-tay)* (to buy), chan**ter** *(shahN-tay)* (to sing) par**ler** *(pahr-lay)* (to speak) don**ner** *(doh-nay)* (to give)

But **aller** (to go) is irregular. Chapter 4 shows how to conjugate **aller** in greater detail.

✔ The group whose infinitive ends in **-ir,** such as: fin**ir** *(fee-neer)* (to finish), chois**ir** *(shwah-zeer)* (to choose)

✔ The smaller but important group whose infinitive ends in **-re,** such as: attend**re** *(ah-tahNdr)* (to wait), vend**re** *(vahNdr)* (to sell)

All these verbs are regular in French in the sense that they follow a definite pattern belonging to each family, and within that family, are conjugated in the same manner with the same ending, depending on the subject and the tenses.

Irregular verbs

An *irregular* verb means that the forms of the verb do not follow the regular pattern for verbs with that ending. You have to make a special effort to memorize the conjugations of these verbs by heart.

The most important ones are the following:

✔ **être** *(ehtr)* (to be)

✔ **avoir** *(ah-vwahr)* (to have)

Not only are they used in many expressions, but they also serve as helping verbs — in making up past tenses.

And here are a few others that you may use often:

- ✔ **faire** *(fehr)* (to do, to make)
- ✔ **venir** *(vuh-neer)* (to come)
- ✔ **pouvoir** *(poo-vwahr)* (to be able to)
- ✔ **savoir** *(sah-vwahr)* (to know)
- ✔ **prendre** *(prahNdr)* (to take)
- ✔ **écrire** *(ay-kreer)* (to write)

The Simple Tenses: Past, Present, and Future

"Tense" simply means "time." So if you want to express an action or a state of being taking place in the present, you use the present tense. If it hasn't happened yet, you use the future tense. And if it took place in the past, you use a past tense.

There are several ways to express the past tense in French, but the simplest and the most common is **le passé composé** *(luh pah-say kohN-po-zay)*. The word **composé** (complex) means that it is made up of more than one component. So for this tense, you use two parts: an auxiliary verb (such as **avoir** or **être**) and the past participle of the action verb (the form which in English would often end with *-ed*.)

Examples:

J'ai chanté. *(zheh shahN-tay)* (I sang.)

Il est parti. *(ee-leh pahr-tee)* (He left.)

If the action is going to take place in the future, the French use a form similar to the English 'to be going to' with the verb **aller** *(ah-lay),* to go

Example:

Demain Sylvie va voyager *(duh-maN seel-vee vah vwah-yah-zhay)* . (Tomorrow Sylvie is going to travel.)

To give you an idea of what a regular verb looks like in these three simple tenses, the following list shows how to conjugate the verb **parler** *(pahr-lay)* (to speak) with the subject pronouns I, you, and he/she.

Présent *(pray-zahN)*

> **Je parle** *(zhuh pahrl)*
>
> **Vous parlez** *(voo pahr-lay)*
>
> **Il/elle parle** *(eel/ehl pahrl)*

Passé composé *(pah-say kohN-po-zay)*

> **J'ai parlé** *(zheh pahr-lay)*
>
> **Vous avez parlé** *(voo-zah-vay pahr-lay)*
>
> **Il a parlé / elle a parlé** *(ee-lah pahr-lay / eh-lah pahr-lay)*

Futur *(few-tewr)*

> **Je vais parler** *(zhuh veh pahr-lay)*
>
> **Vous allez parler** *(voo-zah-lay pahr-lay)*
>
> **Il/elle va parler** *(eel/ehl vah pahr-lay)*

Now you can proudly say: **Bientôt, je vais parler français** *(byaN-to zhuh veh pahr-lay frahN-seh)* (Soon, I am going to speak French.)

The Gender Question

Remembering the gender of nouns may at first seem to be an almost impossible obstacle to speaking French. But don't worry! In this section, we give you some guidelines that make it easier to know right away the gender of many words.

Of course, if you are talking about a man or a woman, the gender is obvious. But if the subject noun or pronoun is a thing or an idea, you have to know the gender (masculine or feminine) of the noun in order to use the right pronoun (**il** or **elle**) as the subject of the verb.

With a few exceptions, the ending of a noun is a rather good indication of its gender. The following list shows some common endings of masculine nouns:

✔ **-age** *(ahzh)*

> **le fromage** *(luh froh-mahzh)* (cheese)
>
> **le nuage** *(luh new-ahzh)* (cloud)
>
> **l'étage** *(lay-tazh)* (a story, a floor)

✔ **-eur** *(uhr)*

l'auteur *(lo-tuhr)* (author)

le bonheur *(luh boh-nuhr)* (happiness)

✔ **-isme** *(eesm)*

le capitalisme *(luh kah-pee-tah-leesm)* (capitalism)

le féminisme *(luh fay-mee-neesm)* (feminism)

✔ **-ment** *(mahN)*

l'appartement *(lah-pahr-tuh-mahN)*

✔ vowels other than **-e**

le cinéma *(luh see-nay-mah)* (movies)

le piano *(luh py-ah-no)* (piano)

le café *(luh kah-fay)* (coffee or coffee shop)

le bureau *(luh bew-ro)* (office or desk)

And here are some common endings for feminine nouns:

✔ **-ade** *(ahd)*

la promenade *(lah proh-muh-nahd)* (walk)

la limonade *(lah lee-moh-nahd)* (lemonade)

✔ **-ance/-ence** *(ahNs)*

la naissance *(lah neh-sahNs)* (birth)

l'indépendance *(laN-day-pahN-dahNs)* (independence)

la différence *(lah dee-fay-rahNs)* (difference)

la patience *(lah pah-sy-ahNs)* (patience)

la science *(lah sy-ahNs)* (science)

✔ **-oire** *(wahr)*

la mémoire *(lah may-mwahr)* (memory)

la victoire *(lah veek-twahr)* (victory)

la poire *(lah pwahr)* (pear)

✔ **-sion/tion** *(syohN)*

l'impression *(laN-pray-sy-ohN)* (impression)

la condition *(lah kohn-dee-sy-ohN)* (condition)

la répétition *(lah ray-pay-tee-sy-ohN)* (repetition)

- -son (zohN)

  la saison (lah seh-zohN) (season)

  la maison (lah meh-zohN) (house)

  la raison (lah reh-zohN) (reason)

- -é/ée (ay)

  la liberté (lah lee-behr-tay) (freedom)

  l'égalité (lay-gah-lee-tay) (equality)

  la fraternité (lah frah-tehr-nee-tay) (fraternity)

  l'idée (lee-day) (idea)

  la pensée (lah pahN-say) (thought)

Now instead of memorizing every single noun's gender, you can make a good guess based on these endings. When you can readily recognize a noun's gender, then you instantly know which third person subject pronoun to use:

- **Il** (masculine)

- **Elle** (feminine)

It's "You" You Know: The Tu/Vous Issue

How you address someone in French depends on how well you know the person. Someone you meet for the first time (unless it is a child) will expect you to address him or her using the more formal **vous** — a polite and respect-ful form of the English *you*.

So start practicing your greetings using **vous** and the corresponding verb form (ending **-ez**) in all circumstances, whether you are addressing one person or more, because **vous** is both singular and plural.

Do not use at first the informal, friendly **tu,** and you will avoid making eti-quette mistakes.

Soon you will become more familiar with French ways and the French lan-guage, and then being able to choose between **tu** and **vous** will become an indication of your degree of integration with French customs.

Remember: In France, you would sound strange at best and impolite at worst using **tu** to address a stranger or a new acquaintance. However, if you go to Quebec, you may soon discover that the familiar **tu** is much more liberally used at all times.

(For more on when and where to use **tu** or **vous**, refer to Chapter 3.)

Numbers

You don't need to juggle numbers like a mathematician right away: Most of the time, you can use plain old cardinal numbers from 0 to around 100 to express the number of units of anything. Knowing these numbers enables you to express, for instance, how much money you have in your wallet, how many sheep you have to count before you fall asleep, how many hours you will have to wait before your plane takes off, how many years you already have spent in your life (be discrete), and so on.

One of the most important and frequent uses of numbers is, of course, to tell time. Chapter 7 explains all about telling time in French.

Because you are just beginning to memorize a few things in French, you can content yourself for now with counting only the first numbers up to 20. (You can cheat and use fingers and toes to help yourself count if necessary.)

1. **un** *(aN)*

2. **deux** *(duh)*

3. **trois** *(trwah)*

4. **quatre** *(kahtr)*

5. **cinq** *(saNk)*

6. **six** *(sees)*

7. **sept** *(seht)*

8. **huit** *(weet)*

9. **neuf** *(nuhf)*

10. **dix** *(dees)*

11. **onze** *(ohNz)*

12. **douze** *(dooz)*

13. **treize** *(trehz)*

14. **quatorze** *(kah-tohrz)*

15. **quinze** *(kaNz)*

16. **seize** *(sehz)*

17. **dix-sept** *(dees-seht)*

18. **dix-huit** *(dee-zweet)*

19. **dix-neuf** *(deez-nuhf)*

20. **vingt** *(vaN)*

Chapter 3

Bonjour! Hello! Greetings and Introductions

. . . .

In This Chapter

▶ Greeting and addressing people

▶ Getting formal or informal

▶ Introducing yourself and friends

▶ Talking about cities, countries, nationalities

▶ Being there: **être** *(ehtr)* (to be)

. . . .

Greetings are the first steps in establishing contact with someone, whatever the language. In many cases, a smile does the job and you just have to wait for the other person to greet you and repeat what he or she just said. However, this chapter presents plenty of very simple French greetings that you may use on different occasions to help you meet people.

Saying Hello and Good-Bye

When you are visiting a foreign country, the locals usually appreciate your effort to speak the language, even just a few words of it. There is nothing easier than saying hello in any language. Actually, the French language has a saying, when refering to something that is really a cinch: **"C'est simple comme bonjour"** *(seh saNpluh kohm bohN-zhoor)* (It's as easy as saying hello). So, go ahead, practice these few greetings and you are in business.

Here are a few examples of common hellos and good-byes:

✔ **Bonjour!** *(bohN-zhoor):* This literally means "Good day," but you can use it when first greeting someone, morning or afternoon, roughly as long as the sun is shining.

In Québec, people also say **Bonjour** when leaving, giving it the true meaning of "good day."

- **Bonsoir!** *(bohN-swahr)* (Good evening!)

   This greeting is used in the late afternoon and the evening to say hello or good-bye.

- **Salut!** *(sah-lew)* (Hi!)

   This is the most informal of all hellos and is also a way of saying good-bye; it can be used at any time of day but not with just anybody. See the section "Getting Formal or Informal" to understand better when to say **Salut.**

- **Au revoir!** *(o-ruh-vwahr* or *ohr-vwahr)* (Good-bye!)

   Like its English counterpart, it applies to any time of day or night.

- **Bonne nuit!** *(bohn new-ee)* (Good night!)

   You say this only when retiring (or when someone retires) for the night, or when putting a child to bed. It can be compared to saying "sleep well."

- **A bientôt!** *(ah-byaN-to)* (See you soon!) (That means anytime soon.)

- **A tout à l'heure!** *(ah- too- tah-luhr)* (See you later!) Use this only when you will see the person the same day.

- **A demain!** *(ah duh-maN)* (See you tomorrow!)

- **Bonne journée!** *(bohn zhoor-nay)* (Have a nice day!)

Getting Formal or Informal

You don't talk the same way to a boss, a friend, or a child. You use different words and phrases, and you are more or less formal, according to how close you are to someone. In French, you can also vary the level of formality by using two ways of saying "you." Depending on whom you are addressing, you can use the informal **tu** *(tew)* or the more formal **vous** *(voo)*. It is important to know the difference because you may, by saying the wrong thing, at best sound a little funny and at worst offend someone.

In general, use the formal **vous** when addressing somebody you have never met, a superior, or an older person. As you get to know that person better, both of you may switch to **tu**. You say **tu** to a young person, a child, or an animal. These are the general rules, but the environment in which you find yourself determines the form of address you use. For example, if you were a young person traveling on the train in France and you met other young people, they would address you as **tu** and expect you to do the same. On the other hand, if you were in a store and the sales clerk looked a lot younger than you were, say, about 25, you should still address her as **vous**. In general, members of the same family, whatever their age, use the **tu** form.

Now, about that greeting, **Salut,** the most informal of all greetings? What form of the pronoun "you" do you think the French use with it? **Tu,** of course!

The **vous** form is used to address one person on a formal level, but it is also a plural form used to address any number of people formally or informally.

If you are not sure what to do, use the **vous** form until the person you are addressing asks you to use the **tu** form. Then you avoid any **faux-pas** *(fo-pah),* [literally "false step"], another Fench word used in English, which means a social blunder. There is even a French verb for saying **tu: tutoyer** *(tew-twa-yay).* So, if you hear: **"On se tutoie, d'accord?"** *(ohN suh tew-twa dah-kohr)* ("Let's say **tu** to each other, okay?") or **"Vous pouvez me tutoyer"***(voo poo-vay muh tew-twa-yay)* ("You can say **tu** to me"), go ahead, feel free to be informal.

Asking "How are you?"

Most of the time, when you meet someone, especially someone you already know, your greeting is followed by the question, "How are you?" You do the same in French, but of course you have several different ways of asking the question, depending on the level of formality between the two speakers.

This way of asking is very formal:

> **Comment allez-vous?** *(koh-mahN-tah-lay voo)* (How are you?)

This way is also very polite:

> **Vous allez bien?** *(voo-zah-lay byaN)* (Are you well?)

A more informal approach is to ask:

> **Comment vas-tu?** *(koh-mahN vah-tew)* (How are you?)

This is the familiar version of the preceding one, using the **tu** form instead of the **vous**.

Rather informal but usable with both **tu** and **vous** are the following:

- ✔ **Comment ça va?** *(koh-mahN sah vah)*
- ✔ **Ça va?** *(sah vah)*

Replying to "How are you?"

Naturally, others expect you to reply to the question, albeit without going into lengthy details about your health, your work, or your private life. A short phrase will do, such as:

- ✔ **Ça va!** *(sah vah)* (I'm okay.)
- ✔ **Ça va bien!/Ça va très bien!** *(sah vah byaN/sah vah treh byaN)* (I'm fine!/I'm very well!)
- ✔ **Bien, merci!/Très bien, merci!** *(byaN mehr-see/treh byaN mehr-see)* (Fine, thank you!/Very well, thank you!)

If you are less enthusiastic, you may say:

Pas mal! *(pah mahl)* (Not bad!)

Even if you feel really bad, no one expects you to answer a simple greeting by saying how things really are for you. Introductions and greetings are for politeness and not for sharing feelings.

Whenever you answer a "How are you?" question, the least you can do is inquire about the well-being of the person you are talking to. You then follow your answer with "And you":

Et vous? *(ay voo)*, which is the formal way,

or

Et toi? *(ay twah)*, a variation of the informal **tu**.

Talkin' the Talk

Here are two dialogues, the first one (formal talk) between a shop-keeper, Monsieur Martin *(muh-syuh mahrtaN)* and his customer, Madame Leblanc *(mah-dahm luh-blahN)*, the second between two teenage friends, Catherine *(kah-treen)* and Michel *(mee-shehl)*.

Madame Leblanc is doing her daily food shopping and goes into Monsieur Martin's butcher shop:

M. Martin: **Bonjour, Madame Leblanc. Comment allez-vous?**
bohN-zhoor mah-dahm luh-blahN koh-mahN tah-lay voo
Hello, Mrs Leblanc. How are you?

M. Leblanc: **Très bien, merci, et vous?**
treh byaN mehr-see ay voo
Very well, thank you, and you?

M. Martin: **Ça va bien, merci.**
sah vah byaN mehr-see
I'm fine, thank you.

Later . . . after Madame Leblanc has bought her **biftek** *(beef-tehk)* (steak), she prepares to leave the store:

M. Martin: **Au revoir, Madame Leblanc. Bonne journée.**
ohr-vwahr mah-dahm luh-blahN bohn zhoor-nay
Good-bye, Mrs Leblanc. Have a nice day.

M. Leblanc: **Au revoir, monsieur.**
ohr-vwahr muh-syuh
Good-bye, sir.

Catherine and Michel are teenagers who meet on the street:

Catherine: **Salut, Michel. Comment ça va?**
sah-lew mee-shehl coh-mahN sah vah
Hi, Michel. How are you doing?

Michel: **Pas mal. Et toi?**
pah mahl ay twah
Not too bad, How about you?

Catherine: **Oh, ça va. . . .**
o sah vah
Oh, I'm okay.

CULTURAL WISDOM

The French are Latin people. Even though they don't speak with their hands as much as the Italians do (or so goes the stereotype), body talk is very important. For instance, they have different ways of saying **Ça va** *(sah-vah)* (I'm okay). You can say it with a big smile or with a sad face, and the person you are talking to can get the meaning from your face rather than your words. Also, the French touch a lot more than the Anglo-Saxons do. The handshake is not restricted to the first meeting between two persons, but most people in an office shake hands every morning when getting to work and every evening when leaving the office. On a more informal level, women friends kiss lightly on each cheek while greeting each other or saying good-bye, and a man and a woman also kiss the same way, whereas men shake hands. Male family members may kiss one another too. If you travel to different parts of France, you may be surprised to discover that, in some areas, people kiss not twice but three times, and sometimes up to four times! It may also be puzzling for an American to observe high school students getting to school in the morning. There too, a large amount of cheek-pecking takes place!

Say you are invited to a dinner party by a French family with children. The parents want to introduce their children to you before they are sent to bed. They may tell the children: **"Dites bonsoir à tout le monde"** *(deet bohN-swahr ah tool mohNd)* ("Say good evening to everyone"). Immediately, the little ones might go around the dinner table giving a kiss to all the guests and expecting a kiss back.

Once more, when you don't know what to do, (kiss or shake), the safest thing is not to take the initiative. Do what the other person is doing and you can't be wrong.

Introducing Yourself and Others

It is not enough to greet people and ask how they are; you also need to introduce yourself and find out what their names are. The purpose of this section is to do just that. You may use either of these phrases:

> **Je m'appelle . . .** *(zhuh mah-pehl)* (My name is . . .)
>
> **Je suis . . .** *(zhuh sew-ee)* (I am . . .)

Facile, non? *(fah-seel nohN)* (easy, isn't it?) Now, that takes care of you. But you may want to know who that person over there is. So you ask:

> **Qui est-ce?** *(Kee ehs?)* (Who is that?)

and you receive the following answer:

> **C'est . . .** *(seh)* (That is . . .)

Now, suppose you want to introduce someone. You say:

> **Je vous présente . . .** *(zhe voo pray-zehNt)* (Let me introduce . . . to you)

or with the informal variation on **tu:**

> **Je te présente . . .** *(zhe tuh pray-zehNt)* (Let me introduce . . . to you)

or else:

> **Voici . . ./Voilà . . .** *(vwah-see/vwah-lah)* (Here is . . . /There is . . .)

and the other person then says:

> **Enchanté!** (man)/**Enchantée!** (woman) *(ahN-shahN-tay)* (Delighted!)

Of course, on the playground or at a gathering of young people, it's a different story, and you may hear:

> **Comment tu t'appelles?** *(ko-mahN tew tah-pehl)* (What's your name?) [informal]

> **Et lui, qui est-ce?/Et elle, qui est-ce?** *(ay lew-ee kee ehs/ay ehl kee ehs)* (And who is he?/And who is she?)

Talkin' the Talk

Marc Sauval *(mahrk so-vahl)*, a businessman from Québec, has come to Paris to attend a meeting. He meets his French counterpart, **Claire Rivet** *(clehr ree-vay)* for the first time.

Marc:	**Bonjour, madame. Je m'appelle Marc Sauval.** *bohN-zhoor mah-dahm zhuh mah-pehl mahrk so-vahl* Hello, ma'am. My name is Marc Sauval.
Claire:	**Ah, monsieur Sauval. Je suis Claire Rivet. Enchantée! Comment allez-vous?** *ah muh-syuh so-vahl zhe sew-ee klehr ree-vay ko-mahN-tah-lay voo* Ah, Mr. Sauval. I am Claire Rivet. Delighted to meet you! How are you?
Marc:	**Très bien, merci.** *treh byaN mehr-see* Very well. Thank you.

Later, in the evening, Claire has invited Marc and his wife to a local restaurant. Marc introduces his wife:

Marc:	**Madame Rivet, je vous présente ma femme, Christine.** *mah-dahm ree-vay zhe voo pray-zahNt mah fahm krees-teen* Mrs Rivet, let me introduce you to my wife, Christine.

Claire:	**Enchantée, madame!**
	ahN-shahN-tay mah-dahm
	Delighted, ma'am!

Christine:	**Enchantée!**
	ahN-shahN-tay
	Delighted!

You have undoubtedly figured out by now that, in French, you use **monsieur** to address a man. But how do you address a woman? In theory, **madame** applies to married women and **mademoiselle** to unmarried women. The English "Ms." has no equivalent in French. Thus, to be on the safe side and in order not to offend anyone, a young girl may be addressed as **mademoiselle,** but you should address any other woman as **madame** (unless you know specifically that she is unmarried and insists on being called **mademoiselle!**).

Remember also that **monsieur** and **madame** can be used on their own and are, most of the time.

Talkin' the Talk

Suppose you are going along with your French friends and their children to a playground where three children are playing on the swings. You may overhear a conversation like this among the kids:

Girl:	**Salut! Comment tu t'appelles?**
	sah-lew ko-mahN tew tah-pehl
	Hi! What's your name?

Boy:	**Julien. Et toi?**
	zhew-lyaN ay twah
	Julien. What about you?

Girl:	**Je m'appelle Sophie. Et lui, qui est-ce?**
	zhuh mah-pehl so-fee ay lew-ee kee ehs
	My name is Sophie. And who is he?

Boy:	**C'est mon frère. Il s'appelle Thomas.**
	seh mohN frehr eel sah-pehl to-mah
	He's my brother. His name is Thomas.

Girl:	**Salut, Thomas!**
	sah-lew to-mah
	Hi, Thomas!

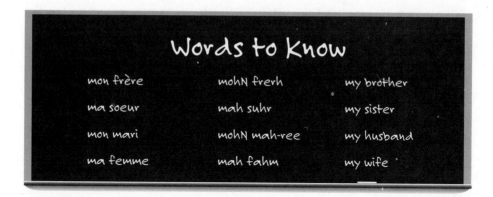

Words to Know

mon frère	mohN frerh	my brother
ma soeur	mah suhr	my sister
mon mari	mohN mah-ree	my husband
ma femme	mah fahm	my wife

When you say in English: "I introduced myself," you are using a reflexive form of the verb "introduce." In French, when you want to say: "My name is," you use a reflexive form of the verb **appeler** *(ah-puh-lay)* (to call). Thus, **je m'appelle** *(zhuh mah-pehl)* means literally, "I call myself."

For reference, the following table shows all the forms of **appeler** in the present tense. (Refer to Chapter 2 for general statements on French verbs.)

Conjugation	*Pronunciation*
Je m'appelle	zhuh mah-pehl
Tu t'appelles	tew tah-pehl
Il/Elle s'appelle	eel/ehl sah-pehl
Nous nous appelons	noo noo zah-puh-lohN
Vous vous appelez	voo voo zah-puh-lay
Ils s'appellent	eel sah-pehl
Elles s'appellent	ehl sah-pehl

Being There: Être (To Be)

After you have met new people, introduced yourself, and learned their names, you may want to know where they're from (what city, what country) and their nationality. To do all this, you need to get familiar with a very useful verb: **être** *(ehtr)* (to be). (Refer to Chapter 2 for general statements on French verbs.) As in English, you use the verb "to be" to describe yourself, to state where you are, and to explain where you are from. As in English, this verb is irregular and admittedly a little difficult, but it is so important and so often used that it's worth putting some effort into memorizing all of its forms and practicing it over and over again so that it becomes second nature. So, **allons-y!** *(ah-lohN-zee)* (let's go) — the following table shows the conjugation of the present tense of **être** *(ehtr)* (to be):

Conjugation	Pronunciation
Je suis	zhuh sew-ee
Tu es	tew eh
Il/elle est	eel ehl eh
Nous sommes	noo sohm
Vous êtes	voo zeht
Ils sont	eel sohN
Elles sont	ehl sohN

If in doubt about whether to use the informal or formal "you," refer to the section of this chapter called "Getting Formal or Informal."

In French, the question is literally "From where are you?" Notice that **de** becomes **d'** in front of a vowel, as in this example:

D'où êtes-vous ? *(doo eht voo)* (Where are you from?)

For more on this, refer to the section on **l'élision** (elision) in Chapter 1.

Now, if you hear the following question:

D'où êtes-vous? or **D'où es-tu?** *(doo eht voo?)* or *(doo eh-tew?)* (Where are you from?) [formal or informal]

You can answer along one of these lines, for instance:

Je suis de New York. Et vous? *(zhuh sew-ee duh New York ay voo)* (I am from New York. What about you?)

Nous sommes de Paris. *(noo sohm duh pah-ree)* (We are from Paris.)

Sounds easy, doesn't it? But notice that the places mentioned in these examples (New York and Paris) are cities. It gets a little more complicated when you start talking about the country you come from because in French, a country can be masculine or feminine: **La France** *(lah frahNs)*, **le Canada** *(luh kah-nah-dah)*.

Some countries are used without an article. You just say **Israël** *(ees-rah-ehl)* or **Madagascar** *(mah-dah-gahs-kahr),* for instance.

Table 3-1 presents a sample list of countries with their genders:

Table 3-1	Genders of Countries	
Feminine:		
La France	lah frahNs	France
La Suisse	lah sew-ees	Switzerland
La Belgique	lah behl-zheek	Belgium
L'Allemagne	lahl-mahNy	Germany
L'Italie	lee-tah-lee	Italy
L'Espagne	lehs-pany	Spain
L'Angleterre	lahN-gluh-tehr	England
L'Algérie	lahl-zhay-ree	Algeria
L'Inde	laNd	India
Masculine:		
Le Canada	luh kah-nah-dah	Canada
Le Danemark	luh dahN-mahrk	Denmark
Le Portugal	luh pohr-tew-gahl	Portugal
Le Japon	luh zhah-pohN	Japan
Le Maroc	luh mah-rohk	Morocco
Le Sénégal	luh say-nay-gahl	Senegal
Le Liban	luh lee-bahN	Lebanon
Les États-Unis	lay-zay-tah-zew-nee	The United States

Notice that all feminine countries end with the letter **e**. One exception is **le Mexique** *(luh mehk-seek)* (Mexico) which, even though it ends in *e,* is masculine.

Paying attention to the gender of countries helps you to understand the variations in the following statements:

- ✔ **Je suis de Paris** (city) *(zhuh sew-ee duh pah-ree):* I am from Paris.

- ✔ **Il est de France** (feminine country) *(ee leh duh frahNs):* He is from France.

✔ **Vous êtes du Canada** (masculine country) *(voo zeht dew kah-nah-dah):*
You are from Canada.

✔ **Nous sommes des Etats-Unis** (plural) *(noo sohm day zay-tah-zew-nee):*
We are from the United States.

But you say: **Elle est d'Israël** *(ehl eh dees-rah-ehl)* (She is from Israel) and **Ils sont de Madagascar** *(eel sohN duh mah-dah-gahs-kahr)* (They are from Madagascar).

Of course sometimes, instead of saying where you are from, you simply want to say where you are. In this case, you use **à** for a city and a different preposition for a country (depending on whether it's masculine or feminine):

✔ **Je suis à Paris** *(zhuh sew-ee ah pah-ree)* (I am in Paris.)

✔ **Montréal est au Canada** (masculine) *(mohN-ray-ahl eh to kah-nah-dah)*
(Montreal is in Canada.)

✔ **Elle est en Suisse** (feminine) *(ehl eh tahN sew-ees)* (She is in
Switzerland.)

In French, as in English, you can say "I come from" as well as "I am from." For example, you can ask:

D'où viens-tu/D'où venez-vous? *(doo vyaN-tew/doo vuh-nay-voo)* (Where do you come from?) [informal and formal]

and the answer may be, for instance:

Je viens de Montréal. *(zhuh vyaN duh mohN-ray-ahl)* (I come from
Montreal.)

For reference, the following table shows the present tense of the verb **venir** *(vuh-neer)* (to come):

Conjugation	Pronunciation
Je viens	zhuh vyaN
Tu viens	tew vyaN
Il/Elle vient	eel/ehl vyaN
Nous venons	noo vuh-nohN
Vous venez	voo vuh-nay
Ils viennent	eel vyehn
Elles viennent	ehl vyehn

Describing Cities

Suppose you want to have a longer exchange with a person who is traveling as you are. What about the city he or she is from: Is it large, small, pretty, international, or . . . ? And what about this person: he may be coming from another country which is quite interesting or maybe she has traveled some more and knows several languages. How are you going to ask all those questions? **Facile!** *(fah-seel)* (easy!) Here are some conversation starters:

- **De quelle ville êtes-vous?** *(duh kehl veel eht-voo)* (Which city are you from?)

- Or **De quelle ville es-tu?** *(duh kehl veel eh-tew),* which is, as you have guessed, the informal form of the above.

- **Où est Montréal?** *(oo eh mohN-ray-ahl)* (Where is Montreal?)

- **Comment est Montréal/Bruxelles/Paris?** *(koh-mahN eh mohN-ray-ahl/brew-sehl/pah-ree)* (How is Montreal/Brussels/Paris?)

- **Est-ce que c'est une petite ville?** *(ehs-kuh seh tewn puh-teet veel)* (Is it a small town?)

And here are some possible answers you could get:

- **Montréal est une ville internationale.** *(mohN-ray-ahl eh tewn veel aNtehr-nah-syo-nahl)* (Montreal is an international city.)

- **C'est au Canada.** *(seh-to kah-nah-dah)* (It is in Canada.)

- **Ce n'est pas une petite ville; c'est une très grande ville.** *(suh neh pah zewn puh-teet veel seh tewn treh grahNd veel)* (It is not a small town; it is a very large city.)

When you want to ask questions in French, most of the time it is enough to put **est-ce que** *(ehs-kuh)* in front of any statement to turn it into a question. For example:

> **Paris est une grande ville.** *(pah-ree eh-tewn grahNd veel)* (Paris is a big city.)

becomes

> **Est-ce que Paris est une grande ville?** *(ehs-kuh pah-ree eh-tewn grahNd veel)* (Is Paris a big city?)

Similarly,

> **Vous venez de Belgique.** *(voo vuh-nay duh behl-zheek)* (You come from Belgium.)

becomes

Est-ce que vous venez de Belgique? *(ehs-kuh voo vuh-nay duh behl-zheek)* (Do you come from Belgium?)

To make a negative statement, French uses a pair of words to mark the negation. Simply stated, **ne** *(nuh)* goes in front of the verb, and **pas** *(pah)* goes after. For example:

- ✔ **Elle <u>ne</u> s'appelle <u>pas</u> Claire.** *(ehl nuh sah-pehl pah klehr)* (Her name is not Claire.)
- ✔ **New York <u>n'</u>est <u>pas</u> une petite ville.** *(New York neh pah zewn puh-teet veel)* (New York is not a small town.)

Words to Know

Où est . . .	oo eh	Where is . . . ?
une petite ville	ewn puh-teet veel	a small town
une grande ville	ewn grahNd veel	a big city
une ville internationale	ewn veel aN-tehr-nah-syo-nahl	an international city

Contrary to English, in French, most adjectives follow the nouns they qualify. But a few very common adjectives always precede the noun. See Chapter 12 for more details.

Also note that the adjective has to agree with the noun it modifies. Thus **petit** *(puh-tee* small) becomes **petite** *(puh-teet)* when associated with a feminine noun as in **une petite ville** *(ewn puh-teet veel)* (a little town).

Speaking the Language

If you are stuck somewhere in a French-speaking country, lost, hungry, or who knows what, and are desperate for some help, you can always ask: Do you speak English? If you get a blank stare in return, go ahead, dive in, and **parlez français** *(pahr-lay frahN-seh)* (speak French)! One of these phrases may help you express your situation:

- **Parlez-vous français?/Est-ce que vous parlez français?** *(pahr-lay voo frahN-seh/ehs-kuh voo pahr-lay frahN-seh)* (Do you speak French?) [formal and plural]

- **Je parle un peu français.** *(zhuh pahrl aN puh frahN-seh)* (I speak French a little.)

- **Je parle bien français.** *(zhuh pahrl byaN frahN-seh)* (I speak French well.)

- **Je ne parle pas du tout français.** *(zhuh nuh pahrl pah dew too frahN-seh)* (I don't speak French at all.)

Notice the way the French sentences above are built as compared to the English translation. The adverb (such as well, a little, or not at all) comes right after the verb instead of being thrown at the end of the sentence.

The verb **parler** *(pahr-lay)* (to speak/to talk) is a good one to know, because, after all, what are you trying to do here if not **parler français**? It also happens (aren't you lucky?) to be an easy verb to conjugate. It's regular and belongs to the **-er** verb family, along with 80 percent of French verbs. (See Chapter 2 for more details on verbs.) Who says French verbs are difficult when most of them are regular? The following table shows the present tense of **parler**:

Conjugation	Pronunciation
Je parle	zhuh pahrl
Tu parles	tew pahrl
Il/elle parle	eel/ehl pahrl
Nous parlons	noo pahr-lohN
Vous parlez	voo pahr-lay
Ils/elles parlent	eel/ehl pahrl

Talkin' the Talk

Two young people, Klaus from Germany and Isabelle from Canada, are on a train going from Paris to Madrid. They meet Pedro and Luisa from Spain. After helping each other with heavy knapsacks, they get acquainted and start talking. They could probably use English as a common language, but they are leaving from Paris and have decided to practice their French. Good for them!

Klaus: **Je m'appelle Klaus; et elle, c'est mon amie Isabelle; et vous?**
zhuh mah-pehl kla-os ay ehl seh mo-nah-mee eesah-behl ay voo
My name is Klaus and this is my friend Isabelle; what about you?

Luisa: **Moi, c'est Luisa et lui, c'est mon ami Pedro. Nous sommes de Madrid.**
mwa seh loo-ee-sah ay lew-ee seh mo-nah-mee peh-dro noo sohm duh mah-dreed
I am Luisa and this is my friend Pedro. We are from Madrid.

Isabelle: **Mais, tu parles très bien français!**
meh tew pahrl treh byaN frahN-seh
But you speak French very well!

Luisa: **Merci, toi aussi.**
mehr-see twa o-see
Thank you. You too.

Isabelle: **C'est normal, je suis québécoise, alors ma langue maternelle, c'est le français.**
seh nohr-mahl zhuh sew-ee kay-bay-kwaz ahlohr mah lahNg mah-tehr-nehl seh luh frahN-seh
It's nothing special, I am from Québec, so my mother tongue is French.

Pedro: **Mais tu parles aussi l'anglais probablement.**
meh tew pahrl o-see lahN-gleh proh-bah-bluh-mahN
But you probably also speak English.

Isabelle: **Bien sûr! Pas vous?**
byaN sewr pah voo
Of course. Don't you?

Klaus: **Moi je le parle.**
mwa zhuh luh pahrl
I speak it.

Luisa: **Moi, je ne parle pas du tout l'anglais, mais Pedro le parle bien.**
mwa zhuh nuh pahrl pah dew too lahN-gleh meh pay-dro luh pahrl byaN
I don't speak English at all, but Pedro speaks it well.

Pedro: **Oh non, pas bien! Un peu seulement.**
o nohN pah byaN an puh suhl-mahN
Oh no, not well! Only a little.

Luisa: **Voici Madrid. Maintenant, il faut parler espagnol!**
vwa-see mah-dreed maN-tuh-nahN eel fo pahr-lay ehs-pah-nyohl
Here is Madrid. Now we have to speak Spanish!

Klaus et Isabelle: **Oh là là!**
o-lah-lah
Oh no!

Words to Know

mon ami	mo-nah-mee	my friend (male)
mon amie	mo-nah-mee	my friend(female)
mais	meh	but
C'est normal.	seh nohr-mahl	It's nothing special. [literally:It's normal.]
alors	ah-lohr	so
ma langue maternelle	mah lahNg mah-tehr-nehl	my mother tongue
moi/toi/lui/elle	mwa/twa/lew-ee/ehl	I/you/he/she (for emphasis)
moi aussi	mwa o-see	me too
bien sûr	byaN sewr	of course
Je le parle.	zhuh luh pahrl	I speak it.
je ne parle pas	zhuhn pahrl pah	I don't speak
seulement	suhl-mahN	only
maintenant	man-tuh-nahN	now
il faut parler	eel fo pahr-lay	we/you have to talk/speak

You may remember that you use **mon** *(mohN)* for "my" (masculine) and **ma** *(mah)* for "my" (feminine), but there are exceptions. The mark of the feminine in French is a final *e,* as you can see in **ami** and **amie**. However, in the case of **ami/amie**, you use **mon** for both the masculine and the feminine form because the word **amie** starts with a vowel. Whenever a word starts with a vowel in French, an alarm rings and funny things happen. This is one of them, and you'll see more as you go along. (Check out Chapter 1 for more on nouns that start with vowels.)

Fun & Games

Here is a list of words which got loose. See if you can put them back where they belong in the text and dialog below.

(elle - je - m'appelle - l'anglais - grande - femme)

Bonjour, je _____ Pierre Lanvin. _____ suis de Marseille. C'est une _____ ville française. Ma _____ s'appelle Monique et _____ est canadienne. Je parle le français, bien sûr et aussi un peu _____.

Answer key: m'appelle - je - grande - femme - elle - l'anglais.

Now fill in the missing words in this dialog between an elderly woman and a teenage boy with a teenage girl.

(voici - vient - bien - ça va - parles - toi.)

- Bonjour, madame Legrand. Comment _____ ?

- Ça va bien, merci Denis. Et _____, comment vas-tu?

- Ça va, merci. Madame Legrand, _____ Lucy. Elle vient des Etats-Unis.

- Oh, bonjour Lucy. Alors tu _____ français?

- Pas très _____, madame

Answer key: ça va - toi - voici - vient - parles - bien.

Part II
French in Action

In this part . . .

We present French in the context of daily life. We show you how to keep up in casual conversations, how to order in a French restaurant, how to shop, how to communicate with coworkers, and much, much more. And we throw in some helpful grammar lessons to boot.

Chapter 4

Getting to Know You: Making Small Talk

* *

In This Chapter

▶ Making small talk in all kinds of situations

▶ Asking simple questions

▶ Getting to know more numbers

▶ Talking about where you live

* *

Small talk usually takes place at the beginning of a conversation with a stranger you have just met, after introducing yourselves and finding out where each of you comes from. Small talk allows you to remain vague, if you so desire, and exchange simple questions and answers. Of course, it can lead to a more serious conversation, but it generally deals with innocuous subjects such as the weather, family, or work. In other words, it is a wonderful way to acquaint yourself with someone else and allows you, as you are sitting in your airplane seat, to decide whether you want to pursue the conversation with the stranger next to you or go back to the great book you are reading.

There are several ways in French to designate small talk. One of them is: **parler de tout et de rien** *(pahr-lay duh too ay duh ryahN)* (talk about everything and nothing).

Asking Key Questions

In order to start a conversation in any language, you have to use some key question words. Here are the basic French ones:

✔ **Qui?** *(kee)* (Who?)

✔ **Qu'est-ce que?** *(kes-kuh)* (What?)

✔ **Où?** *(oo)* (Where?)

- **Quand?** *(kahN)* (When?)
- **Pourquoi?** *(poor-kwa)* (Why?)
- **Comment?** *(ko-mahN)* (How?)
- **Combien?** *(kohN-byaN)* (How much?)
- **Quel/Quelle?** (m. and f.) *(kehl)* (Which?)

Here are a few examples of how to use these French question words in simple sentences — you can also use some of them on their own occasionally — just like in English.

- **Qui est-ce?** *(kee ehs)* (Who is it?)
- **Qu'est-ce que tu fais?** *(kehs-kuh tew feh)* (What are you doing?) [informal]
- **Où habitez-vous?** *(oo ah-bee-tay-voo)* (Where do you live?) [formal or plural]
- **Quand part l'avion?** *(kahN pahr lah-vyohN)* (When does the airplane leave?)
- **Pourquoi allez-vous à Paris?** *(poor-kwa ah-lay-voo ah pah-ree)* (Why are you going to Paris?)
- **Comment s'appelle la petite fille?** *(koh-mahN sah-pehl lah puh-teet fee-y)* (What is the little girl's name?)
- **Comment s'appelle . . .?** *(koh-mahN sah-pehl)* (What's . . . name?)
- **Quel est son prénom?** *(keh-leh sohN pray-nohN)* (What's his/her first name?)
- **Combien coûte le billet?** *(kohN-byaN coot luh bee-yeh)* (How much is the ticket?)
- **Quel hôtel préférez-vous?** *(kehl oh-tehl pray-fay-ray-voo)* (Which hotel do you prefer?)

You should add the following statements to the questions I mention previously. These statements are the basics of small talk and are indispensable when you are fairly new at a foreign language:

- **Je ne comprends pas.** *(zhuhn kohN-prahN pah)* (I don't understand.)
- **Je ne sais pas.** *(zhuhn seh pah)* (I don't know.)
- **Pardon/Excusez-moi.** *(pahr-dohN/eks-kew-zay-mwa)* (Excuse me.)
- **Je suis désolé/désolée.** *(zhuh sew-ee day-zoh-lay)* (I am sorry.)

If you ever find yourself in a foreign country trying to get directions from one of the locals who starts babbling at you with incredible speed, you can imagine how useful the previous few sentences are.

Talkin' the Talk

After arriving in Paris from New York, Amanda Hull gets on her connecting flight to Nice. She is very tired because of spending the night on the plane. She collapses in her seat and gets ready to fall asleep. But minutes after, she is awakened by the following words:

Patrick Barnet: **Pardon, madame, quel est le numéro de votre place?**
pahr-dohN mah-dahm kehl eh luh new-may-ro duh voh-truh plahs
Excuse me, ma'am. What is your seat number?

Amanda Hull: **Je ne sais pas. Attendez! Oh, c'est le 24B ; excusez-moi. Je suis désolée.**
zhuhn seh pah ah-tahN-day o seh luh vaNt-kahtr bay eks-kew-zay-mwa zhuh sew-ee day-zoh-lay
I don't know. Wait! Oh it's number 24B. Excuse me. I am sorry.

Patrick Barnet: **Ce n'est pas grave!**
suh neh pah grahv
That's okay.

As you must have figured out, Amanda has taken the wrong seat. She apologizes profusely and moves to her assigned seat, but is now quite awake. Why not then have a conversation with this nice young man who seems eager to talk? After the usual introductions, they continue chatting.

Patrick Barnet: **Où allez-vous?**
oo ah-lay-voo
Where are you going?

Amanda Hull: **Je vais d'abord à Nice, puis à Toulon voir ma fille.**
zhuh veh dah-boh-rah nees pwee ah too-lohN vwar mah fee-y
I am going to Nice first, then to Toulon to visit my daughter.

Patrick Barnet: **Vous venez souvent en France?**
voo vuh-nay soo-vahN ahN frahNs
Do you often come to France?

Amanda Hull: **Oh oui, j'adore la France.**
o wee zhah-dohr lah frahNs
Oh yes, I love France.

Patrick Barnet:	**Quand repartez-vous pour les Etats-Unis?**
	kahN ruh-pahr-tay-voo poor lay-zay-tah-zew-nee
	When are you going back to the States?
Amanda Hull:	**Dans un mois. Et vous, pourquoi allez-vous à Nice?**
	dahN-zaN mwa ay voo poor-kwa ah-lay voo-zah nees
	In a month. And you, why are you going to Nice?
Patrick Barnet:	**Pour le travail.**
	poor luh trah-vay
	For work.

Pay attention to two little words that you see over and over again in French. Both are unpretentious but very important:

- **et** *(ay)* (and) You must never link **et** with the next word (no liaison). Here is an example: **Il est beau et intelligent** *(ee-leh bo ay aN-teh-lee-zhahN)* (He is handsome and intelligent.)

- **dans** *(dahN)* (in) — used for time and space. Notice in these examples that **dans** can have slightly different meanings depending on the context. Sorry, you can seldom translate word for word from French to English or vice-versa!

  - **Dans un mois** *(dahN-zaN mwa)* (In a month)

  - **Dans l'avion** *(dahN lah-vyohN)* (On the plane)

Words to Know

l'avion	lah-vyohN	the airplane
je vais/vous allez	zhuh veh/voo zah-lay	I go/you go
souvent	soo-vahN	often
j'adore	zhah-dohr	I love
partir/repartir	pahr-teer/ruh-pahr-teer	to leave / to go back
dans un mois	dahN zahN mwa	in a month
le travail	luh trah-vahy	work

Posing Simple Questions

Here is a list of simple questions you may want to use when meeting some-one. Some you have seen before; others are new. They all use the formal **vous** because, unless you are very young, you are more likely to use the **vous** when meeting someone for the first time (see Chapter 3 for more details).

- **Comment vous appelez-vous?** *(koh-mahN voo-zah-play-voo)* (What's your name?)
- **Quel âge avez-vous?** *(keh-lah-zhah-vay-voo)* (How old are you?)
- **Où habitez-vous?** *(oo ah-bee-tay-voo)* (Where do you live?)
- **Est-ce que vous êtes marié?** *(ehs-kuh voo-zeht mah-ryay)* (Are you married?)
- **Avez-vous des enfants ?** *(ah-vay-voo day-zahN-fahN)* (Do you have children?)
- **Qu'est-ce que vous faites (dans la vie)?** *(kehs-kuh voo feht dahN lah vee)* (What do you do [for a living]?)
- **Pour quelle compagnie travaillez-vous?** *(poor kehl kohN-pah-nyee trah-va-yay-voo)* (What company do you work for?)
- **Parlez-vous français?** *(pahr-lay-voo frahN-seh)* (Do you speak French?)
- **Aimez-vous voyager?** *(ay-may-voo vwa-yah-zhay)* (Do you like to travel?)
- **Quand partez-vous?** *(kahN pahr-tay-voo)* (When are you leaving?)
- **Quel temps fait-il aujourd'hui?** *(kehl tahN feh-teel o-zhoor-dwee)* (What is the weather like today?)

Chatting about the Family

If you're going to talk about your family, you need to know these common words:

- **le mari** *(luh mah-ree)* (husband)
- **la femme** *(lah fahm)* (wife)
- **les parents** *(lay pah-rahN)* (parents)
- **le père** *(luh pehr)* (father)
- **la mère** *(lah mehr)* (mother)
- **les enfants** *(lay-zahN-fahN)* (children)

- ✔ **le fils** *(luh fees)* (son)
- ✔ **la fille** *(lah fee-y)* (daughter)
- ✔ **le frère** *(luh frehr)* (brother)
- ✔ **la soeur** *(lah suhr)* (sister)
- ✔ **les petits-enfants** *(lay puh-tee-zahN-fahN)* (grandchildren)

Talkin' the Talk

 Let's go back on that plane and listen to Patrick and Amanda:

Patrick: **Votre fille habite en France?**
vohtruh fee-y ah-bee-tahN frahN
Does your daughter live in France?

Amanda: **Oui, son mari est français.**
wee sohN mah-ree eh frahN-seh
Yes, her husband is French.

Patrick: **Et vous, êtes-vous française ou américaine?**
ay voo eht-voo frahN-seh-zoo ah-may-ree-kehn
And you, are you French or American?

Amanda: **Les deux! Mon père est américain et ma mère est française.**
lay duh mohN pehr eh-tah-may-ree-caN ay mah mehr eh frahN-sehz
Both! My father is American, and my mother is French.

Patrick: **Alors vous parlez bien l'anglais et le français?**
ah-lohr voo pahr-lay byaN lahN-gleh ay luh frahN-seh
Then you speak English and French well?

Amanda: **Bien sûr et mes enfants et mes petits-enfants aussi.**
byaN sewr ay may-zahN-fahN ay may puh-tee-zahN-fahN o-see
Of course, and my children and grandchildren too.

Patrick: **Quelle chance! Moi je parle seulement français.**
kehl shahNs mwa zhuh pahrl suhl-mahN frahN-seh
How lucky! I only speak French.

Words to Know

habiter	ah-bee-tay	to live
les deux	lay duh	both
quelle chance!	kehl shahNs	how lucky! (Literally: what luck)
seulement	suhl-mahN	only

In French, there are two verbs that correspond to the English to live: **habiter** *(ah-bee-tay)* and **vivre** *(veevr)*. Most of the time, these verbs are interchangeable, but **habiter** is limited to space, whereas **vivre** refers to time as well as space.

For example, you need to use **vivre** for this statement:

> **Nous vivons au vingt-et-unième siècle.** *(noo vee-vohN o vaN-tay-ew-nyehm syehkl)* (We live in the twenty-first century.)

Vivre is an irregular verb, so when you talk about space, stick to **habiter** for now because it is regular and easy to use.

Making Small Talk on the Job

In French, when you state your profession, you just say: **Je suis professeur** *(zhuh sew-ee proh-feh-suhr)* (I am a teacher or a professor), or **il est ingénieur** *(ee-leh-taN-zhay-nyuhr)* (he is an engineer), without using an article (**un**) like you would in English (I am a teacher; he is an engineer). This construction is just as you would say: **Je suis petit** *(zhuh sew-ee puh-tee)* (I am small) or **Il est intelligent** *(ee-leh-taN-teh-lee-zhahN)* (he is intelligent).

Notice that some professions have only one form for the masculine and the feminine. The professions that end with an *e* — **dentiste** — stay the same as a rule. For the other professions, it is more a remnant of the sexist days when a doctor and a professor were males. Even the French Academy was not able to find an acceptable feminine version of **médecin**. Recently, a lot of noise was made in the French government by some women members who demanded to be called **Madame la Ministre** (Ms. Minister) — to make it more female because it's a word ending in *e* anyway — instead of **Madame le Ministre**. They won!

The following are some useful job terms and job-related expressions:

- **Qu'est-ce que vous faites dans la vie?** *(kes-kuh voo feht dahN lah vee)* (What do you do for a living?)
- **professeur** *(pro-feh-suhr)* (high school teacher or college professor)
- **informaticien/informaticienne** *(aN-fohr-mah-tee-syaN/aN-fohr-mah-tee-syehn)* (computer scientist)
- **secrétaire** *(suh-cray-tehr)* (secretary)
- **médecin** *(mayd-saN)* (physician)
- **infirmier/infirmière** *(aN-feer-myay/aN-feer-myehr)* (nurse)
- **avocat/avocate** *(ah-vo-kah/ah-vo-kaht)* (lawyer)
- **ingénieur** *(aN-zhay-nyuhr)* (engineer)
- **serveur/serveuse** *(sehr-vuhr/sehr-vuhs)* (waiter/waitress)
- **dentiste** *(dahN-teest)* (dentist)
- **retraité/retraitée** *(ruh-treh-tay)* (retired person)

Talkin' the Talk

Back on the plane, Amanda has shown Patrick a few pictures of her family, and suddenly realizes that she has talked a lot about herself, but knows nothing of him, except that he is going to Nice **pour le travail** *(poor luh trah-va-y)* (for work).

Amanda: **Où travaillez-vous?**
oo trah-va-yay voo
Where do you work?

Patrick: **Mon bureau est à Paris, mais je vais souvent à Nice en voyage d'affaires.**
mohN bew-ro eh-tah pah-ree meh zhuh veh soo-vahN ah nees ahN vwa-yazh dah-fehr
My office is in Paris, but I often go to Nice on business trips.

Amanda: **Pour quelle compagnie travaillez-vous?**
poor kehl kohN-pah-nyee trah-va-yay voo
What company do you work for?

Patrick: **Pour une compagnie d'informatique.**
poo-rewn kohN-pah-nyee daN-fohr-mah-teek
For a computer science company.

Amanda:	**C'est une grande compagnie?**
	seh-tewn grahNd kohn-pa-nyee
	Is it a large company?
Patrick:	**Non, elle est très petite. Il y a seulement dix employés.**
	nohN eh-leh treh puh-teet eel ee-yah suhl-mahN dee-zahN-plwa-yay
	No, it is very small. There are only ten employees.

Words to Know

le voyage d'affaires	luh vwa-yahzh dah-fehr	business trip
mon bureau	mohN bew-ro	my office
l'informatique	laN-fohr-mah-teek	computer science
une compagnie	ewn kohn-pah-nyee	a company
grand/grande	grahN/grahNd	big, tall, large
petit/petite	puh-tee/puh-teet	small, short
il y a	ee-lee-yah	there is/there are
un employé/une employée	aN nahN-plwa-yay/ ew nahN-plwa-yay	an employee
un collègue/une collègue	aN koh-lehg/ewn koh-lehg	a co-worker

Going to Town with the Verb Aller

The verb **aller** *(ah-lay)* — to go — is almost as important as the verbs **être** *(ehtr)* (to be) and **avoir** *(ah-vwahr)* (to have) (see Chapter 3), and it is especially sneaky because it hides as an **-er** verb but is actually extremely irregular. Here it is:

Conjugation	Pronunciation
Je vais	zhuh veh
Tu vas	tew vah
Il/Elle va	eel/ehl vah
Nous allons	noo-zah-lohN
Vous allez	voo-zah-lay
Ils/Elles vont	eel/ehl vohN

Talking about the Weather

Another great topic for small talk is, of course, **le temps** *(luh tahN)* (the weather). As a matter of fact, one way to designate small talk in French is **parler de la pluie et du beau temps** *(pahr-lay duh lah plew-ee ay duh bo tahN)* (Literally: to talk about the rain and the nice weather). In countries of great weather contrasts, like Canada, it is a constant topic of conversation. Under more temperate climates, like that of France, the weather is still a favorite topic, especially if you want to complain about it. Here are some useful phrases:

- **Quel temps fait-il?** *(kehl tahN feh-teel)* (What is the weather like?)
- **Il fait chaud.** *(eel feh sho)* (It's warm/hot.)
- **Il fait froid.** *(eel feh frwah)* (It's cold.)
- **Il fait doux.** *(eel feh doo)* (It's mild.)
- **Il fait beau.** *(eel feh bo)* (The weather is nice.)
- **Il fait mauvais.** *(eel feh mo-veh)* (The weather is bad.)
- **Il fait du vent.** *(eel feh dew vahN)* (It's windy.)
- **Il fait du soleil.** *(eel feh dew soh-lehy)* (It's sunny.)
- **Il pleut.** *(eel pluh)* (It's raining.)
- **Il neige.** *(eel nehzh)* (It's snowing.)
- **La température est de 20 degrés.** *(lah tahN-pay-rah-tew-reh duh vaN duh-gray)* (It is 20 degrees.)

CULTURAL WISDOM

Making sense of Celsius

In Québec(Canada) and in other French speaking countries in Europe, the temperature is not stated in Fahrenheit, but in Celsius (centigrades). Thus, when you hear **La température est de 25 degrés** (*la tahN-pay-rah-tewr eh duh vaN t-saNk duh-gray*) (The temperature is 25 degrees), don't run and get your winter coat and gloves, it is actually quite nice out (about 77 degrees F).

To figure things out without getting into complicated calculations, just remember this: Water boils at 100 degrees C and freezes at 0 degrees C. So when it is around 0 degrees C, plus or minus, it is time to bundle up! Also, if you can stand it, you won't have to bother about calculations when the thermometer goes down to –40 degrees (F or C): the numbers are the same. But then, who cares anyway?

You cannot talk about the weather without knowing the names of the seasons:

- ✔ **au printemps** (*o praN-tahN*) (in spring)
- ✔ **en été** (*ahN-nay-tay*) (in summer)
- ✔ **en automne** (*ahN-no-tohn*) (in fall)
- ✔ **en hiver** (*ahN-nee-vehr*) (in winter)

GRAMMATICALLY SPEAKING

Have you noticed that all the weather phrases start with **il**? You are familiar with **il** (**il s'appelle, il habite**), but this **il** has a different meaning. It does not refer to a male person or a masculine object. It is impersonal, like the English *it* in *it's raining*. It is not difficult to use: As far as conjugation and verb agreements go, there is just one **il**, and the verb form which follows it is the same for any **il** or **elle**.

Talkin' the Talk

Our friends' airplane is sailing along and the captain has just made an announcement over the public address system:

> **A Nice, il fait beau et chaud et la température est de 30 degrés.**
> *ah nees eel feh bo ay sho ay lah tahN-pay-rah-tew-reh duh trahNt duh-gray*
> In Nice, the weather is nice and warm and the temperature is 30 degrees.

Patrick:	**A Nice, il fait toujours beau!**
	ah nees eel feh too-zhoor bo
	In Nice, the weather is always nice!

Amanda:	**Même en hiver?**
	meh-mahN-nee-vehr
	Even in winter?

Patrick:	**En hiver, il pleut un peu, mais il fait doux. Et à New York?**
	ahN-nee-vehr eel pluh aN puh me-zeel feh doo ay ah New York
	In winter, it rains a little, but it is mild. And in New York?

Amanda:	**En hiver, il fait très froid et il neige, et en été il fait très chaud et humide.**
	ahN-nee-vehr eel feh treh frwa ay eel nehzh ay ahN-nay-tay eel feh treh sho ay ew-meed
	In winter it is very cold and it snows, and in summer it is very hot and humid.

Patrick:	**Et au printemps et en automne?**
	ay o praN-tahN ay ahN-no-tohn
	What about spring and fall?

Amanda:	**Le temps est agréable.**
	luh tahN eh-tah-gray-ahbl
	The weather is pleasant.

Doing the Numbers

Refer to Chapter 2 to brush up on numbers up to 20. But if the weather is very hot, you probably need to know higher numbers. And what about buying that lovely scarf — it will surely cost more than 20 francs! With what follows, you can handle almost everything, from buying your daily **baguette** *(bah-geht)* (loaf of bread), to purchasing your dream house on the Riviera.

- **vingt** *(vaN)* (20)
- **vingt-et-un** *(vaN-tay-aN)* (21)
- **vingt-deux** *(vahNt-duh)* (22)
- **vingt-trois** *(vahNt-trwa)* (23)

and so on . . .

- **trente** *(trahNt)* (30)
- **trente-et-un** *(trahN-tay-aN)* (31)

  and so on . . .
- **quarante** *(kah-rahNt)* (40)
- **cinquante** *(saN-kahNt)* (50)
- **soixante** *(swa-sahNt)* (60)
- **soixante-dix** *(swa-sahNt-dees)* (70)
- **quatre-vingts** *(kah-truh vaN)* (80)
- **quatre-vingt dix** *(kah-truh-vaN-dees)* (90)
- **cent** *(sahN)* (100)
- **mille** *(meel)* (1,000)
- **un million** *(aN mee-lyohN)* (1,000,000)
- **un milliard** *(aN mee-lyahr)* (1,000,000,000)

If you travel to Switzerland or to Belgium, you may be happy to know that the old — and easier forms of **septante** *(sehp-tahNt)* (70) and **nonante** *(noh-naNt)* (90) are commonly used instead of the strange French **soixante-dix** *(swah-sahNt-dees)* and **quatre-vingt dix** *(kah-truh vaN-dees)*. In some remote part of Switzerland, they use the forms **huitante** *(ew-ee-tahNt)* or **octante** *(ohk-tahNt)* (80).

Words to Know

d'abord	dah-bohr	first
puis	pew-ee	then
toujours	too-zhoor	always
même	mehm	even
un peu	aN puh	a little
agréable	ah-gray-ahbl	pleasant

One last piece of cultural tidbit on the weather: In every language, the weather is the source of many proverbs. Here is one of those French proverbs:

> **Une hirondelle ne fait pas le printemps.** *(ew-nee-rohN-dehl nuh feh pah luh praN-tahN)* (*Literally:* One swallow does not make the spring.)

In France, you can expect cold weather soon when the swallows start gathering on the electric wires, ready to take off to warmer climates, and when you see them coming back, you know that spring is close, but not quite there.

Talking about Where You Live

As people get more friendly, they may want to exchange addresses or phone numbers. And that introductory question covered earlier comes along: **Où habitez-vous?** *(oo ah-bee-tay-voo)* (Where do you live?). Or it can be:

- ✔ **Quelle est votre adresse?** *(keh-leh voh-tra-drehs)* (What is your address?)
- ✔ **Donnez-moi votre numéro de téléphone.** *(doh-nay-mwa voh-truh new-may-ro duh tay-lay-fohn)* Give me your phone number.

You may occasionally talk about your home. These words and phrases come in handy:

- ✔ **Nous habitons dans une maison.** *(noo-zah-bee-tohN dahN-zewn meh-zohN)* (We live in a house.)
- ✔ **Moi, j'habite dans un appartement.** *(mwa zhah-beet dahN-zaN-nah-pahr-tuh-mahN)* (I live in an apartment.)
- ✔ **Le jardin** *(luh zhahr-daN)* (The yard)

In this day and age, you are likely to want and give an e-mail address. The French language has a word for it: **l'adresse électronique** *(lah-dreh-say-lehk-tro-neek),* but it is so much more convenient to say e-mail that everybody says it; recently it has even been frenchified as **le mel** *(luh mehl)*!

Of course, French also has a word for that little sign now so familiar to most of us: @. The French call it **aroba** *(ah-ro-bah)*. But once more, hardly anybody uses this word; they prefer to say **à** or simply "at"; Finally, the dot is **point** *(pwaN)*, which means, among many other things, the period at the end of a sentence.

Talkin' the Talk

Back on the plane which is about to land. Amanda has found out that Patrick often does business in Toulon. He is about the same age as her daughter and her husband. Wouldn't it be lovely if they met? Patrick gets his address book out.

Patrick: **Comment s'appelle votre fille?**
     koh-mahN sah-pehl voh-truh fee-y
     What's your daughter's name?

Amanda: **Anne Texier. Le prénom de son mari est Olivier.**
     ahn tehk-syay luh pray-nohN duh sohN mah-ree eh
     oh-lee-vyay
     Anne Texier. Her husband's name is Olivier.

Patrick: **Et quelle est son adresse?**
     ay kehl eh sohN-nah-drehs
     And what is her address?

Amanda: **Elle habite 5 rue Basire à Toulon. Vous voulez le code postal?**
     ehl ah-beet saNk rew bah-see-rah too-lohN voo voo-lay luh cohd pohs-tahl
     She lives on 5 Basire Street in Toulon. Do you want the zip code?

Patrick: **Pourquoi pas?**
     poor-kwa pah
     Why not?

Amanda: **C'est 83000.**
     seh kah-truh vahN trwa meel
     It's 83000.

Patrick: **Et son numéro de téléphone?**
     ay sohN new-may-ro duh tay-lay-fohn
     And her phone number?

Amanda: **le 04 94 37 08 56**
     luh zay-ro kahtr kah-truh-vahN-kah-tohrz trahNt-seht
     zay-ro-ew-eet saN-kahNt-sees
     Zero four Ninety-four Thirty-seven Zero eight Fifty-six.

Words to Know

le nom	luh nohN	last name
le prénom	luh pray-nohN	first name
l'adresse	lah-drehs	address
le numéro de téléphone	luh new-may-ro duh tay-lay-fohn	phone number
vous voulez?	voo voo-lay	do you want?
le code postal	luh cohd pohs-tahl	zip code
Pourquoi pas?	poor-kwa pah	Why not?

France is divided into 95 **départements** (*day-pahr-tuh-mahN*), administrative sections. Each one has a name and a number according to its alphabetical order: 01 is **Ain** *(aN)*, 83 is **Var** *(vahr)*. The former **Seine** *(sehn)* **département** (75), which included Paris and its suburbs, has been split into five new ones. Paris has kept the number 75 and the others have been thrown at the end of the list. The **département** number makes up the first two digits of the zip code (**le code postal** *[luh cohd pohs-tahl]*) and the last two digits of cars' license plates.

Canada has the same telephone system as the United States: A local area code (**l'indicatif** *[laN-dee-kah-teef]*) followed by the seven digits of a personal phone number. In France, you now have to dial the area code each time you make a call, even locally. In fact, there are only a total of five area codes for all of France, Paris being 01. This code is followed by eight numbers which are stated in groups of two. When you call from abroad, skip the first 0 and dial the number directly after the code for France, which is 33.

For example, if you were to call Anne Texier from the United States, you would dial 011 33 4 94 37 08 56.

If you were to call her from anywhere in France, even from the same town, Toulon, you would dial 04 94 37 08 56.

Talkin' the Talk

Just before landing, Amanda wants to make sure that Patrick will be familiar with her children, **les Texier** *(lay tayk-syay)* the Texiers, when he meets them. She pulls a picture out of her bag and proceeds to describe it:

Amanda: **Voilà la maison de ma fille et de son mari.**
vwa-lah lah meh-zohN duh mah fee-y ay duh sohN mah-ree
Here is my daughter's and her husband's house.

Patrick: **C'est une belle maison!**
say-tewn-behl meh-zohN
It's a beautiful house!

Amanda: **Oui, elle est petite mais charmante et elle a un grand jardin.**
wee ehl eh puh-teet meh shahr-mahNt ay eh-lah aN grahN zhahr-daN
Yes, it is small but charming and it has a big yard.

Patrick: **Et qui sont ces personnes sur la photo?**
ay kee sohN say pehr-sohn sewr lah fo-to
And who are these people on the picture?

Amanda: **Le petit garçon, c'est mon petit-fils, Thibault; il a 4 ans.**
luh puh-tee gahr-sohN seh mohN puh-tee fees tee-bo ee-lah kah-trahN
The little boy is my grandson Thibault; he is 4.

Patrick: **Et là?**
ay lah
And there?

Amanda: **Là, c'est Emilie; elle a 2 ans. Et ici, c'est moi et je ne vous dis pas mon âge!**
lah seh ay-mee-lee eh lah duh-zahN ay ee-see seh mwa ay zhuh nuh voo dee pah mo-nazh
Over there is Emilie; she is 2. And here, it's me, and I don't tell you my age!

Words to Know

charmant	shahr-mahN	charming
ces personnes	say pehr-sohn	these people
sur	sewr	on; on top of
la photo	lah fo-to	the picture
le garçon	luh gahr-sohN	the boy
la fille	lah feey	the girl
mon petit-fils	mohN puh-tee fees	my grandson
ma petite-fille	mah puh-teet feey	my granddaughter

Remember that an adjective varies in gender (and number) according to the noun it qualifies. Said more simply, if a noun is feminine, you usually add an *e* at the end of the adjective that goes along with it. For example:

- ✔ **un petit appartement** *(aN puh-tee-tah-pahr-tuh-mahN)* (a small apartment)
- ✔ **une grande maison** *(ewn grahNd meh-zohN)* (a big house)

But this does not always work! In French, there is a saying that **l'exception confirme la règle** *(layk-sayp-syohN kohN-feerm lah rehgl)* (the exception confirms the rule). Thus, the feminine of **beau** *(bo)* is **belle** *(behl)* (beautiful). This is just one example of several exceptions.

Did you notice in the preceding dialog, that, in French, you don't ask, "How old are you?" but something like, "What age do you have?" (**Quel âge as-tu?** *[keh-lahzh ah-tew]*) using the verb **avoir** *(ah-vwahr)* (to have), instead of **être** *(ehtr)* (to be). The logical answer is then, for instance, "I have 12 years": **J'ai douze ans** *(zheh doo-zahN)* (I am 12).

When you want to talk about a family as a whole, you may, in English, refer to Mr. and Mrs. Miller as the Millers, or Mr. and Mrs. White as the Whites. This cannot be done in French because proper names do not change, and you may not add an s to mark the plural. So **Monsieur et Madame Texier** *(muh-syuh ay mah-dahm tehk-syay)* are **Les Texier** *(lay tehk-syay)*.

Fun & Games

En quelle saison sommes-nous? (In which season are we?)

Answers:

A._____

B._____

C._____

D._____

Chapter 5

Bon Appétit! Dining Out and Going to the Market

. . . .

Chapter

for your bread and butter — and water, too

restaurant reservations, ordering, and paying the check

ing for food

g comparisons

. . . .

*E*xploring the food and eating habits of another country is one of the most pleasant ways to discover its culture. When the subject is French food and restaurants, this exploration is especially enjoyable. This chapter is undoubtedly the most appetizing and probably one of the most useful if you are planning to visit a French-speaking country or if you just want to impress your date by ordering in French at the hot, new bistro in your town.. Whether you want to eat in a fancy two- or three-star restaurant or eat bread and cheese sitting on a park bench, you need to know how to select, order, and then enjoy (which we promise will be easy)!

All About Meals

What better way to enjoy what you are going to eat than to start with an empty stomach. Then you can say, **"J'ai faim"** *(zheh faN)* (I'm hungry) or **"J'ai soif"** *(zheh swaf)* (I'm thirsty), and the glorious world of French gastronomy is yours!

French food is probably the most famous and the most praised in the world. And you don't have to go to Paris to enjoy it. In the United States, French restaurants and specialty food shops are often very expensive. But just across the border, you can find total satisfaction at reasonable prices in Montreal.

The meals

In the United States, people eat breakfast, lunch, and dinner. Wouldn't it be simple if only three words designated **les repas** *(lay ruh-pah)* (the meals) in all French-speaking countries? Well, it simply isn't so. Québec has kept some of the 17th century French of its first settlers and uses the words that were used then (as do the people in some parts of the French countryside):

✔ The word for "breakfast" is:

  • **le déjeuner** *(luh day-zhuh-nay)* in Québec

  • **le petit déjeuner** *(luh puh-tee day-zhuh-nay)* in France

  • **Le déjeuner** (in Québec) is probably a remnant from the d... when farm workers ate a big hearty meal in early morning... big meal at midday, and only hot soup with bread at the e... day. Then breakfast was more a **déjeuner** (meal) than a **pe... uner** (little meal). Also, the Quebecois are North American... thus more used to a big breakfast than the French are. So, if... meeting someone for **le déjeuner** in Montreal, don't wait unt... lunch time! Unless your hosts invited your for **le brunch** — n... explanation necessary, right? — they won't be expecting you...

✔ The word for "lunch" is:

  • **le dîner** *(luh dee-nay)* in Québec

  • **le déjeuner** *(luh day-zhuh-nay)* in France

✔ The word for "dinner" is:

  • **le souper** *(luh soo-pay)* in Québec

  • **le dîner** *(luh dee-nay)* in France

These nouns are also verbs; to have lunch or dinner is **déjeuner**, **dîner**, or **souper**.

After coming home from school, children enjoy **le goûter** *(luh goo-tay)* (mid-afternoon snack), which usually consists of bread and butter, jam, or chocolate. If you suddenly find yourself hungry between meals, you can always have **un casse-croûte** *(kahs-kroot)* (a snack, *literally:* break the crust) like a crêpe at a stand in Paris, a hot dog sold by a street vendor in Montreal, or anything in between. Even out in the middle of the country, you may be lucky enough to find a café where you can get **une omelette** *(ew-nom-leht)* (an omelet) or **un sandwich** *(aN sahn-dweesh)* (a sandwich).

A note about breakfast

As we mention earlier, a Canadian breakfast looks much like its American or British counterpart. The French breakfast, on the other hand, is more like what hotels call a continental breakfast. Many French don't even eat the famous **croissant** *(krwa-sahN)* with their morning coffee; they're often satisfied with just a quick espresso before boarding the train or the subway. Nowadays, like North American children, many French children have cereal and milk, **les céréales et le lait** *(lay say-ray-ah-lay luh lay)* for breakfast. Still, the traditional French breakfast is usually made up of the following:

- **le café** *(luh kah-fay)* (coffee)

- **le café au lait** *(luh kah-fay o leh)* (coffee with hot milk)

- **le café crème** *(luh kah-fay crehm)* (coffee with a little milk)

- **le thé nature** *(luh tay nah-tewr)* (plain tea)

- **le thé au lait** *(luh tay o leh)* (tea with milk)

- **le thé au citron/le thé citron** *(luh tay o see-trohn/luh tay see-trohn)* (tea with lemon)

- **le pain** *(luh pahN)* (bread)

- **le pain grillé** *(luh pahN gree-yay)* (toast)

- **les tartines** *(lay tahr-teen)* (slices of bread with some kind of spread)

- **le beurre** *(luh buhr)* (butter)

     la margarine *(lah mahr-zhah-reen)* (margarine), not as popular as butter but used nevertheless

- **la confiture** *(lah kohn-fee-tewr)* (jam)

- **le croissant** *(luh krwa-sahN)* (croissant — crescent-shaped)

- **le pain au chocolat** *(luh pan o sho-ko-lah)* (same dough as a croissant, but a different shape and with a chocolate bar inside)

- **le chausson aux pommes** *(luh sho-sohN o pohm)* (applesauce-filled danish)

- **le pain aux raisins** *(luh pahN o ray-zan)* (a sort of raisin bread)

You can find all of these mouth-watering goodies in any **pâtisserie** *(pah-tees-ree)* (confectioner's shop) or **boulangerie** *(boo-lahn-zhree)* (bakery) throughout France. If you aren't sure what something is, you can always simply point to it in the window and be delightfully surprised at whatever delicious confection you discover!

Coffee break

When you order coffee from a café or a restaurant in France, you get **un express** *(aN nehks-prehs)* (an espresso) in a small cup. Only at breakfast do you get a medium-size pot of coffee with hot milk on the side, **un café au lait** *(aN kah-fay o leh)*. Beware, though, this coffee is strong — nothing like the washed-down version people drink on this side of the Atlantic. If you want milk in your coffee at any other time of the day, you have to order **un café crème** *(an kah-fay krehm)*. Of course, you can also order one of the following:

✔ **un double express** *(aN doob-lehks-prehs)* (a double espresso)

✔ **un grand crème** *(aN grahn krehm)* (a large coffee with milk)

> *Note:* Large doesn't mean large in the American sense, but more exactly double, which is the equivalent of two small espresso cups.

✔ **un déca; un décaféiné** *(aN day-kah; aN day-kaf-fay-ee-nay)* (a decaf coffee)

If you're really desperate for those gallons of weak coffee, many large hotels in Paris do offer **un café américain** *(aN kah-fay ah-may-ree-kan)* (American coffee). You can also ask anywhere for **de l'eau chaude** *(duh lo shod)* (hot water) and carry your instant coffee powder with you.

A note about lunch

Until the mid-1960s, lunch was the big meal of the day in France. Fathers came home from work and children came home from school to sit to a four- or five-course meal prepared by the mother. After a two-hour break, everybody went back to their activities. Children still have a two-hour break for lunch, and many of them still go home. But with many women working outside the house, most active people spend much less time on their lunch break and don't have time to come home. They also eat more lightly at midday.

Eating at home: Setting the table

As in North America, the biggest meal of the day in most French homes nowadays is dinner. French families usually eat dinner around 7:30 or 8:00 p.m. Following are the items used to **mettre le couvert** *(meh-truh luh coo-vehr)* (set the table):

✔ **une assiette** *(ewn ah-see-yeht)* (a plate)

✔ **un verre** *(aN vehr)* (a glass)

✔ **les couverts** *(lay koo-vehr)* (silverware)

✔ **une fourchette** *(ewn foor-sheht)* (a fork)

✔ **une cuillère** *(ewn kwee-yehr)* (a spoon)

✔ **un couteau** *(aN koo-to)* (a knife)

✔ **une serviette** *(ewn sehr-vee-yeht)* (a napkin)

✔ **le sel et le poivre** *(luh seh-lay luh pwavr)* (salt and pepper)

After dessert, people move away from the table to have their coffee. They then use the following:

✔ **une tasse** *(ewn tahs)* (a cup)

✔ **une soucoupe** *(ewn soo-koop)* (a saucer)

✔ **une petite cuillère** *(ewn puh-teet kwee-yehr)* (a teaspoon)

✔ **le sucre** *(luh sewkr)* (sugar)

Going Out to a Restaurant

You may not be lucky enough to share a French family's dinner, but the words from the preceding section may come in handy when you go to a restaurant. In most big cities like Paris or Montreal, restaurants line the streets. Many popular or well-known restaurants require a reservation, though — as much as two months in advance in some cases! This section walks you through every aspect of dining out.

French law requires that all restaurants post their menus — with prices — outside, so you won't have any costly surprises when you get in.

Talkin' the Talk

M. Miller is visiting Paris with his wife. They've decided to splurge one evening and go out to a very good restaurant. To find a restaurant, they consulted the **Guide Michelin** *(geed mee-shlahN)*. (The **Guide Michelin** is the restaurant lover's bible. A new edition of this internationally-known red book — the one with stars for food quality and forks for the level of formality — is published annually and can make or break a restaurant overnight.) They've chosen a wonderful little restaurant not far from the famous cathedral, **Notre Dame** *(noh-truh dahm)*. M. Miller gets on the phone and talks to **la réceptionniste** *(lah ray-sehp-syo-neest)* (the receptionist):

M. Miller:	**Bonjour, je voudrais réserver une table.** *bohn-zhoor zhuh voo-dreh ray-zehr-vay ewn tah-bl* Hello, I would like to reserve a table.
Réceptionniste:	**Bien sûr monsieur, pour quand?** *byan sewr muh-syuh poor kahn* Of course, sir, when (would you like to)?
M. Miller:	**Pour samedi prochain.** *poor sahm-dee pro-shan* (For) next Saturday.
Réceptionniste:	**Ah je suis désolée, monsieur, nous sommes fermés le samedi.** *ah zhuh sew-ee day-zo-lay mo-syuh noo sohm fehr-may luh sahm-dee* Oh, I'm sorry, sir, we're closed on Saturdays.
M. Miller:	**Alors vendredi.** *ah-lohr vahn-druh-dee* Friday, then.
Réceptionniste:	**D'accord, pour déjeuner ou pour dîner?** *dah-kohr poor day-zhuh-nay oo poor dee-nay* Very well, for lunch or dinner?
M. Miller:	**Pour dîner.** *poor dee-nay* (For) dinner.
Réceptionniste:	**Pour combien de personnes?** *poor kohn-byand-pehr-sohn* For how many?
M. Miller:	**Pour deux personnes.** *poor duh pehr-sohn* For two people.
Réceptionniste:	**Et à quelle heure?** *ay ah-keh-luhr* And at what time?
M. Miller:	**A huit heures.** *ah wee-tuhr* Eight o'clock.

Réceptionniste:	**C'est à quel nom?**
	seh-tah kehl nohN
	What is the name?

M. Miller:	**Miller, M-I-L-L-E-R.**
	mee-lehr ehm-ee-ehl-ehl-uh-ehr
	Miller, M-I-L-L-E-R.

Réceptionniste:	**Très bien monsieur, une table pour deux personnes vendredi 16 à 20 heures. A bientôt.**
	treh byan muh-syuh ewn tahbl poor duh pehr-sohn vahn-druh-dee seh-zah van-tuhr ah byaN-to)
	Very well, sir, a table for two, Friday the 16th, at 8:00 p.m. See you then.

You may be asked to spell your name when you make any kind of reservation, so be sure to check the letters of the alphabet and their pronunciations in Chapter 1.

Talkin' the Talk

It's now Friday the 16th, and the Millers arrive at the restaurant a few minutes before 8:00 p.m. **Le maître d'hôtel** *(luh meh-truh-do-tehl)* (the head waiter) greets them at the door.

Le maître d'hôtel:	**Bonsoir, monsieur. Bonsoir, madame.**
	bohN-swar muh-syew bohN-swar mah-dahm
	Good evening, sir. Good evening, madame.

M. Miller:	**Bonsoir, nous avons une réservation au nom de Miller.**
	bohN-swar noo-zah-vohN ewn ray-sehr-vah-syohN o nohN duh mee-lehr
	Good evening, we have a reservation under the name of Miller.

Le maître d'hôtel:	**Votre table est là-bas à côté de la fenêtre.**
	voh-truh tahb-leh lah-bah ah ko-tay duh lah fuh-nehtr
	Your table is over there, next to the window.

M. Miller:	**Parfait! Merci.**
	pahr-feh mehr-see
	Perfect! Thank you.

Le maître d'hôtel: **Et voici le menu et la carte des vins.**
ay vwa-see luh muh-new ay lah kahr-tuh
day vahn
Here is the menu and the wine list.

Words to Know

nous sommes fermés	(noo sohm fehr-may)	we're closed
d'accord	(dah-kohr)	okay; all right
c'est à quel nom?	(seh-tah kehl nohn)	what's the name?
là-bas	(lah-bah)	over there
à côté de . . .	(ah ko-tay duh)	next to . . .
la fenêtre	(lah fuh-nehtr)	the window
parfait!	(pahr-feh)	perfect!

Perusing the menu

In most restaurants in France, you may order from a **menu à prix fixe** *(muh-new ah pree feeks)* (set-price menu), or **à la carte** *(ah-lah kahrt)*. There are usually several set menus which you can choose from, depending on the size of your appetite or of your wallet, with a selection of between two and four appetizers, entrées, and desserts. When you order à la carte, you may choose anything. If you want a meal with several courses, ordering from a set menu generally costs less. In many restaurants, the **prix fixe** menu includes an appetizer, a main course, cheese or dessert, a drink (water, wine, or beer), and coffee.

Un apéritif *(aN-nah-pay-ree-teef)* is not just any drink, but more specifically a "drink before the meal." **L'apéritif** *(lah-pay-ree-teef)* (which comes from the Latin verb for "to open") is supposed to open the meal and the appetite. The French like fairly mild alcoholic drinks — kir, sweet wines like sherry or port, and so on — as **apéritif,** but they drink regular wine during the meal and not before as some Americans do. The French may consume hard liquors also, but there is usually less emphasis on sophisticated cocktails than you may notice in the United States. In general, an **apéritif** is reserved for special occasions like family gatherings or dinner parties.

Talking with the waiter

You may want to ask the waiter a few questions about the dishes on the menu. Actually, the more sophisticated the restaurant, the less likely you are to understand its menu! The art of giving unusual names to dishes is almost as elaborate as the art of actually preparing them. And don't think that you're the only one who doesn't understand. The average French restaurant-goer doesn't either. Your best bet is to ask the waiter.

Talkin' the Talk

John and Diana are in a French restaurant. They look at the menu and cannot understand much. So they call the waiter:

John: **Les blancs de volaille au sabayon de poireau, qu'est-ce que c'est?**
lay blahN duh voh-lay o sah-bah-yohN duh pwa-ro kes-kuh-seh
What are the "blancs de volaille au sabayon de poireau"?

The waiter: **Ce sont des blancs de poulet avec une sauce aux poireaux et aux petits légumes.**
suh sohN day blahN duh poo-leh ah-ve-kewn so-so-pwah-ro ay o puh-tee lay-gewm
They're white chicken meat with a leek sauce and small vegetables.

Diana: **C'est bon?**
seh bohN
Is it good?

The waiter: **C'est délicieux. C'est une spécialité de la maison.**
seh day-lee-syuh seh-tewn-spay-syah-lee-tay duh lah meh-zohN
It's delicious. It's a house specialty.

You can also ask for the waiter's recommendation by saying, **"Qu'est-ce que vous recommandez?"** *(kes-kuh voo ruh-koh-mahn-day)* (What do you recommend?)

When you're all set and ready to order, you need to have these phrases handy:

- ✔ **comme entrée, je prends . . .** *(koh-mahn-tray zhuh prahn)* (for the first course, I'll have . . .)
- ✔ **je voudrais . . .** *(zhuh voo-dreh)* (I would like . . .)
- ✔ **pour moi . . .** *(poor mwah)* (Literally: for me . . .)
- ✔ **et ensuite . . .** *(ay ahn-sweet)* (and then . . .)
- ✔ **et comme boisson . . .** *(ay kohm bwa-sohn)* (and to drink . . .)
- ✔ **et comme dessert . . .** *(ay kohm day-sehr)* (and for dessert . . .)

The questions **Qu'est-ce que vous voulez boire?** *(kes-kuh voo voo-lay bwar)* and **Qu'est-ce que vous voulez comme boisson?** *(kes-kuh voo voo-lay kohm bwa-sohn)* both mean "What do you want to drink?" The second question more literally translates, "What do you want as a drink?" The phrase with **"comme"** *(kohm)* (as), followed by a noun, is very commonly used in French, not only for food items, but also each time you are asked to express a preference for something or other. For example, you may ask a friend, **"Qu'est-ce que tu aimes <u>comme</u> films?"** *(kes-kuh tew ehm kohm feelm)* (What kind of movies do you like?)

You no longer address the waiter as **garçon** *(gahr-sohN),* which is considered condescending since it means "boy," but as **monsieur** *(muh-syuh)* (sir). In case it is **une serveuse** *(ewn sehr-vuhz)* a waitress, you say **madame** *(mah-dahm)* (ma'am), or **mademoiselle** *(mahd-mwa-zehl)* (miss), if she is very young.

Check Chapter 1 for the definition of **un faux-ami** *(an fo-zah-mee)* (a false friend).The French word **entrée** *(ahn-tray)* (entrance; way in) is such a word. Because it leads in to the meal, the **entrée** is the first course, not the main course as it is in the United States. What Americans call the entree, the French call **le plat principal** *(luh plah pran-see-pahl)* (the main course).

Understanding what's on the menu

Following is a sample of some of the things you may find in a French restaurant. Remember, different restaurants may give these things different names, so if you're unsure, ask the waiter.

✔ **les entrées** *(lay-zahn-tray)* (appetizers)

- **le pâté/la terrine** *(luh pah-tay/lah teh-reen)* (pâtés; meat paste)
- **le saumon fumé** *(luh so-mohn few-may)* (smoked salmon)
- **la salade verte** *(lah sah-lahd vehrt)* (literally: green salad, salad with lettuce only)
- **les crudités** *(lay krew-dee-tay)* (mixed raw vegetables)

✔ **les viandes** *(lay vyahnd)* (meats):

- **le boeuf** *(luh buhf)* (beef)

  You can order your steak **saignant** *(seh-nyahn)* (rare), **à point** *(ah pwan)* (medium), or **bien cuit** *(byan kwee)* (well done).

- **le veau** *(luh vo)* (veal)
- **le poulet** *(luh poo-leh)* (chicken)
- **le porc** *(luh pohr)* (pork)
- **l'agneau** *(la-nyo)* (lamb)
- **les poissons** *(lay pwa-sohn)* (fish)

✔ **le riz** *(luh ree)* (rice)

✔ **les pâtes** *(lay paht)* (pasta)

What a difference an accent can make! **Le pâté** *(luh pah-tay)* is a meat paste, usually made from pork meat and spices, which is eaten as an appetizer with bread. On the other hand, **les pâtes** *(lay paht)* are the familiar pasta. So watch out for that accent when you order, or you might be surprised.

✔ **les légumes** *(lay lay-gewm)* (vegetables):

- **les pommes de terre** *(lay pohm duh tehr)* (potatoes)
- **les haricots verts** *(lay ah-ree-ko vehr)* (green beans)
- **les petits pois** *(lay puh-tee pwa)* (peas)
- **les champignons** *(lay sham-peen-yohN)* (mushrooms)

✔ **les fromages** *(lay fro-mahzh)* (cheeses)

✔ **les desserts** *(lay deh-sehr)* (dessert):

- **la glace** *(lah glahs)* (ice cream)
- **la crème** *(lah krehm)* (pudding)
- **le gâteau au chocolat** *(luh gah-to o sho-ko-lah)* (chocolate cake)

• **la tarte aux pommes** *(lah tahr-to-pohm)* (apple pie)

The French eat ice-cream and they do eat apple pie too, but they don't eat them together, which is funny, considering that the **"a la mode"** added to apple pie is a French phrase (which means "in fashion," by the way)! French apple pies are also very different from their American counterpart. They are very thin and do not have a top crust. They look more like what Americans would call a tart.

A word about the salad

You don't get a choice of dressing. Salad is served already seasoned with **une vinaigrette** *(ewn vee-neh-greht),* which is a combination of **la moutarde** *(lah moo-tahrd)* (Dijon mustard), **l'huile** *(lew-eel)* (oil), and **le vinaigre** *(luh vee-nehgr)* (vinegar).

What are you "taking" for dinner?

In the case of drink or food, French uses the verb **prendre** *(prahndr)* (to take) instead of **avoir** *(ah-vwahr)* (to have). Following are a couple of examples:

✔ **Pour le petit déjeuner, je prends du pain et de la confiture.** *(poor luh puh-tee day-zhuh-nay zhuh prahn dew pahn ay duh lah kohn-fee-tewr)* (I have bread and jam for breakfast.)

✔ **Moi, je prends le steak frites.** *(mwa zhuh prahn luh stehk freet)* (I'll have the steak with french fries.)

Prendre is an irregular verb:

Conjugation	Pronunciation
je prends	zhuh prahn
tu prends	tew prahn
il/elle prend	eel/ehl prahn
nous prenons	noo pruh-nohn
vous prenez	voo pruh-nay
ils/elles prennent	eel/ehl prehn

Words to Know

les poireaux	lay pwa-ro	leeks
vous voulez . . . ? [formal, plural]	voo voo-lay	Do you want . . . ?
tu veux . . . ? [informal]	tew vuh	Do you want . . . ?
la boisson	lah bwa-sohn	drink
et ensuite . . .	ah ahn-sweet	and then . . .
c'est bon!	seh bohn	It's good!
c'est délicieux!	seh day-lee-syuh	It's delicious!

Talkin' the Talk

Julie *(zhew-lee)*, a young woman from Québec, and her friend Mike, visiting from the United States, are walking up **la rue St Denis** *(lah rew saN duh-nee)* St. Dennis Street after a long morning of sight-seeing in **le vieux Montréal** *(luh vyuh mohn-ray-ahl)* (the old Montreal). They're getting hungry, and the street is lined with restaurants.

Julie: **Je meurs de faim, pas toi?**
           zhuh muhr duh fan pah twa
           I'm starving, aren't you?

Mike: **Moi aussi! Tu veux un sandwich?**
           mwah o-see tew vuh aN sahn-dweesh
           Me too! Do you want a sandwich?

Julie: **Oh non, il y a un tas de bons petits restaurants pas chers ici. Et puis je suis fatiguée.**
           o nohn ee-lee-yah an tah duh bohn puh-tee rehs-to-rahn pah shehr ee-see ay pew-ee zhuh sew-ee fah-tee-gay
           Oh no, there are plenty of good cheap little restaurants here. And I am tired.

Mike: **Bon, d'accord. Alors, on mange dehors!**
bohn dah-kohr ah-loh-rohn mahnzh duh-or
Well, okay. Let's eat outside then!

 After looking at a few places, they settle on a little bistro (which Julie knows well) with a lovely terrace. They sit down and **le serveur** *(luh sehr-vuhr)* (the waiter) brings them the menu.

Le serveur: **Vous voulez boire quelque chose?**
voo voo-lay bwar kehl-kuh shoz
Would you like something to drink?

Julie: **Un verre de vin blanc, s'il vous plaît.**
an vehr duh van blahn seel-voo-play
A glass of white wine, please.

Mike: **Et pour moi, une bière.**
ay poor mwa ewn byehr
And for me, a beer.

A few minutes later, the waiter comes back with the drinks.

Le serveur: **Voilà vos boissons. Vous êtes prêts ?**
vwa-lah vo bwa-sohn voo-zeht preh
Here are your drinks. Are you ready to order?

Julie: **Oui, je voudrais une soupe aux pois et une salade verte.**
wee zhuh voo-dreh ewn soo-po-pwa ay ewn sah-lahd vehrt
Yes, I would like pea soup and a green salad.

Mike: **Moi, je prends la tourtière.**
mwa zhuh pran lah toor-tyehr
I'll have the potpie.

Le serveur: **Et comme boisson, la même chose?**
ay kohm bwa-sohn lah mehm shoz
Would you like the same thing to drink?

Mike: **Oui, merci.**
wee mehr-see
Yes, thank you.

How cheesy!

Most French people eat **le fromage** *(luh fro-mazh)* (cheese) with every meal. France is said to have a different cheese for each day of the year. In fact, France has many sayings about the importance of cheese. For instance,

"Un repas sans fromage est comme une journée sans soleil."

aN ruh-pah san fro-mahzh eh kohm ewn zhoor-nay sahn soh-lay

"A meal without cheese is like a day without sun."

French-speaking people like to emphasize the way they feel. So, instead of simply saying "I am very hungry" or "I am very thirsty," they will tell you that they are dying of hunger or thirst: **Je meurs de faim** *(zhuh muhr duh fan)*, **je meurs de soif** *(zhuh muhr duh swaf)*.

Eating and drinking

Manger *(mahn-zhay)* (to eat) is a regular **-er** verb. (Chapter 1 shows you how to conjugate regular verbs.) **Boire** *(bwahr)* (to drink), however, is another matter. The following table shows you how to conjugate this irregular verb:

Conjugation	*Pronunciation*
je bois	zhuh bwa
tu bois	tew bwa
il/elle boit	eel/ehl bwa
nous buvons	noo bew-vohn
vous buvez	voo bew-vay
ils/elles boivent	eel /ehl bwav

Here's a list of drinks people commonly order in a restaurant:

- **un verre de vin** *(aN vehr duh van)* (a glass of wine)
- **une bouteille de bière** *(ewn boo-tehy duh byehr)* (a bottle of beer)
- **une carafe d'eau** *(ewn kah-rahf do)* (a carafe of water)
- **une tasse de thé** *(ewn tahs duh tay)* (a cup of tea)

French flavor the Canadian way

You can savor the local Quebecois specialties in Montreal restaurants. You may want to try the following if you have a chance to visit:

✔ **La soupe aux pois** *(lah soo-po-pwah)* (yellow pea soup)

✔ **la tourtière** *(lah toor-tyehr)* (a hearty meat pie made from different kinds of meats and chopped potatoes)

✔ **la truite** *(lah trweet)* (trout), for which Québec is famous

✔ **la tarte au sucre** *(lah tahr-to-sewkr)* (maple-sugar pie), a deliciously rich pie made from the famous maple syrup that is Canada's treasure

✔ **le cidre** *(luh seedr)* (alcoholic apple cider) is available in **les brasseries** *(lay brah-sree)* (taverns and cafés)

People seldom order wine by the glass in France. More often they order wine as **un quart** *(aN kahr)* (25cl, or a quarter of a liter), **une demi-bouteille** *(ewn duh-mee boo-tehy)* (33cl) or **une bouteille** *(ewn boo-tehy)* (75cl). They order the house wine in **une carafe** *(ewn kah-rahf)* or **un pichet** *(ewn pee-sheh)* (a jug).

You usually don't have water on the table unless you say, **"Une carafe d'eau, s'il vous plaît"** *(ewn kah-rahf do seel-voo-play)* (a pitcher of water, please). Many people prefer bottled water and ask for it by its brand name, **une bouteille d'Evian, de Vittel,** or **de Perrier** *(ewn boo-tehy day-vyahN duh vee-tehl* or *duh peh-ryay).*

Finishing the meal

In France, don't expect the waiter to come to you with the check if you haven't asked for it. To bring the check before you ask is considered pushy and impolite. Call the waiter when you're ready. In the meantime, sit back and relax.

In France, the tax and a 15 percent tip are included in the price list: **le pour-boire est compris** *(luh poor-bwar eh kohn-pree)* (the tip is included). What you see is what you get. Of course, you may tip extra if you so desire, especially in a very good restaurant, but in cafés and ordinary restaurants, you don't have to.

In Canada, a tax is added to your check and the waiter expects to be tipped in addition (about 15 percent).

Le pourboire *(luh poor-bwar)* (the tip) is a funny word in French. It literally means "in order to drink." This very old word dates from the 17th century when it was customary to give a tip so the recipient could go and buy himself a drink (alcoholic supposedly). The name has remained, but its function has changed; today many waiters and theater ushers are paid only with tips.

Talkin' the Talk

Julie and Mike are thoroughly enjoying their meal and relaxing when the waiter comes along.

Le serveur: **Vous voulez un dessert?**
voo voo-lay aN deh-sehr
Would you like dessert?

Julie: **Non, merci. Deux cafés seulement et l'addition.**
nohn mehr-see duh kah-fay suhl-mahn ay lah-dee-syohn
No, thank you, just two coffees and the check.

The waiter comes back with the check, and Mike takes out his credit card.

Mike: **Vous prenez les cartes de crédit?**
voo pruh-nay lay kahrt duh cray-dee
Do you take credit cards?

Le serveur : **Bien sûr, monsieur.**
byaN seur muh-syah
Of course, sir.

CULTURAL WISDOM

Lighting up

In most of Europe, smoking in restaurants is still common practice, and France is no exception in spite of a law that was passed some years ago restricting smoking in public places. More and more restaurants, especially the large ones, have a smoking and a non-smoking section, but it's far from the norm. In most tiny places where the next table almost touches yours, be prepared to see — and smell — your neighbor lighting a cigarette while you are eating.

Words to Know

un tas de . . .	aN tah duh	a lot of . . .
cher/pas cher	shehr/pah shehr	expensive/cheap
fatigué	fah-tee-gay	tired
d'accord	dah-kohr	all right; okay
dehors	duh-ohr	outside
le serveur	luh sehr-vuhr	the waiter
la serveuse	lah sehr-vuhz	the waitress
quelque chose	kehl-kuh shoz	something
le vin blanc	luh van blahn	white wine
le vin rouge	luh van roozh	red wine
la bière	lah byehr	beer
l'eau	lo	water
vous êtes prêts?	voo-zeht preh	Are you ready?
la même chose	lah mehm shoz	the same thing
l'addition	lah-dee-syohn	the check
le pourboire	luh poor-bwar	the tip
laisser un pourboire	leh-say an poor-bwar	to leave a tip
la carte de crédit	lah kahr-tuh duh cray-dee	credit card
accepter	ah-ksehp-tay	to accept
manger	mahn-zhay	to eat
boire	bwar	to drink

Finding the restrooms

Before leaving the restaurant, you may want to visit the restroom, in which case you ask **"Où sont les toilettes, s'il vous plaît?"** *(oo sohn lay twah-leht seel voo-pleh)*. In French restaurants, the restrooms are usually located **en bas** *(ahn bah)* (downstairs) by the telephone booths. Don't forget to take some change — usually a 1 franc piece — along with you; you often have to pay to get in! In most places, the pictogram is self-explanatory, but you may also see **Dames** *(dahm)* (women) or **Hommes** *(ohm)* (men) written on the door.

An Article on Articles

In French, a noun is almost always preceded by a little word called an article that tells you whether the noun is masculine, feminine, singular, or plural. **Le** *(luh)*, **la** *(lah)*, **l'** *(ehl ah-pohs-trohf)*, and **les** *(leh)* are called definite articles because they refer to an object or a person already mentioned, like "the" does in English. **Le** refers to a masculine object, **la** to a feminine object, and **l'** to an object starting with a vowel, which can be masculine or feminine. **Les** is the common plural form.

The definite article also accompanies nouns that are used in a general meaning. *Note:* English has no article in that case. For example, in English you say "coffee" or "love," but French speakers say **le café** *(luh kah-fay)* or **l'amour** *(lah-moor)*.

Un *(aN)*, **une** *(ewn)*, and **des** *(deh)* refer to undertermined objects, just like "a" does in English. These words are called indefinite articles. In the singular, French has, of course, a masculine form (**un**), a feminine form (**une**), and a plural common form (**des**). Following are some examples of how French speakers use indefinite articles:

- ✔ **Paris est une grande ville. La ville est belle.** *(pah-ree eh-tewn grahnd veel lah vee-leh behl)* (Paris is a big city. The city is beautiful.)

- ✔ **Je voudrais un café. Le café est bon.** *(zhuh voo-dreh-zaN kah-fay luh kah-fay eh bohn)* (I would like a cup of coffee. The coffee is good.)

- ✔ **Il y a des maisons dans la rue. Les maisons sont rouges.** *(ee-lee-yah day may-zohn dahn lah rew lay meh-zohn sohn roozh)* (There are houses on the street. The houses are red.)

Table 5-1 lists the variations of definite and indefinite articles in French.

Table 5-1	Definite and Indefinite Articles in French		
Masculine	*Feminine*	*Vowel*	*Plural*
le	la	l'	les
un	une	un/une	des
du	de la	de l'	des

The French language has a specific article that refers to a part of something as opposed to the whole. You can translate this article as "some" or sometimes "a piece of." Sound complicated?

As you may guess, the article has a masculine form **du** *(dew),* a feminine form **de la** *(duh lah),* and a plural form **des** *(deh).* You also have a singular form when the following noun starts with a vowel **de l'** *(duhl)* Here are a few examples:

- ✔ **Je voudrais du pain et du fromage.** *(zhuh voo-dreh dew pan ay dew fro-mahzh)* (I would like [some] bread and [some] cheese.)

- ✔ **Si tu as soif, bois de l'eau!** *(see tew ah swaf bwa duh lo)* (If you are thirsty, drink (some)water.)

- ✔ **Il mange souvent de la salade.** *(eel mahnzh soo-vahn duh lah sah-lahd)* (He often eats salad.)

Buying Food at the Market

Outdoor markets are a delight. They're especially nice in small, country villages, where you can enjoy the local fare and delight in the noises, smells, and accents. But big cities have wonderful markets, too. Certain Paris districts have a market twice a week in the morning, rain or shine. Montréal is famous for its outdoor all-day markets during the summer months. The largest places and many small town squares also have **les halles** *(lay ahl)* (an indoor market). What better way to try out your French? After all, you can point to what you want and maybe learn the right word from a friendly vendor.

Vendors in an outdoor market sell almost everything. In many of them, you can even find clothes, shoes, kitchen utensils, and, of course, flowers. Here's a brief list of things you may find:

✔ **la viande** *(lah vyahnd)* (meat)

✔ **le poisson** *(luh pwa-sohn)* (fish)

✔ **les fruits** *(lay frwee)* (fruit)

- **la pomme** *(lah pohm)* (apple)

- **la banane** *(lah banaN)* (banana)

- **la poire** *(lah pwar)* (pear)

- **la pêche** *(lah pehsh)* (peach)

- **l' orange [f.]** *(lor ahnzh)* (orange)

- **la fraise** *(lah frehz)* (strawberry)

✔ **les légumes** *(lay lay-gewm)* (vegetables)

- **la laitue** *(lah leh-tooeh)* (lettuce)

- **la tomate** *(lay to-maht)* (tomato)

- **la carotte** *(lah kah-roht)* (carrot)

- **l'oignon [m.]** *(loyhn-ohN)* (onion)

✔ **la fleur** *(lah fluhr)* (flower)

Talkin' the Talk

Friday morning is **le jour du marché** *(luh joor dew mahr-shay)* (market day). **Madame Arnaud** *(mah-dah-mahr-no)* takes her nephew **Thibaud** *(tee-bo)* along with her to go shopping at the local outdoor market.

Mme Arnaud: **Qu'est-ce que tu aimes comme fruits?**
kes-kuh tew ehm kohm frwee
What kind of fruit do you like?

Thibaud: **Tous! Mais à cette saison, je préfère les pêches.**
toos meh ah seht seh-zohn zhuh pray-fehr lay pesh
All of them, but at this time of year, I prefer peaches.

Mme Arnaud : **Est-ce qu'il y a des pêches ici?**
ehs-kee-lee-yah day peh-shee-see
Are there peaches here?

Thibaud :	**Oui, mais là-bas, elles sont plus belles et moins chères.**
	wee meh lah-bah ehl sohn plew beh-lay mwan shehr
	Yes, but over there, they're nicer and cheaper.

Madame Arnaud and **Thibaud** wait in line at the fruit stand. When their turn comes, **Madame Arnaud** addresses **le vendeur** *(luh vahn-duhr)* (the vendor).

Mme Arnaud:	**Donnez-moi un kilo de pêches s'il vous plaît.**
	doh-nay mwa ewn kee-lo duh pesh seel-voo play
	Give me two pounds [literally: 1 kilogram] of peaches please.

Le vendeur:	**Choisissez!**
	shwa-zee-say
	Take your pick!

Mme Arnaud:	**Celle-ci . . . celle-là . . .**
	sehl-see sehl-lah
	This one here . . . that one there . . .

Le vendeur:	**Voilà madame, et avec ça?**
	vwa-lah mahdahm ay ah-vehk sah
	Here you are, ma'am, anything else?

Mme Arnaud:	**C'est tout. Ça fait combien?**
	seh too sah feh kohn-byan
	That's all. How much is it?

Le vendeur:	**Huit francs.**
	ew-ee frahn
	Eight francs.

Talking about weights and measures

French-speaking countries use the metric system. The basic unit of weight is the gram and you usually buy fruit, vegetables, or meat in multiples of the basic gram:

- **un gramme** *(aN gram* [1g.]) (1lb. = 453.60 g)

- **un kilogramme/un kilo** *(aN kee-lo-grahm/aN kee-lo)* (1kg = 1000 g, about 2.2 lb.)

- **une livre** *(ewn leevr)* (a pound = 500 g, about 1.1lb.)

As far as liquid measures go, the basic unit is **le litre** *(luh leetr)* (the liter), which equals 1.06 quarts in the United States. A liter is equal to 100 cl, **centilitres** *(sahn-tee-leetr)* (centiliters).

Making comparisons

To make a comparison between two objects or two people, the French language uses the following for all adjectives and adverbs, whether long or short:

- ✔ **plus . . . que** *(plew . . . kuh)* (more . . . than)
- ✔ **moins . . . que** *(mwan . . . que)* (less . . . than)
- ✔ **aussi . . . que** *(o-see . . . kuh)* (as . . . as)

Here are a few examples:

- ✔ **La France est moins grande que le Canada.** *(lah frahn-seh mwan grahnd kuh luh kah-nah-dah)* (France is smaller than Canada.)
- ✔ **On mange plus souvent des fruits en été qu'en hiver.** *(ohn mahnzh plew soo-vahn day frwuh-ee ahn-nay-tay kahn-nee-vehr)* (One eats fruit more often in summer than in winter.)
- ✔ **Les poires sont aussi chères que les pêches.** *(lay pwahr sohN-to-see shehr kuh lay pehsh)* (Pears are as expensive as peaches.)

You may not use the "plus" construction for the adjective **bon** *(bohN)* (good). Just as in English, it has its own form, **meilleur** *(meh-yuhr)* better.

> **Les fruits du marché sont meilleurs que les fruits du supermarché.** *(lay frew-ee dew mahr-shay sohN meh-yuhr kuh lay frew-ee dew sew-pehr-mahr-shay)* (Fruit at the market is better than fruit at the supermarket.)

Words to Know

tous	toos	all of them
mais	meh	but
là-bas	lah-bah	over there
donnez-moi	do-nay-mwa	give me
celui-ci [m]/celle-ci [f]	suh-lwee-see/sehl-see	this one
celui-là [m]/celle-là [f]	suh-lwee-lah/sehl-lah	that one
voilà	vwah-lah	there you go
et avec ça?	ay ah-vahk sah	anything else?
c'est tout	seh too	that's all
ça fait combien ?	sah feh kohn-byan	how much is it?
ça fait 10 francs	sah feh dee frahn	it costs 10 francs

Getting to know a few useful verbs for the market

When shopping, you frequently use the verbs **acheter et vendre** *(ah-shuh-tay ay vahndr)* (to buy and to sell). **Acheter** is a regular verb with a slight irregularity: **Il achète** *(ee-la-sheht)* (He buys).

Vendre is an irregular verb with the following conjugation:

Conjugation	Pronunciation
je vends	zhuh vahn
tu vends	tew vahn
il/elle vend	eel/ehl vahn
nous vendons	noo vahn-dohn
vous vendez	voo vahn-day
ils/elles vendent	eel/ehl vahnd

Aimer *(ay-may)* (to like; to love) is a very important verb for shopping, and as a regular **-er** verb, it's easy to conjugate.

Préférer *(pray-fay-ray)* (to prefer) is also an **-er** verb but with a slight irregularity: The **je**, **tu**, **il**, and **ils** forms make the second syllable sound like *(eh)* instead of *(ay)*. For example, **je préfère** *(zhuh pray-fehr)*.

Donner *(do-nay)* (to give) is another regular **-er** verb.

Choisir *(shwa-zeer)* (to choose) is a regular **-ir** verb. (See Appendix A for conjugating regular **-ir** verbs.)

Going to the Supermarket and the Food Stores

When you don't have time to go to the outdoor market, or you can't find what you need at the little store, the supermarket comes in handy. France has some huge supermarkets that line the highways as you enter a city. Some of them are so large that they are called **hypermarchés** *(ee-pehr-mahr-shay)* (hypermarkets) instead of **supermarchés** *(sew-pehr-mahr-shay)* (supermarkets). Here, you can find absolutely everything: food, clothes, computers, large appliances, and sometimes even cars! They're certainly convenient, but if you visit France and have some time on your hands, go discover the little food stores. You're sure to enjoy them.

Following are some of **les petits magasins** *(lay puh-tee mah-gah-zaN)* (the little [food] stores):

- **la boulangerie** *(lah boo-lahn-zhree)* (the bakery) which sells bread and pastries
- **la pâtisserie** *(lah pah-tees-ree)* (the confectioner's shop) which specializes in cakes and pastries, usually of a higher quality and does not sell bread
- **la boucherie** *(lah boo-shree)* (the butcher shop)
- **la charcuterie** *(lah shahr-kew-tree)* (butcher shop that specializes in pork and prepared foods)
- **l'épicerie** *(lay-pees-ree)* (the grocery store [more like a general store])
- **la crèmerie** *(lah kraym-ree)* (the dairy product and cheese store)
- **le marchand de fruits et légumes** *(luh mahr-shan duh frew-ee zay lay-gewm)* (the produce vendor)

Here are examples of this vocabulary in action:

> ✔ **On achète du pain à la boulangerie.** *(oh-nah-sheht dew pan ah lah boo-lahn-zhree)* (Bread is bought at the bakery.)

> ✔ **L'épicier vend du café, du thé et des épices.** *(lay-pee-syay vahn dew kah-fay dew tay ay day-zay-pees)* (The grocer sells coffee, tea, and spices.)

A fairly large number of people — mostly older — still go shopping for food every morning in France. They walk from store to store buying everything they need for the day's meals. It's also not unusual for the French — especially in big cities — to buy bread twice a day. French bread is made without preservatives and doesn't keep well, so buying in small quantities more often makes better sense. Plus, French bread tastes so good when it's freshly baked!

Fun & Games

Identify as many fruits and vegetables **du marché** *(dew mahr-shay)* (at the market) as possible:

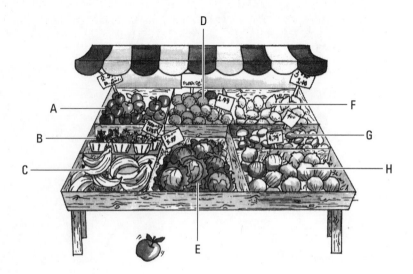

A. _____

B. _____

C. _____

D. _____

E. _____

F. _____

G. _____

H. _____

Answer key: A. les pommes; B. les fraises; C. les bananes; D. les oranges; E. les laitues; F. les citrons; G. les champignons; H. les oignons.

You have just ordered a glass of water, coffee, pea soup, salad, steak, and potatos for lunch at a charming café. Identify everything on the table to make sure your waiter hasn't forgotten anything:

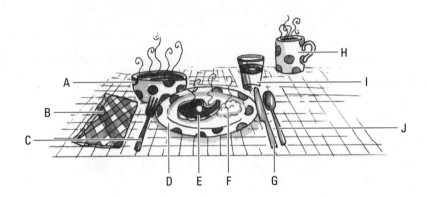

A. _____

B. _____

C. _____

D. _____

E. _____

F. _____

G. _____

H. _____

I. _____

J. _____

Chapter 6

Shopping Made Easy

. . . .

In This Chapter

▶ "Just looking" at the store

▶ Asking for help

▶ Trying things on

▶ Recognizing sizes, colors, materials, items

▶ Using superlatives

. . . .

*L*e shopping *(luh shoh-peeng)* — what a fun thing to do when you are in a foreign country! Of course, you want to bring back that special souvenir, that little typical something or other. And think of those French perfumes, those lovely designer scarves or handbags, the wonderful French songs that you absolutely must have on a CD or cassette. Beware though — these things don't come cheap! But, after all, **une fois n'est pas coutume** *(ewn fwa neh pah koo-tewm)* (one occurrence does not make a rule). You are here in a shopper's paradise, in Paris, Montreal, Geneva, or Brussels, and you may not come back for a long time, so go ahead, enjoy, and shop till you drop. These cities are not usually places where you will make a good deal or be happy because you have bargained to death. But you will have the best of the best.

Going to Stores

If you don't know where to start or even if you don't have the slightest idea of what you want to bring back, **un grand magasin** *(ewn grahN mah-gah-zaN)* (a department store), may be a good choice. The two most famous ones in Paris, **le Printemps** *(luh pran-tahN)* and **les Galeries Lafayette** *(lay gah-lree lah-fah-yeht)* are located a couple of blocks from each other on the same boulevard. How convenient! You are likely to find something you want in either one. In my opinion, they are very similar, but many people swear by one or the other. In Montreal's Ogilvy's, you can find a collection of designers' boutiques which rival anything in Paris or London, and Eaton's, also on the rue Sainte-Catherine (St. Catherine Street), is the largest department store in the city. These are just a few examples of what is available in either city.

Of course, department stores are not the only places you can go to shop. They are just the easiest, because everything is there together and you can browse without being bothered. You can also do this easily in one of the many shopping malls, **les centres commerciaux** *(lay sahN-truh ko-mehr-syo).* These malls, which are a fairly recent phenomenon in Europe, are developing ouside of big cities, but also more and more inside them and are very popular with the locals. They give you the advantage of medium-size boutiques (often part of a chain) with the ease of having everything located in one spot. Last but not least, don't forget that the French language has given to the world the word **boutique** *(boo-teek).* From simple to fancy, from trinkets to designer clothes, they offer everything. But your browsing may be hindered by the over-attentive presence of the salesclerk. On the other hand, you are likely to receive good professional advice.

Here's a list of other types of stores and the items you can find in them:

✔ **A la librairie, on achète des livres**. *(ah lah lee-breh-ree ohN-nah-sheht day leevr)* (At the bookstore, you buy books.)

✔ **A la bijouterie, on achète des bijoux.** *(ah lah bee-zhoot-ree ohN nah-sheht day bee-zhoo)* (At the jewelry store, you buy jewels.)

✔ **Au bureau de tabac** (France), **à la tabagie** (Québec), **on achète des cigarettes, des timbres et des cartes postales.** *(o bew-ro duh tah-bah / ah lah tah-bah-zhee ohN-nah-sheht day see-gah-reht day taN-bray day kahrt pohs-tahl)* (At the tobacco shop, you buy cigarettes, stamps, and postcards.)

✔ **A la dépanneuse** (Québec), **on trouve de tout!** *(ah lah day-pah-nuh-zohN troov duh too)* (At the convenience store, you can find everything!)

Dépanner *(day-pah-nay)* means "to help out" and people in France and in Québec understand it that way, but use it for different purposes. In Québec, **une dépanneuse** *(ewn day-pah-nuhz)* is one of those convenience stores which are open all the time and where you can stop when you run out of bread or milk. In France, **une dépanneuse** *(ewn day-pah-nuhz)* is a tow-truck. They both help you out, don't they?

When you decide to go shopping, you probably want to call ahead to find out about the store's hours. These questions can help:

✔ **A quelle heure ouvrez-vous/fermez-vous?** *(ah keh-luhr oo-vray-voo/fehr-may-voo)* (At what time do you open/close?)

✔ **Quelles sont vos heures d'ouverture?** *(kehl sohN vo-zuhr doo-vehr-tewr)* (What are your opening hours?)

✔ **Etes-vous ouverts le dimanche?** *(eht voo oovehr luh dee-mahNsh)* (Are you open on Sundays?)

Pay attention to opening hours. Canada is pretty much the same as the United States. But in France, all department stores and malls are closed on Sundays. Many stores — mostly food stores — close at lunch time, especially outside of big cities, though this is less and less the case. Most stores are closed on Mondays, but department stores usually stay open.

Just browsing

So you have found out when the department store is open and decide to go take a look; no buying, just browsing. You start on the first floor, **le rez-de-chaussée** *(luh ray duh sho-say)* and go wandering between the stands, **les rayons** *(lay ray-yohN)* smelling this, touching that until you hear a saleslady, **une vendeuse** *(ewn vahN-duhz)* in back of you asking:

> **Je peux vous aider?** *(zhuh pew voo-zayday)* (Can I help you?)

At this point, you are really enjoying yourself and want to go on doing so without being bothered. So you answer:

> **Non, merci, je regarde seulement.** *(nohN mehr-see zhuh ruh-gahrd suhl-mahN)* (No thank you, I am just looking.)

Getting around the store

Time to get more serious! You have that long shopping list to get through. But this store is a maze! Fortunately, here is the information counter, **les renseignements** *(lay rahN-seh-nyuh-mahN)*. There will most likely be someone there who speaks English, but who cares? If you know the following phrases, you can certainly find your way around.

- ✔ **Pardon, madame où sont les parfums?** *(pahr-dohN mah-dahm oo sohN lay pahr-faN)* (Excuse me, ma'am, where are the perfumes?)
- ✔ **Ici, au rez-de chaussée.** *(ee-see o ray duh sho-say)* (Here, on the ground floor.)
- ✔ **Les vêtements pour dames, s'il vous plaît?** *(lay veht-mahN poor dahm seel voo pleh)* (Ladies'clothes, please.)
- ✔ **C'est au troisième étage.** *(seh-to trwa-zyeh-may-tazh)* (It is on the third floor.)
- ✔ **Excusez-moi, je cherche les compact disques.** *(eks-kew-zay-mwa zhuh shehrsh lay kohN-pakt deesK)* (Excuse me, I am looking for CDs.)
- ✔ **Ils sont au sous-sol, à côté des livres.** *(eel sohN-to-soo-soh-lah-ko-tay day leevr)* (They are in the basement, next to the books.)

Many ways to ask, many possible answers . . .

Getting assistance

You have reached the floor where you want to go, by escalator, **les escaliers roulants** *(lay-zehs-kah-lyay roo-lahN)*, or elevator, **l'ascenseur** *(lah-sahN-suhr)*. You start looking around, but now you really need help. It's time to look for a clerk. (Unfortunately, often at those times they have all disappeared!)

- ✔ **Pouvez-vous m'aider s'il vous plaît ?** *(poo-vay voo may-day seel-voo-play)* (Can you help me please?)

- ✔ **Je voudrais un renseignement** *(zhuh voo-dreh aN rahN-seh-nyuh-mahN)* (I would like some information.)

- ✔ **Je cherche . . .** *(zhuh shehrsh)* (I am looking for . . .)

The French language does not make a distinction between the notions represented by "I can" and "I may." They are both translated by **je peux** *(zhuh puh)*. The verb is **pouvoir** *(poo-vwar)* and it is irregular. You conjugate the present tense as follows:

Conjugation	*Pronunciation*
Je peux	zhuh puh
Tu peux	tew puh
Il/elle peut	eel/ehl puh
Nous pouvons	noo poo-vohN
Vous pouvez	voo-poo-vay
Ils/Elles peuvent	eel/ehl puhv

This verb **pouvoir** is always followed by an infinitive. Notice that when there is an object pronoun, it is placed between the conjugated form of **pouvoir** and the infinitive:

- ✔ **Est-ce que vous pouvez <u>me</u> renseigner ?** *(ehs-kuh voo poo-vay muh rahN-say-nyay)* (Can you give <u>me</u> some information?)

- ✔ **Je peux <u>l'</u>essayer** *(zhuh puh lay-say-yay)* (I can try <u>it</u> on.)

For more on object pronouns, go to Chapter 13.

Talkin' the Talk

Cécile is in a department store with her friend Marie. They are looking at dresses. Cécile has spotted one that she likes. The saleslady, **la vendeuse** (lah vahN-duhz) comes to them:

La vendeuse: **Je peux vous aider, mesdames?**
zhuh puh voo-zay-day may-dahm
Can I help you, ladies?

Cécile: **Oui, s'il vous plaît. Avez-vous cette robe en 36?**
wee seel voo play ah-vay-voo seht roh-bahN trahNt-sees
Yes, please. Do you have this dress in size 36?

La vendeuse: **Attendez un instant. Oui, nous l'avons. La voilà.**
ah-tahN-day aN-naNs-tahN wee noo lah-vohN lah vwah-lah
Wait a moment. Yes, we have it. There it is.

Cécile: **Est-ce que je peux l'essayer?**
ehs-kuh zhuh puh lay-say-yay
May I try it on?

La vendeuse: **Mais bien sûr, madame. Les cabines d'essayage sont au fond à gauche.**
meh byaN sewr mah-dahm lay kah-been day-say-yahzh sohN-to-fohN ah gosh
But, of course ma'am. The fitting-rooms are in the back on the left.

A few minutes later, Cécile gets out of the fitting room with the dress on and wants her friend's opinion.

Cécile: **Qu'est-ce que tu en penses?**
kes-kuh tew ahN pahNs
What do you think of it?

Mary: **Je ne sais pas . . . elle est un peu trop grande, je crois.**
zhuhn-seh pah . . . eh-leh-taN puh tro grahNd zhuh crwah
I don't know . . . it's a little too big, I think.

Cécile: **Moi, je trouve qu'elle ne me va pas du tout.**
mwa zhuh troov kehl nuh muh vah pah dew too
I think it does not fit me at all.

Est-ce que vous l'avez en plus petit?
ehs-kuh voo lah-vay ahN plew puh-tee
Do you have it in a smaller size?

La vendeuse: **Non, je suis désolée; c'est la plus petite taille.**
nohN zhuh swee day-zo-lay seh lah plew puh-teet ta-y
No, I am sorry, it is the smallest size.

Cécile: **Tant pis!**
tahN pee
Too bad!

Words to know

attendez un instant	ah-tahN-day aN-naNs-tahN	wait a moment
aider	ay-day	to help
essayer	ay-say-yay	to try
les cabines d'essayage	lay kah-been day-say-yazh	the fitting rooms
au fond	o fohN	in the back
à gauche	ah gosh	on the left
à droite	ah drwaht	on the right
Je trouve/pense	zhuh troov/pahNs	I think
un peu	aN puh	a little
trop	tro	too much
pas du tout	pah dew too	not at all
Tant pis	tahN pee	too bad

Shopping for Clothes

Clothes shopping involves all kinds of issues, including finding the right size, finding the right material, and finding the right color.

Finding the right fit

In Canada, clothes sizes are the same as in the United States. In Europe, you may find different ways of measuring, depending on the country. Here are the rough equivalents for sizes of women's clothes:

Canadian and U.S. sizes	6	8	10	12	14	16	18	20
French sizes		36	38	40	42	44	46	48	50

For men's jacket and suit sizes, use the following approximate conversions:

Canadian and U.S. sizes	38	40	42	44	46	48	50
French sizes		48	50	52	54	56	58	60

Of course, if everything else fails, you always have the possiblity of asking for **petit** *(puh-tee)*, **moyen** *(mwa-yaN)*, **large** *(lahrzh)*, or **extra-large** *(ehks-trah lahrzh)* small, medium, large, or extra-large.

In French, size is **la taille** *(lah ta-y)*. But, often, you don't even have to say the word, as in these examples:

- **Je fais du 36** *(zhuh feh dew trahNt-sees)* (I am a [size] 36.)
- **Je voudrais essayer une robe en 40** *(zhuh voo-dreh ay-say-yay ewn roh-bahN kah-rahNt)* (I would like to try a dress in [size] 40.)
- **Est-que vous l'avez en plus petit?** *(ehs-kuh voo lah-vay ahN plew puh-tee)* (Do you have it in a small[er size]?)

English has only one word for clothes and shoe sizes, but French has two words: **la taille** works for height and clothes, and **la pointure** *(lah pwaN-tewr)* is for shoes.

For women's shoe sizes, use this chart:

Canadian and U.S. sizes	5	6	7	8	9	10
French sizes	36	37	38	39	40	41

Here are the size conversions for men's shoes:

Canadian and U.S. sizes	7.5	8	8.5	9	9.5	10	10.5	11	11.5	12
French sizes		38	39	40	41	42	43	44	45	46	47

Use the following phrases to describe how something fits:

- ✔ **Ça me va** *(sah muh vah)* (It fits me.) This phrase varies, of course according to the person you are talking about. You can say:

- ✔ **Ça te va bien** *(sah tuh vah byaN)* (It fits you well.) [informal]

- ✔ **Ça lui va mal** *(sah lwee vah mahl)* (It fits him/her poorly.)

- ✔ **Ça ne nous va pas** *(sah nuh noo vah pah)* (It does not fit us.)

- ✔ **Ça vous va très bien** *(sah voo vah treh byan)* (It fits you very well.) [formal]

- ✔ **Ça ne leur va pas du tout** *(sah nuh luhr vah pah dew too)* (It does not fit them at all.)

Talkin' the Talk

Vincent is looking for a sports jacket. He enters one of the little boutiques in a **chic** *(sheek)* area of the city, **une boutique de vêtements pour hommes** *(ewn boo-teek duh veht-mahN poo-rohm)* (a men's clothing store). At this time of year, many clothes are on sale (**en solde** *[ahN sohld]*). He is immediately greeted by a clerk and presents his request.

Vincent: **Je cherche une veste.**
zhuh shehr-shewn vehst
I am looking for a jacket.

Le vendeur: **Quel genre de veste voulez-vous, monsieur, un blazer, un veston habillé?**
kehl zhahNr duh vehst voo-lay-voo muh-syuh aN blah-zehr aN vehs-tohN ah-bee-yay
What type of jacket do you want, sir, a blazer, a dressed-up suit jacket?

Vincent: **Non plutôt une veste de sport.**
nohN plew-to ewn vehs-tuh duh spohr
No, rather a sports jacket.

Le vendeur: **En quelle taille?**
ahN kehl tay
In what size?

Vincent: **En général, je porte du 50.**
ahN zhay-nay-rahl zhuh pohr-tuh dew saN-kahNt
Usually, I wear a [size] 50.

Le vendeur: **Nous avons ce modèle, ou celui-ci en pure laine.**
noo-zah-vohN suh moh-dehl oo suh-lwee-see ahN
pewr lehn
We have this style or this one in pure wool.

Vincent: **Je préfère une couleur plus foncée.**
zhuh pray-fehr ewn koo-luhr plew fohN-say
I prefer a darker color.

Vincent chooses a jacket that he tries on.

Le vendeur: **Oh, celle-ci vous va à merveille! Et elle est très à la mode.**
o sehl-see voo vah ah mehr-veh-y ay eh-leh treh-zah
lah mohd
Oh this one looks great on you! And it's very much in fashion.

Vincent: **Oui, vous avez raison et elle est en solde! Alors je la prends.**
wee voo-zah-vay ray-zohN ay eh-leh-tahN sohld ah-
lohr zhuh lah prahN
Yes, you're right, and it's on sale! Then I'll take it.

Words to Know

une veste	ewn vehst	a jacket (for men and women)
un veston	an vehs-tohN	a man's suit jacket
un blazer	an blah-zehr	a blazer
porter	pohr-tay	to wear
en laine	ahN lehn	made of wool
la couleur	lah koo-luhr	the color
foncé	fohN-say	dark
clair	klehr	light-colored
Ça vous va à merveille	sah voo vah ah mehr-veh-y	It looks great on you
C'est à la mode	seh-tah lah mohd	It's in fashion
la caisse	lah kehs	the cash-register
les soldes	lay sohld	sales [France]
l'aubaine	lo-behn	sales [Quebec]
le magasin	luh mah-gah-zaN	the store

Clothing materials

When talking about materials, you use **en** after the verb or **de** after the noun, as in these examples:

▸ **Cette veste est <u>en</u> laine. C'est une veste <u>de</u> laine.** *(seht vehs-teh-tahN lehn seh-tewn vehst-uh duh lehn)* (This jacket is [made] of wool. It is a wool jacket.)

✔ **Je voudrais un foulard <u>de</u> soie.** *(zhuh voo-dreh aN foo-lahr duh swa)* (I would like a silk scarf.)

✔ **Est-ce que ces chaussures sont <u>en</u> cuir?** *(ehs-kuh say sho-sewr sohN-tahN kweer?)* (Are these shoes [made of] leather?)

By the way, here's a list of clothing materials, just in case you need to know them:

✔ **la laine** *(lah lehn)* (wool)

✔ **la soie** *(lah swah)* (silk)

✔ **le coton** *(luh ko-tohN)* (cotton)

✔ **le velours côtelé** *(luh vuh-loor kot-lay)* (corduroy) [France]

✔ **le corduroy** *(luh kohr-dew-rwah)* (corduroy) [Québec]

✔ **le cuir** *(luh kweer)* (leather)

Getting dressed

Here's a list of **vêtements pour dames** *(veht-mahN poor dahm)* (women's clothes):

✔ **une robe** *(ewn rohb)* (a dress)

✔ **une jupe** *(ewn zhewp)* (a skirt)

✔ **un tailleur** *(aN tah-yuhr)* (a suit)

✔ **une veste*** *(ewn vehst)* (a jacket)

✔ **un pantalon*** *(an pahN-tah-lohN)* (slacks)

✔ **un jean*** *(ewn dzheen)* (jeans)

✔ **un manteau** *(aN mahN-to)* (a coat)

✔ **un imperméable*** *(aN-naN-pehr-may-ahbl)* (a raincoat)

✔ **un chemisier** *(an shuh-mee-zyay)* (a blouse)

✔ **un foulard** *(an foo-lahr)* (a scarf)

✔ **une chemise de nuit** *(ewn shuh-meez duh nwee)* (a night gown)

✔ **une robe de chambre** *(ewn rohb duh shahNbr)* (a dressing gown)

✔ **un maillot de bains** *(an mah-yo duh baN)* (a bathing suit) [France]

✔ **un costume de bains** *(an kohs-tewm duh baN)* (a bathing suit) [Québec]

✔ **des sous-vêtements* [m]** *(day soo-veht-mahN)* (underwear)

*These terms are also used for men's clothing.

And now for the **vêtements pour hommes** *(veht-mahN poo-rohm)* (men's clothes):

- ✔ **un complet** *(aN kohN-pleh)* (a suit) [France]
- ✔ **un habit** *(aN-nah-bee)* (a suit) [Québec]
- ✔ **un veston** *(aN vehs-tohN)* (a suit jacket)
- ✔ **une chemise** *(ewn shuh-meez)* (a shirt)
- ✔ **une ceinture** *(ewn saN-tewr)* (a belt)
- ✔ **des chaussettes** (f) *(day sho-seht)* (socks)
- ✔ **un pardessus** *(aN pahr-duh-sew)* (an overcoat)
- ✔ **un chapeau** *(aN sha-po)* (a hat)
- ✔ **une cravate** *(ewn krah-vaht)* (a tie)

French has borrowed many English words for clothes. But they sometimes have a different meaning. Here are a few:

- ✔ **le tee-shirt** *(luh tee-shuhrt)* (tee-shirt)
- ✔ **le sweat** *(luh sweet)* (sweat-shirt) Notice the pronunciation.
- ✔ **le jogging** *(luh zhoh-geeng)* (warm-up suit)
- ✔ **le pull** *(luh pewl)* (sweater)
- ✔ **le slip** *(luh sleep)* (underpants)
- ✔ **les baskets** *(lay bahs-keht)* (sneakers)

Now for shoes:

- ✔ **les sandales** *(lay sahN-dahl)* (sandals)
- ✔ **les bottes** *(lay boht)* (boots)
- ✔ **les chaussures à talons** *(lay sho-sew-rah tah-lohN)* (high-heeled shoes)
- ✔ **les baskets** *(lay bahs-keht)* (sneakers)
- ✔ **les chaussons** *(lay sho-sohN)* (slippers)
- ✔ **une paire de chaussures** *(ewn pehr duh sho-sewr)* (a pair of shoes)

When you're picking out clothes, what's more important than the color?

- ✔ **noir/noire** *(nwahr)* (black)
- ✔ **marron** *(mah-rohN)* (brown)
- ✔ **blanc/blanche** *(blahN/blahNsh)* (white)
- ✔ **bleu/bleue** *(bluh)* (blue)

✔ **rouge/rouge** *(roozh)* (red)

✔ **vert/verte** *(vehr/vehrt)* (green)

✔ **jaune** *(zhon)* (yellow)

✔ **orange** *(oh-rahNzh)* (orange)

The adjective of color always follows the noun:

✔ **un pantalon noir** *(an pahN-tah-lohN nwahr)* (black pants)

✔ **des chaussures vertes** *(day sho-sewr vehrt)* (green shoes)

Talkin' the Talk

After walking up and down the streets of Montreal, Nicole Verdier decides to go to the Place Bonaventure to buy a pair of shoes. It is a very large underground shopping mall right in the center of the city and it is connected with other underground malls. It is almost impossible not to find what you need there. After looking in the windows of several stores, Nicole sees a pair she really likes. **Elle entre dans le magasin** *(ehl ahN-truh dahN luh mah-gah-zaN)*, she enters the store.

Nicole: **Bonjour, je voudrais voir les chaussures noires là dans la vitrine.**
bohN-zhoor zhuh voo-dreh vwahr lay sho-sewr nwahr lah dahN lah vee-treen
Hello, I would like to see the black shoes there in the window.

La vendeuse: **Bien sûr, madame, en quelle pointure?**
byan sewr mah-dahm ahN kehl pwaN-tewr
Of course, ma'am, in what size?

Nicole: **Je fais du 38.**
zhuh feh dew trahN-tweet
I am a 38.

La vendeuse: **Je regrette. En 38, nous les avons seulement en marron.**
zhuh ruh-greht ahN trahN-tweet noo lay-zah-vohN suhl-mahN ahN mah-rohN
I am sorry. In 38, we only have them in brown.

Nicole: **Bon, montrez-moi les marron.**
bohN mohN-tray mwah lay mah-rohN
Okay, show me the brown ones.

Nicole puts the shoes on. **Aïe!** *(ah-y)* (Ouch!)

Nicole: **Elles sont trop étroites. Vous les avez en plus larges ?**
ehl sohN tro-pay-trwaht voo lay-zah-vay ahN plew lahrzh
They are too narrow. Do you have them in a wider size?

La vendeuse: **Ah non, madame. Voulez-vous voir un autre modèle ?**
ah nohN mah-dahm voo-lay-voo vwah-raN-no-truh mo-dehl
No, ma'am. Do you want to see another style?

Nicole is not satisfied and moves on to another store.

Nicole: **Combien coûtent celles-ci?**
kohN-byaN koot sehl-see
How much are these?

La vendeuse: **Cent cinquante dollars.**
sahN saN-kahNt doh-lahr
One hundred fifty dollars.

Nicole: **C'est un peu cher, mais elles sont très jolies et puis je dois absolument acheter des chaussures aujourd'hui. Allez, je les prends.**
say-taN puh shehr meh ehl sohN treh zho-lee ay pwee zhuh dwah ahb-so-lew-mahN ah-shu-tay day sho-sewr o-zhoor-dwee. ah-lay zhuh lay prahN
It is a little expensive, but they are very pretty, and I absolutely must buy shoes today. Okay, I'll take them.

La vendeuse: **C'est une très bonne décision, madame.**
seh-tewn treh bohn day-see-zyohN mah-dahm
It's a very good decision, ma'am.

Canada's currency is the dollar. But things in Canada are actually cheaper than they look for an American visitor because a U.S. dollar is worth about one and a half times a Canadian dollar. Thus a $150.00 pair of shoes in Canada costs $100.00 US dollars; to which you have to add the tax, of course!

Je dois *(zhuh dwah)*, when it means "I must," is followed by an infinitive. For example:

Je dois acheter des chaussures aujourd'hui. *(zhuh dwah a-shuh-tay day sho-sew-ro-zhoor-dwee)* I must buy shoes today.

Here is the verb **devoir** *(duh-vwahr)*, infinitive of the verb "must":

Conjugation	Pronunciation
Je dois	zhuh dwah
Tu dois	tew dwah
Il/elle doit	eel/ehl dwah
Nous devons	noo duh-vohN
Vous devez	voo duh-vay
Ils/elles doivent	eel/ehl dwahv

When **devoir** has the meaning of "to owe," a noun can follow it:

> **Je dois cinq cents francs à Catherine**. *(zhuh dwah saN sahN frahN ah kah-treen)* (I owe Catherine 500 francs.)

Words to Know

voir	vwahr	to see
la pointure	lah pwaN-tewr	shoe size
montrer	mohN-tray	to show
étroit	ay-trwah	narrow
large	larzh	wide
un autre	aN-notr	another
Combien coûte . . . ?	kohN-byaN koot	How much is . . . ?
joli	zho-lee	pretty
aujourd'hui	o-zhoor-dwee	today
absolument	ahb-so-lew-mahN	absolutely

Using Superlatives

When you want to say something is the best — or the most awful — you use a superlative in French as well as in English. In an earlier dialog in this chapter, the saleslady tells Cécile that the dress she is trying on is **la plus petite taille** *(lah plew puh-teet ta-y)* (the smallest size she has). Superlatives are constructed in two ways in French: with the adjective before the noun or with the adjective after the noun.

When the adjective precedes the noun

When the adjective goes in front of the noun (see Chapter 12 for the placement of adjectives), the construction is pretty much the same as in English. For example:

- **C'est la moins jolie robe.** *(seh lah mwaN zho-lee rohb)* (It is the least pretty dress.)
- **Eaton's est le plus grand magasin de Montréal.** *(Eaton's eh luh plew grahN mah-gah-zaN duh MohN-ray-ahl)* (Eaton's is the largest department store in Montreal.)

When the adjective follows the noun

The superlative construction is slightly different when you use one of those adjectives which follow the noun. For example:

- **C'est le garçon le plus intelligent de l'école.** *(seh luh gahr-sohN luh plew-zan-teh-lee-zhahN duh lay-kohl)* (He is the most intelligent boy in the school.)
- **Elle achète la robe la moins chère de la boutique.** *(eh-lah-shet lah rohb lah mwaN shehr duh lah boo-teek)* (She buys the least expensive dress in the store.)

Just as in English you may not use "the most" or "the least" for the adjective "good," you may not do it in French either. There is a special word, **le meilleur** *(luh meh-yuhr)* (the best). Here is how you use it:

> **On trouve le meilleur chocolat en Suisse.** *(ohN troov luh meh-yuhr sho-ko-lah ahN sew-ees)* (The best chocolate is found in Switzerland.)

Fun & Games

The following French words have been scrambled. They are all color words. Unscramble them!

LUBE

RION

ENAJU

GUROE

CANLB

TREV

Answer key: bleu, noir, jaune, rouge, blanc, vert

Try to identify all of the items of clothing that are indicated in the following drawing.

You can find the answers in this chapter.

Chapter 7

Going Out on the Town

In This Chapter

▶ Telling time

▶ Touring a museum

▶ Catching a movie

▶ Attending a play

▶ Going to a concert

▶ Heading to a nightclub

*W*hen you visit a new city or town, have fun trying out as much of the local entertainment as possible. In France, there is something for everyone. The French work hard, but also know how to relax. From museums and theater to nightclubs and movies, your stay in France will be one filled with culture and fun. All you need to do in Paris is grab a newspaper, either **Pariscope** *(pah-ree-skohp)* or **Officiel des Spectacles** *(oh-fee-see-ahl day spehk-tahk-luh)* for local listings of cultural activities. Or you can call **Info-Loisir** *(aN-fo loh-wah-zeer),* a recording that keeps tabs on what's going on in Paris (English tel. 01 49 52 53 56; French tel. 01 49 52 53 55). You can also watch for schedules of events on the green, cylindrical kiosks posted around the city. Of course, it's always helpful to know how to tell time in French so that you don't miss the show!

Paris Sélection *(pah-ree say-lek-see-ohn)* (available from tourist offices) is a free monthly listing of concerts, festivals, and shows. **Pariscope** and **L'Official des Spectacles** and **Le Bulletin** *(luh bewl-taN)* in Brussels are weekly guides to cultural events.

Telling Time in French

In Europe, as well as French-speaking Canada, the use of the 24-hour clock, or military time, is universal. This may be a little confusing at first, but with a little practice, it will become quite natural. Imagine a clock (not digital) numbered traditionally from 1:00-12:00. If 12:00 is midnight, you have 1:00 a.m., 2:00 a.m., 3:00 a.m., etc. However, if you keep counting to 24, 1:00 p.m. becomes 13:00, 2:00 p.m. is 14:00, 3:00 p.m. is 15:00, etc.

Instead of using a colon to separate the hour from the minutes (that is, 11:30), in French you use a lowercase "h." For example, 11:30 becomes 11h30. Also, if you see that a movie starts at 10h30, it is safe to say it begins at 10:30 a.m. However, if it begins at 22h30, it begins at 10:30 p.m. Remember, in French, there is no need to distinguish between a.m. or p.m. because they use the 24-hour clock.

Words to Know

Il est huit heures.	eel ay weet uhr	It's 8 a.m.
Il est dix neuf heures.	eel ay dees nuhf uhr	It's 7 p.m.
Et quart	ay kahr	quarter past
Et demi(e)	ay duh-mee	half past
Moins vingt	mwahN vahN	twenty (minutes) to
Moins le quart	mwahN luh kahr	quarter to

In French, to say what time it is, simply add the number of minutes to the hour. Here are some examples:

- **Il est 11h (onze heures).** *(eel ay ohNz uhr)* It's 11:00 (a.m.).

- **Il est 11h30 (onze heures trente).** *(eel ay ohNz uhr trahNt)* It's 11:30 (a.m.).

- **Il est 16h (seize heures).** *(eel ay sehz uhr)* It's 4:00 (p.m.).

- **Il est 16h10 (seize heures dix).** *(eel ay sehz uhr dees)* It's 4:10 (p.m.).

To express time before the hour ("It's 10 minutes to 2:00."), the French use **moins** *(mwahN)*, which means "minus." Here are a couple examples of that usage:

- ✔ **Il est huit heures moins dix.** *(eel eh weet uhr mwahN dees)* It's 7:50.

- ✔ **Il est dix heures moins vingt cinq.** *(eel eh deez uhr mwahN vahN sayNk)* It's 9:35.

As in English, the French also use quarter after, **et quart** *(ay kahr);* half-past, **et demi** *(ay duh-mee);* and quarter till, **moins le quart** *(mwahN luh kahr).* Here are some examples:

- ✔ **Il est 9h15 (neuf heures et quart).** *(eel eh nuhv uhr ay kahr)* It's 9:15 (a.m.).

- ✔ **Il est une heures moins le quart.** *(eel eh ewn uhr mwahN luh kahr.)* It's 12:45 (p.m.).

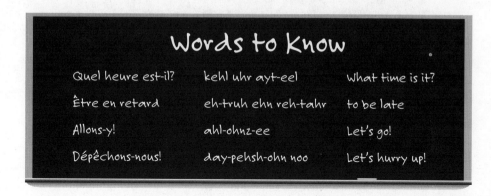

Words to Know

Quel heure est-il?	kehl uhr ayt-eel	What time is it?
Être en retard	eh-truh ehn reh-tahr	to be late
Allons-y!	ahl-ohnz-ee	Let's go!
Dépêchons-nous!	day-pehsh-ohn noo	Let's hurry up!

Talkin' the Talk

The following dialog is between Pierre *(pee-air)* et Claire *(klehr),* who are running late.

Pierre: **Claire, quelle heure est-il?**
klehr kehl uhr eh-teel
Claire, what time is it?

Claire: **Il est 10h10 (dix heures dix).**
eel eh deez uhr dees
It's 10:10 am.

Pierre:	**Il est 10h10 (dix heures dix)?**
	eel eh deez uhr dees
	It's 10:10 am?

Claire:	**Oui, nous sommes en retard.**
	wee noo sohmz ehN ruh-tahr
	Yes, we're late.

Pierre:	**Oh non! Allons-y! Dépêchons-nous!**
	oh nohN ahl-onz ee day-pesh-ohN nu
	Oh no! Let's go! Hurry up!

Words to Know

Il y a 10 (dix) minutes	ill ee ah dees mee-noot	10 minutes ago
Dans 20 (vingt) minutes	dahN vahN mee-newt	in 20 minutes
Commencer	kohm-ahN-say	to begin

Talkin' the Talk

The following dialog is between Jean-Paul *(zhahN-pohl)* and Marc *(mahrk)*, who are trying to take a tour at **Versailles** *(vehr-sah-ee)*.

Jean-Paul:	**À quelle heure commence l'excursion?**
	ah kehl uhr kohm-ahNs lehks-kewr-zee-ohN
	What time does the tour begin?

Marc:	**À 13h (treize heures).**
	ah trehz uhr
	At 1:00 (p.m.).

Jean-Paul:	**Dommage! Il y a dix minutes.**
	dohm-ahzh eel ee ah dee mee-newt
	Rats! Ten minutes ago!

Marc:	**C'est ça. Il y en a une autre dans 30 (trente) minutes.**
	say sah eel ee ahN nah ewn ohtruh dahN trahNt mee-noot
	That's okay. There's another one in 30 minutes.
Jean-Paul:	**Bon. Attendons au café.**
	bohN ah-tahN-dohN oh kahfay
	Good. Let's wait at the café.

Visiting Museums

You can visit many different museums in Paris. Perhaps the most famous is **Le Louvre** *(luh loo-vruh)*. Originally built as a royal fortress, the Louvre is now home to artifacts dating from 5000 B.C. to 1848. Originally built as a palace, the Louvre is now home to some of the most famous sculptures and paintings in the world, including the winged *Victory of Samothrace*, the *Venus de Milo*, and Leonardo da Vinci's *Mona Lisa* (**La Joconde**) *(lah zhoh-kohNd)*. You can also see original 12th century fortress foundations and drawbridge supports.

The Louvre is open from 9 a.m. to 6 p.m. and closed on Tuesdays. Admission is free on the first Sunday of the month. The museums in Paris are closed on different days. It's wise to check this out beforehand and arrange your visits accordingly. What a disappointment to save visiting **Le Musée D'Orsay** *(luh mew-zay dohr-seh)* until the last day of your trip, only to discover that it's closed on Tuesdays!

The Musée D'Orsay was originally a hotel and later was transformed into a train station. In 1986, it was converted into a museum dedicated to French art from 1848 to 1914. Its collection includes the Impressionist paintings formerly housed in the **Jeu de Paume** *(zhuh duh pom)*. It's also home to the world's finest collection of **van Gogh** *(vahn guhg)* paintings outside the van Gogh museum in Amsterdam. In addition, the Musée D'Orsay is one of the only air-conditioned museums in France!

Be sure to check out the museum admission fees. Although admission fees range between 25F (F= French franc) to 50F (approximately $5 to $10), don't be embarrassed to ask for a discount. Students (including college students) showing a valid ID are admitted at a discounted fee. In some museums, those under age 18 enter free, with those 18 to 25 and over 60 paying half price. In other museums, children under age 7 are free, and those from age 7 to 17 and students pay a reduced rate. Some museums charge less on Sundays.

You can also buy a museum pass, a **Carte Musées et Monuments** *(kahrt mew-zay ay mohN-yoo-mehN)*, available at museum ticket offices, tourist offices, and main **métro**, or subway, stations, which can add to your savings. This pass offers admission to 65 museums in the Paris area. It may also be combined with a visit to Versailles. Not only will you save money, but you'll be the envy of other tourists standing in line to buy admission. Summer lines at museums can be a half hour long, and lines at Versailles have been known to be as long as an hour and a half. For more information, contact the **Association InterMusées** *(ah-soh-see-ah-see-ohN aN-tehr-mew-zhay)* 25, rue du Renard (tel. 01 44 78 45 81; fax 44 78 12 23; http://www.intermusees.com).

You may also tour many of the **châteaux** *(shah-toh)* (castles) of France. **Versailles** is quite impressive and worth a day trip. In 1694, Louis XIII built Versailles as a hunting lodge. His son, Louis XIV, turned it into the official residence of the French monarchy. You may visit the State Apartments, the Hall of Mirrors, and the Royal Chapel on your own. However, the guided tours are not only more informative but can also get you into many parts of the palace not open to the casual visitor. There are 5–9 guided visits offered. In the summertime, there are special Saturday night fireworks displays.

The Treaty of Versailles, ending World War I, was signed in the Hall of Mirrors.

Fontainebleau *(fohN-tehn-bloh)* is another famous chateau turned museum. Originally built as a hunting lodge during the midle ages, it was continually renovated by the French aristocracy for over 700 years. Fontainebleau's heyday began with the French Renaissance King, **François I**. *(frahN-swah preh-mee-ay)*. It was also where Napoléon set up court in the early 19th century. It was also here that the emperor signed his abdication papers in 1814.

There are also many châteaux along the **Loire** *(lwahr)* river valley. Here you can tour such fairy tale castles as **Chambord** *(shahN-bohr)*, **Blois** *(blwah)*, **Chenonceau** *(shuh-nohN-soh)*, **Azay-le-Rideau** *(ah-zay luh ree-doh)*, and **Chinon** *(shee-nohN)*.

While touring museums, please remember that many works of art were not made to withstand the intensity of modern tourism. That's why you see the warning **Photos au flash interdites** *(photo oh flash aN-tehr-deet)* (no flash photography). There are also many museum guides and guards to "remind" you, should you forget. Also, museums are in a constant state of change. Works of art and even complete exhibits are moved or rooms are renovated. Sometimes, as is the case with many **châteaux** *(sha-toh)* or castles, complete rooms or even wings do not allow tourists and have signs posted that read **"Défense d'entrer"** *(day-fahNs dahN-tray)* (no admittance).

Talkin' the Talk

The following dialog is between Paul *(pohl)* and Marie *(mah-ree)*, the guide at the Louvre.

Paul: **Bonjour. Y a-t-il des réductions pour des étudiants?**
          bohN-zhoor ee ah teel day ray-dewk-syohN poor dayzay-tewd-ee-ahN
          Hello. Are there any discounts for students?

Marie: **Oui, si vous avez votre carte d'identité, c'est moitié prix.**
          wee see vooz ahvay vohtruh kahrt dee-dehN-tee-tay-say mwah-tyay pree
          Yes, if you have your ID card, it's half price.

Paul: **Avez vous un guide en anglais?**
          ahvay voo aN geed ahN nahN-glay
          Do you have a guide book in English?

Marie: **Mais bien sûr, monsieur.**
          may bee-ehN syur muh-zhyur
          But of course, sir.

Paul: **Et aussi, à quelle heure est la prochaine visite guidée?**
          ay oh-see ah kehl uhr ay lah proh-shehn veez-eet gee-day
          Also, what time is the next guided visit?

Marie: **Elle commence dans quinze minutes.**
          ehl kohm-aNs dahN kahN meen-ewt
          It starts in 15 minutes.

Paul: **Bon. Deux adultes et un étudiant, s'il vous plaît.**
          BohN duhz ahd-ewlt ay aN nay-tew-dyahN seel voo play
          Good. Two adults and one student (ticket) please.

Words to Know

Y a-t-il des réductions pour? . . .	ee ah teel day ray-dewk-syohN poor	Are there any discounts for? . . .
Carte d'identité	kahrt dee-dehn-tee-tay	Identification card
Moitié prix	mwah-tyay pree	half price
La prochaine visite guidée	lah proh-shehn veez-eet gee-day	the next guided tour

Going to the Theater

French theater has been world famous for centuries and offers something for every taste and budget, from classical productions to the **avant-garde** *(ahv-ahNt gahrd)* (modern). Four of France's five national theaters are located in Paris. (The fifth one is in Strasbourg.) Reservations at one of the national theaters should be made at least two weeks in advance, unless you plan on trying to pick up some last minute "rush" tickets. These are usually on sale (and at a discount to students) 45 minutes before the show starts. Again, like the museums, watch the schedules. Many theaters do not have performances on Monday and many close during the months of July and August.

There are four well-known ticket services in Paris. These provide the service of buying tickets without having to go to the theater box office in advance. In addition, some offer discount tickets, though there are restrictions.

- ✔ **Kiosque Info Jeune** *(kee-osk aN-fo zhuhn):* 2 branches (25, boulevard Bourdon; 101, quai Branly). This is a youth information service and you must be under 26 for discounts. In addition to selling theater tickets at half-price, it also distributes free passes to concerts, plays and exhibits.

- ✔ **Kiosque-Théâtre** *(kee-osk tay-aht-ruh):* 2 branches (25, place de la Madeleine; Châtelet-les-Halles). This is considered the best discount box office, selling discount tickets the day of the show. There is a 16F per seat commission.

- ✔ **Alpha FNAC: Spectacles** *(ahl-fa fnahk spehk-tahk-lu):* 4 branches (136, rue de Rennes; Forum des Halles, 1-7, rue Pierre Lescot; 26-30, avenue des Ternes; 71, boulevard St-Germain). Offers tickets for theater, concerts, and festivals.

- ✔ **Virgin Megastore** *(lower level):* 1 branch (52, avenue Champs Elysées). No discounts.

Men and women are expected to "dress" to go to the theater. Men should wear dark suits and women should wear dresses. Openings call for more formal attire, such as tuxedos and long dresses.

Don't forget to tip the usher. It is customary to tip 10F in France and 20F in Belgium.

Talkin' the Talk

The following dialog is between Elise *(ay-leez)* a French student, and Steven, an American exchange student.

Elise:	**Je veux aller au théâtre ce soir. Et toi?** *zhuh vuhz ahl-ay oh tay-ahtruh suh swahr ay twah* I'd like to go to the theater tonight. And you?
Steven:	**Oui, d'accord. Qu'est-ce qu'on joue?** *wee sah vah kes kohN zhoo* Sure. What's playing?
Elise:	***Tartuffe*, une comédie de Molière.** *tar-tewf ewN kohm-ay-dee duh mohl-ee-ehr* *Tartuffe*, a comedy by Molière.
Steven:	**Je ne connais pas beaucoup le français. Ça va me plaire?** *zhuh nuh kohNay pah boh-koo luh frahN-say sah vah muh plehr* I don't know a lot of French. Will I like it?
Elise:	**Oui, bien sûr. C'est rigolo.** *we byaN syur say ree-goh-loh* Yes, of course. It's very funny.
Steven:	**À quelle heure commence-t-elle?** *ah kehl uhr kohm-ahNs tehl* What time does it start?
Elise:	**À 20h. Allons-y.** *ah vahN uhr ahl-ohNzee* At 8:00 p.m. Let's go.

Words to Know

Le théâtre	luh tay-ahtruh	the theater
Qu'est-ce qu'on joue?	kes kohN zhoo	What's playing?
Une comédie	ewn kohm-ay-dee	comedy
Je ne connais pas beaucoup de français.	zhuh nuh kohnay pahboh-koo duh frahN-seh	I don't know a lot of French.
Rigolo	ree-goh-loh	funny

Talkin' the Talk

The following dialog continues from the previous dialog, with Elise buying tickets **au guichet** *(oh gee-shay)* (at the box office) from "Le monsieur" *(luh muh-suhr)*, the ticket seller.

Elise: **Bonsoir. Je voudrais deux places à l'orchestre, s'il vous plaît.**
bohN swahr zhuh voo-dray duh plahs ah lohr-kes-truh seel voo play
Good evening. I'd like two orchestra seats, please.

Le monsieur: **Tout est complet à l'orchestre.**
toot ay kohm-play ah lohr-kes-truh
The orchestra seats are sold out.

Elise: **Au balcon, s'il vous plaît.**
oh bahl-kohN seel voo play
The balcony, please.

Le monsieur: **Il y a deux places au premier rang au balcon.**
eel ee ah duh plahs oh prehm-ee-ay rahN oh bahl-kohN
There are two seats in the front row of the balcony.

Elise: **C'est parfait! Combien coûtent les billets?**
say pahr-fay kohm-byaN koot lay bee-yay
That's perfect! How much will the tickets be?

Le monsieur: **Ils coûte 400F, s'il vous plaît.**
eel koot kaht-ruh sehN frahNk seel voo play
That will be 400 francs, please.

Elise: **Le lever du rideau est à quelle heure?**
luh luh-vay dew ree-doh ayt ah kehl uhr
What time does the curtain go up?

Le monsieur: **Dans une demi-heure.**
dahN ewn duh-mee uhr
In half an hour.

Elise: **Merci, monsieur.**
mehr-see muh-syuh
Thank you, sir.

Words to Know

La place	lah plahs	seat
À l'orchestre	ah lohr-kes-truh	orchestra seats
Au balcon	oh bahl-kohN	balcony
Tout est complet	toot ay kohm-play	sold out
Le premier range	luh prehm-ee-ay rahN	front row
C'est parfait!	say pahr-fay	That's perfect!
Combien coute les billets?	kohm-bee-ehn koot lay bee-yay	How much do the tickets cost?
Le rideau se lève.	luh ree-doh suh lehv	The curtain goes up.
Une demie heure	oon deh-mee uhr	half hour

Going to the Movies

Sometimes after a hectic day of sightseeing, it's very relaxing to go to the movies and just sit. Don't be surprised, however, when the movie begins in French and there are no subtitles! It's especially fun to go to a movie that's been dubbed in French and watch the actors' mouths speaking English and hearing French come out.

When the first movie about a train pulling up in to a station debuted in 1895, the audience ran out of the theater screaming in terror, afraid they were going to be run over.

The cinema, invented by Frenchmen **Auguste** (*oh-gewst*) and **Louis Lumière** (*Loo-ee Lew-mee-ehr*), had its debut in Paris. The French film industry has always seen itself as an artistic venue first and an industry second. The French cinema is so popular that over 300 films are shown in Paris per week, more than any other city in the world. French cinemas sell tickets with specific seat assignments. On Mondays and Wednesdays, look for discounts, often around 10F. Some cinemas also offer discounts to students, seniors, and families. Many theaters show a series of commercials and previews (**la séance**) (*lah say-ahNs*) for as long as a half hour before the show.

Check Pariscope or L'Officiel des Spetacles for weekly schedules, prices, and reviews. Films marked **VO** (*vay oh*) (**version originale**) (*vehr-zee-ohN ohr-eezh-ee-nahl*) means that the film is shown in its original language, with French subtitles. **Version française** (*vehr-zee-ohN frahN-sehz*) (**VF**) (*vay ef*) means that the film has been dubbed in French. This is an increasingly rare practice.

Talkin' the Talk

The following dialog joins Madame and Monsieur Dumont and their son Ben as they try to decide what to do today.

M. Dumont: **Je veux visiter un musée.**
zhuh vuh veez-ee-tay aN mewzay
What shall we do today? I'd like to visit a museum.

Mme. Dumont: **Non, non, non. Je veux visiter une cathédrale.**
nohN noh noh zhuh vuh veez-ee-tay ewn kah-tay-drahl
No, no, no. I'd like to visit a cathedral.

Ben:	**Ah non, pas de musées, pas de cathédrales!** *ah nohN pah duh mew-zay pas duh kah-tay-drahl* No museums, no cathedrals.
M. Dumont:	**D'accord. Voulez-vous aller au cinéma?** *dah-kohr voolay vooz ahlay oh see-nay-mah* Okay. Do you want to go to the movies?
Ben:	**Super! Un film d'aventure!** *sew-pehr aN feelm dah-vahN-tewr* Great! An adventure film!
Mme. Dumont:	**J'aime mieux les documentaires.** *zhehm myuh lay doh-kew-mahN-teh* I like documentaries better.
Ben:	**Non, un dessin animé!** *nohN aN day-saN an-nee-may* No, a cartoon!
M. Smith:	**C'est moi qui décide. Je voudrais voir un western!** *say mwah kee day-seed zhuh voo-dray vwhar aN vehstehrn* I'll decide! I want to see a Western!

Words to Know

Je veux visiter. . . .	zhuh vuh veez-ee-tay	I want to visit. . . .
Au cinéma	oh see-nay-mah	at the movies
Un dessin animé	aN day-sehn ahn-ee-may	a cartoon
Un documentaire	aN doh-kyoo-mehn-tahr	a documentary
Un film d'aventure	aN feelm dah-vehn-tyoor	an adventure film
Un western	aN vestehrn	a Western
J'aime mieux	zhehm mee-yuh	I prefer
C'est moi qui décide	say mway kee day-seed	I'll decide
Je voudrais voir	zhuh vood-dray vwahr	I want to see

Going to a Concert

No matter what language you speak, music is international. If you're feeling overwhelmed by having to speak French all the time, try going to a concert. While there, you won't have to talk for a few hours, and can relax and enjoy the music without worrying about making someone understand you.

Do not shout **"Encore"** *(ahN-kohr)* at a French concert unless you want the performers to play the entire piece again. Instead, say **"Bis"** *(bees),* which means that you want them to play some more.

Talkin' the Talk

The following dialog joins Michèle *(mee-shel)* and Georges *(zhohrzh)* at a café. Georges is reading *Pariscope,* trying to find some musical entertainment for tonight.

Georges:	**Michèle, aimes-tu les orchestres de chambre?** *mee-shel ehm tew layz ohr-kes-truh doo shahNbr* Michele, do you like chamber music?
Michele:	**Non, c'est ennuyeux.** *nohN say ahN-nwee-yuh* No, it's boring.
Georges:	**La musique techno?** *lah mew-zeek tehk-noh* Techno music?
Michele:	**Non, c'est bizarre.** *nohN say beez-ahr* No, it's weird.
Georges:	**Le rap?** *luh rahp* Rap?
Michele:	**Non, c'est trop bruyant.** *nohN say troh brew-ee-yahN* No, it's too noisy.
Georges:	**La musique rock?** *lah mew-seek rohk* Rock 'n' roll?

Michele: **Non, c'est trop moderne.**
             nohN say troh moh-dehrN
             No, it's too modern.

George: **Alors, quel type de musique aimes-tu?**
             ah-lohr kehl teep duh mew-seek ehm tew
             Then, what type of music do you like?

Michele: **J'adore la musique classique.**
             zhah-dohr la mew-seek klah-seek
             I love classical music.

George: **Eh, bien. Il y a une symphonie de Mozart au parc ce
             soir. Veux-tu y aller?**
             *ay byan eel ee ah ewn saN-fohn-ee duh mo-zahr oh
             pahrk suh swahr vuh tew ee ahl-ay*
             Good. There's a Mozart symphony in the park
             tonight. Do you want to go?

Michele: **Certainement! Prenons un pique-nique!**
             ser-tehn-uh-mahN! pruh-nohN aN peek-neek
             Absolutely! Let's take a picnic!

Words to Know

Une symphonie	ewn saN-fohn-ee	a symphony
La musique classique	lah mew-seek klah-seek	classical music
La musique moderne	lah mew-seek moh-dehrn	modern music
La musique rock	lah mew-seek rohk	rock music
La musique de jazz	lah mew-seek duh zhahz	jazz music
La musique techno	lah mew-seek tehk-no	techno music
Le rap	luh rahp	rap music
Un orchestre de chambre	aN ohr-kes-truh duh shahNbr	a chamber orchestra
Aimer	eh-may	to like
Ennuyeux	ahN-nwee-yuh	boring
Bizarre	beez-ahr	weird, bizarre
Bruyant	brew-ee-yahN	noisy
Moderne	moh-dehrn	modern

The verb **jouer** *(zhoo-ay)* is a regular **-er** verb, meaning "to play." It must be used with either the preposition **de** *(duh)* or **au** *(oh)*. When jouer is used with instruments, you use the preposition **de**. The preposition **au** is used when referring to playing games or to theatrical, cinematic, or musical performances. See Table 7-2 for some examples of the use of "jouer."

Table 7-2	Using the Verb *Jouer* (to Play)	
Word	*Pronunciation*	*Meaning*
Je joue du piano.	*zhuh zhoo dew pee-ahnoh*	I play the piano.
Tu joues de la guitare.	*tew zhoo duh lah gee-tahr*	You play the guitar.
Nous jouons aux échecs.	*noo zhoo-ohN ohz ayshek*	We play chess.
Vous jouez de la trompette.	*voo zhoo-ay duh la trohN-peht*	You play the trumpet.
Elles jouent du violon.	*ehl zhoo dew vee-oh-lohN*	They play the violin.

Words to Know

Le piano	luh pee-ahn-oh	piano
Le violon	luh vee-oh-lohN	violin
La trompette	lah trohN-peht	trumpet
La guitare	la gee-tahr	guitar
Les échecs	lays ayshehk	chess
Les dames	lay dahm	checkers

Going to a Nightclub

If you're not exhausted after a full day of sight-seeing, you may want to try visiting a more lively setting. Most large cities have plenty of nightclubs that offer everything from live music to dancing.

Many Parisian clubs are officially private. This means they have the right to pick and choose their clientele. In general, word of mouth and weekly journals are the best guide to the current scene. Europeans also tend to dress up more for a night on the town than do their North American counterparts. Wearing black is **de rigeur** *(duh ree-guhr)* (compulsory). Some smaller places in the **Quartier Latin** *(kahr-tee-ay lah-taN)* in Paris will admit almost anyone as long as they are wearing black. To be admitted in to one of the more exclusive clubs, you may need to accompany a regular (and wear black!).

The drinking age in France is 18. Women often receive discounts or are admitted free. The best advice is not to go alone, unless you're looking for a lot of attention. Weekday admission is much cheaper and not nearly as crowded. However, the most action happens on weekends and very, very late. The peak time for any club is around 2 to 3 a.m.!

Paris also has a very active **Centre Gai et Lesbien** *(sahN-truh gay ay layz-bee-aN)* (Gay and Lesbian Community). It centers around the chicest part of the city known as **Le Marais** *(luh mahr-ay).* For the most comprehensive guide to Paris' gay and lesbian nightlife, check out these guides and magazines: **Guide Gai** *(geed gay),* **Illico** *(eel-ee-koh),* **Le Guide Paris** *(luh geed pahr-ee),* **Lesbia** *(lehz-bee-ah),* and **Têtu** *(teh-tew). Pariscope* also has an English-language section called *A Week of Gay Outings.*

 CULTURAL WISDOM

The word **disco** *(dees-koh)* or **discothèque** *(dees-koh-tehk)* in English usually conjures up images of the music scene of the 1970s — *Saturday Night Fever* and the Bee Gees, for example. However, in French, it means a dance club with popular dance music.

Talkin' the Talk

Ready for some practice conversation before you hit the nightclubs? The following dialog joins Paul and Denise as they are finishing dinner and deciding what type of nightlife to pursue.

Paul: **Veux-tu aller en boîte? Nous pouvons danser.**
vuh too ahl-ay ahN bwat noo poo-vohN dahn-say
Do you want to go to a disco? We could go dancing.

Denise: **Non, merci. Je suis trop fatiguée.**
noh mehr-see zhuh swee troh fah-tee-gay
No, thanks. I'm too tired.

Paul: **Bon. Allons au club pour regarder une revue.**
bohN ahl-ohnz oh kloob poor ruh-gahr-day ewn ruh-vew
Okay. Let's go to a club to watch a show.

Denise: **D'accord. Faut-il réserver?**
dah-kohr foh-teel rayz-ehr-vay
Okay. Do we need reservations?

Paul: **Nous allons devoir faire la queue.**
noozah-lohN duh-vwahr fehr lah kuh
We'll have to stand in line.

Denise: **À quelle heure commence le spectacle?**

ah kehl uhr kohm-ahNs luh spehk-tahk-luh
What time does the show start?

Paul: **À 23h.**
               ah vahN trwah zuhr
               At 11:00 (p.m.).

Denise: **Oh non! C'est trop tard!**
               oh nohN say troh tahr
               Oh no! That's too late!

Words to Know

Danser	dahN-say	to dance
Une disco/discothèque	ewn dees-koh/ dees-koh-tehk	a disco
Je suis trop fatiguée.	zhuh swee troh fah-tee-gay	I'm too tired.
Un club	aN kloob	a club
Une revue	ewn ruh-vew	a review/show
À quelle heure commence le spectacle?	ah kehl uhr kohm-ahns luh spehk-tahk-luh	What time does the show start?
Faut-il réserver?	foh-teel ray-zehr-vay	Is a reservation necessary?
C'est trop tard.	say troh tahr	That's too late.

In addition to tipping the usher at a concert, theater, or movie, you also are expected to tip the attendant in the public restrooms. This attendant is such a familiar character of the French scene that she has a name: **dame pipi** *(dahm pee-pee)*.

FUN & GAMES

Matching: Draw a line between the matching pairs.

8:00 a.m.	Il est quinze heures trente.
9:15 p.m.	Il est sept heures moins dix.
3:30 p.m.	Il est dix heures vingt cinq.
10:25 a.m.	Il est neuf heures et quart.
6:50 a.m.	Il est huit heures.

Chapter 8

Enjoying Yourself: Recreation

. . . .

In This Chapter

▶ Playing sports

▶ Hitting the ski slopes

▶ Heading for the beach

▶ Going camping

. . . .

All work and no play makes **Jacques un garçon ennuyeux** *(zhahk aN gahr-sohN ahN-nwee-yuh)* (Jack a dull boy). Whether you're playing or watching sports, going to the beach, or camping, you're sure to have a good time if you know some of the language.

Today, the French are much more sports minded than in the past. Young people regulary join teams and compete in sports such as **le basket** *(luh bahs-keht)* (basketball), **le football** *(luh foot-bol)* (soccer), and **le rugby** *(luh rewg-bee)* (rugby). Individual sports such as **la natation** *(lah nah-tah-see-ohN)* (swimming), **le tennis** *(luh teh-nees)* (tennis), **la randonnée** *(lah rahN-doh-nay)* (hiking), **le cyclisme** *(luh see-kleez-muh)* (cycling), **la voile** *(lah vwahl)* (sailing) and **la planche à voile** *(lah plahNsh ah vwahl)* (windsurfing) are also popular. A few of the popular North American sports such as football (**le football américain**) *(luh foot-bol ah-may-ree-kaN),* baseball, and hockey remain uncommon in Europe.

The modern Olympic Games (**les Jeux Olympiques**) *(lay zhuhz oh-laN-peek)* were revived in the late 19th century by **Pierre de Coubertin** *(pee-ehr duh koo-behr-taN).*

Since the universities are built solely around academics, there are no official collegiate teams. Many students join sports clubs. These clubs are a good way to meet new people and make new friends. They are also open to foreign students.

Each sport has a **Fédération** *(fay-day-rah-see-ohN)* that supplies all information regarding affiliated clubs and associations. The **Fédération** also sponsors regional and national public events. **La Fédération française de football** *(la fay-day-rah-see-ohN frahN-sehz duh foot-bol)* (the French football federation) sponsors **Les Championnats de France** *(lay shahN-pee-oh-nah duh frahNs)* (the French championships) every year for amateurs and professionals, and **La Coupe de France** *(lah koop duh frahNs)* (the French cup) for professionals.

Among the most popular **sports-spectacles** *(spohr spehk-tahk-luh)* (spectator sports) are **le football** (soccer), **les courses de chevaux** *(lay koors duh shuh-voh)* (horse racing), and **les courses automobiles** *(lay koors o-to-mo-beel)* (automobile racing). The best known horse race is **le Grand Prix de Longchamp** *(le grahN pree duh lohNg-shahN)* in Paris. As for **les courses automobiles,** there are two extremely famous ones: **24 heures du Mans** *(vaNt kat-ruhr dew mahN)* and **le Rallye de Monte-Carlo** *(luh rah-lee duh mohN-tay kahr-lo).*

First held in 1903, **Le Tour de France** *(luh toor duh frahNs)* is the largest **course du cycliste** *(koors duh see-kleest),* or cycling race, in the world. Every summer, cyclists from all over the world bike over 1,500 miles (4,000 km). The race begins in a different city each year, but always ends in Paris. The course is very demanding, traveling through the Alps and Pyrenees mountain regions and under difficult weather conditions. **Le maillot jaune** *(luh mah-yo zhon)* (the yellow T-shirt) is awarded to the winner.

Playing Sports

It seems that every nation has a national pastime. Baseball is as American as apple pie and hot dogs. Here's a breakdown of some Francophone pastimes.

- France and Belgium: cycling and soccer
- Southern France: rugby
- Switzerland: skiing
- Canada: hockey

Words to Know

le basket (ball)	luh bahs-keht (bol)	basketball
le tennis	luh teh-nees	tennis
le foot (ball)/ le soccer-(Canada)	luh foot (bol)/ luh soh-kuhr	soccer
le football américain	luh foot-bol ah-may-ree-kaN	American football
le coup d'envoi	luh koo dahN-vwah	kick-off
un club de sport	aN kluhb duh spohr	a sports club
une equipe	ewn ay-keep	a team
gagner	gahn-yay	to win
marquer un point	mahr-kay aN pwaN	to score a point
manquer	mahN-kay	to miss
un but	aN bewt	a goal
égalité	ay-gah-lee-tay	tied score

The French use two different verbs when talking about playing sports: **faire de** *(fehr duh)* for individual sports and **jouer au** *(zhew-ay o)* for team sports. **Faire** *(fehr)*, an irregular verb, uses the preposition **de** *(duh)*, and its variants whereas **jouer**, a regular **-er** verb, uses the preposition **au** *(o)* and its variants. See Tables 8-1 and 8-2 for the correct ways to use these verbs.

Table 8-1	Conjugating the Verb *Faire* (to Do)	
Conjugation	*Pronunciation*	*Meaning*
Je fais du tennis.	zhuh fay dew teh-nees	I play tennis.
Tu fais du tennis.	too fay dew teh-nees	You play tennis.
Elle fait du tennis.	ehl fay dew teh-nees	She plays tennis.

(continued)

Table 8-1 *(continued)*		
Conjugation	*Pronunciation*	*Meaning*
Nous faisons du tennis.	noo fayz-ohN dew teh-nees	We play tennis.
Vous faites du tennis.	voo feht dew teh-nees	You play tennis. (formal/plural)
Ils font du tennis.	eel fohN dew teh-nees	They play tennis.

Table 8-2	Conjugating the Verb *Jouer* (to Play)	
Conjugation	*Pronunciation*	*Meaning*
Je joue au basket.	zhuh zhoo o bahs-keht	I play basketball.
Tu joues au basket.	tew zhoo o bahs-keht	You play basketball.
Il joue au basket.	eel zhoo o bahs-keht	He plays basketball.
Nous jouons au basket.	noo zhoo-oN o bahs-keht	We play basketball.
Vous jouez au basket.	voo zhoo-ay o bahs-keht	You play (formal/plural) basketball.
Elles jouent au basket.	ehl zhoo o bahs-keht	They play basketball.

Talkin' the Talk

The following dialog occurs at a soccer game. We join the conversation just as Marc sits down next to Paul.

Marc: **Zut! J'ai manqué le coup d'envoi!**
zewt zhay mahn-kay luh koo dehn-vwah
Darn! I missed the kick-off!

Paul: **Tu n'as pas manqué beaucoup. Ils sont à égalité.**
tew nah pah mahn-kay bo-koo eel sohN tah ay-gahl-ee-tay
You didn't miss much. The score's tied.

Marc: **Oh, excellent. Joues-tu au foot?**
           oh ex-say-lahN zhoo tew o foot
           Oh, excellent. Do you play soccer?

Paul: **Non, je joue au basket.**
           nohN zhuh zhoo o bahs-ket
           No, I play basketball.

Marc: **Je joue au basket aussi. Je cherche une équipe.**
           zhuh zhoo o bahs-ket o-see zhuh shersh ewn ay-keep
           I play basketball, too. I'm looking for a team.

Paul: **Nous jouons au club local.**
           noo zhoo-ohN o klewb loh-kahl
           We play at a local club.

Marc: **Eh, regarde! Il marque un but!**
           ay ruh-gahrd eel mark aN bewt
           Hey, look! He scored a goal!

Paul: **Super! Nous gagnons!**
           sew-pehr noo gahn-yohN
           Super! We won!

Going Skiing

Whether you're in Switzerland, France, or Canada, you can find plenty of
opportunities for both downhill (**ski**) (*skee*) and cross-country (**ski de fond**)
(*skee duh fohN*) skiing. In France, the Alps are the best for downhill skiing and
the Pyrenees for cross-country. Resorts in France tend to be modern and efficient; in Switzerland the emphasis is on tradition and character. Switzerland
has nearly 200 villages and small towns equipped for downhill skiing. And
Montreal skiing conditions are billed as the "best in the East." You can even
cross-country ski through the **Parc du Mont-Royal** (*park dew mohN-rwah-yahl*)
in Montreal proper.

Words to Know

un forfait	aN fohr-fay	a lift pass
les conditions	lay kohN-dee-see-ohN	conditions (ski)
la neige	lah nehzh	snow
poudreuse	pood-ruhz	powdery
Il fait très frois	eel fay treh frwah	It's very cold
rester	rehs-tay	to stay
acheter	ahsh-tay	to buy

Talkin' the Talk

The following dialog is between Antoine *(ahN-twahn)* and his girl-friend, Françoise, *(frahN-swahz)* who have come to the mountains to ski.

Françoise: **Il fait très froid aujourd'hui.**
              eel fay treh frwah oh-zhood-wee
              It's really cold today.

Antoine: **Oui! Et il y a beaucoup de neige.**
              wee ay eel ee ah bo-koo duh nehzh
              Yes! And there's a lot of snow.

Françoise: **Mais, bien sûr. Il a neigé hier soir.**
              may byaN sewr eel ah nehzh-ay ee-ehr swahr
              But of course. It snowed last night.

Antoine: **La neige est poudreuse, aussi.**
              lah nehzh ay pood-ruhz oh-see
              The snow is powdery, too.

Françoise: **Oui, les conditions sont excellentes.**
              wee lay kohN-dee-see-ohN sohN tay-ksay-lahNt
              Yes, the conditions are excellent.

Antoine: **Reste ici. J'achète les forfaits.**
rehst ee-see zhah-sheht lay fohr-fay
Stay here. I'll buy the lift passes.

If you re-read Antoine's last line in the preceding dialog, notice that he says "Stay here." Who's he talking to? Obviously, he's telling Françoise to stay there. The subject of his sentence is implied, yet we still know to whom he is speaking. This is called the imperative.

The imperative, or command, form of a verb may be used only with the **tu** (you, informal/singular), **vous** (you, formal/plural), and **nous** (we) forms of the verb. You cannot give yourself a command, nor can you give he, she, or they one either. The subject of the verb is not used, only implied. Table 8-3 shows some examples. Note that the last two examples show that the imperative may be used with all verbs, not just **-er** verbs.

Table 8-3	Using the Imperative Form of Verbs	
Word	*Pronunciation*	*Meaning*
Tu restes ici.	tew rehst ee-see	You stay here.
Reste ici! (drop the final s with -er verbs)	rehst ee-see	Stay here!
Vous ne parlez pas.	voo nuh pahrlay pah	You don't talk.
Ne parlez pas!	nuh pahrlay pah	Don't talk!
Nous mangeons des frites.	noo mahN-zhoN day freet	We are eating some fries.
Mangeons des frites!	mahN-zhoN day freet	Let's eat some fries!
Allons-y!	ahl-ohNz-ee	Let's go (there)!
Finis ton lait!	fee-nee tohN lay	Finish your milk!

Words to Know

Je voudrais . . .	zhuh voo-dray . . .	I'd like . . .
louer	loo-ay	to rent
l'équipement	lay-keep-mahN	equipment
les leçons de ski	lay luh-sohN duh skee	skiing lessons
les skis	lay skee	skis

Talkin' the Talk

In this dialog, Antoine is buying lift tickets from Anne at the ski resort.

Antoine: **Je voudrais deux forfaits pour une journée, s'il vous plaît.**
zhuh voo-dray duh fohr-fay poor ewn zhoo-nay seel voo play
Two one-day passes, please.

Anne: **Voulez-vous louer de l'équipement, monsieur?**
voo-lay voo loo-ay duh-lay-keep-mahN muh-syuh
Do you want to rent some equipment, sir?

Antoine: **Oui, je voudrais louer des skis, s'il vous plaît.**
wee zhuh voo-dray loo-ay day ski seel voo play
Yes, I'd like to rent some skis, please.

Anne: **Voulez-vous des leçons de ski?**
voo-lay voo day luh-sohN duh ski
Will you need lessons?

Antoine: **Non, merci.**
nohN mehr-see
No, thank you.

Anne: **Ça coûte 600F (francs), s'il vous plaît.**
sah koot see sahN frahN seel voo play
That will be 600 francs, please.

Did you notice the new verb tense in the preceding dialog? Antoine and Anne are strangers, so they use the conditional verb tense. The conditional verb tense is used in formal situations, as well as in cases in which you want to imply that the action of the verb depends on certain circumstances. For example, you might say, "We'll go on a picnic, if it's not raining." In that sentence, the condition is "if it's not raining."

The following table shows the conditional tense for the verb **vouloir** *(vool-wahr)* (to wish or to want). The conditional translation for the verb vouloir becomes "would like."

Conjugation	*Pronunciation*
je voudrais	zhuh voo-dray
tu voudrais	too voo-dray
il/elle voudrait	ehl voo-dray
nous voudrions	noo voo-dree-ohn
vous voudriez	voo vew-dree-yay
ils/elles voudraient	eel voo-dree-ohn

Going to the Beach

La Côte d'Azur *(lah kot dah-zewr)* (the azure coast), also known as the French Riviera, is situated on the southern coast of France, along the Mediterranean. Its numerous beaches are quite crowded during the months of July and August. Swimming is quite safe because most beaches are supervised by lifeguards.

Topless sunbathing is accepted on most French beaches, and there are also nudist beaches, primarily around **Saint-Tropez** *(sahN troh-pay)* and **l'île du Levant** *(leel dew lehv-ahN)*. Before disrobing completely, look around to see what is acceptable! As they say, "When in Rome . . ."!

If you see a sign posted that reads "**Baignade interdite**" *(bah-nyahd aN-tehr-deet)*, beware. That means no swimming!

If you do something to or for yourself, you use a reflexive verb. Reflexive verbs are regular verbs that attach a pronoun to show who received the action of the verb. The action of a reflexive verb is always performed by the subject. The pronoun is usually implied in English. The following table shows the use of the reflexive verb **se baigner** *(suh-beh-nyay)* (to swim).

Conjugation	*Pronunciation*
je me baigne	zhuh muh beh-ny
tu te baignes	too tuh beh-ny
il/elle se baigne	eel suh beh-ny
nous nous baignons	noo noo beh-ny-ohN
vous vous baignez	voo voo beh-ny-ay
ils/elles se baignent	eel se beh-ny

Here are a couple other examples of uses of reflexive verbs:

- **Les enfants s'amusent sur la plage.** *(layz ahN-fahN sah-mewz sewr lah plazh)* (The children have fun on the beach.)
- **Nous nous promenons au bord de la mer.** *(noo noo proh-mehn-ohn oh bohr duh lah mehr)* (We walk [ourselves] along the beach.)

So, now that we know how to have a good time, **allons à la plage!** *(ahlon ah lah plahzh)* (let's go to the beach!).

Words to Know

les vagues	lay vahg	waves
nager	nahzh-ay	to swim
oublier	oo-blee-ay	to forget
se dépêcher	suh day-pehsh-ay	to hurry
bronzer	brohn-zay	to tan
la crème solaire	lah krehm soh-lehr	sunscreen
le tuba	luh tew-bah	snorkel
les palmes	lay pahlm	flippers
la plage	lah plazh	the beach
s'amuser	sah-mew-zay	to have fun

Talkin' the Talk

The following dialog is between Mme. Lafarge *(mah-dahm lah-fahrzh)* and her two sons Gaston *(gahs-tohN)* and Henri *(ahN-ree).* They are spending the day at the beach.

Gaston et Henri: **Au revoir, maman! Nous allons nager.**
ohr-vwahr, mah-mahN noo zah-lohN nah-zhay.
Bye, mama! We're going swimming.

Mme. Lafarge: **Attendez! Vous oubliez la crème solaire.**
ah-tahN-day vooz oo-blee-ay lah krehm soh-lehr
Wait! You forgot your suncreen.

Gaston: **Oh, maman! Dépêche-toi!**
oh mah-mohn day-pehsh-twah
Oh, mama! Hurry up!

Henri: **Gaston, regarde les très grandes vagues!**
gahstohn ruh-gahrd lay tray grahnd vahg
Gaston, look at those really big waves!

Gaston: **C'est super! Maman, as-tu mon tuba et mes palmes?**
seh sew-pehr mah-mahN ah-tew mohN tew-bah ay may pahlm
Wow! Mama, do you have my snorkel and flippers?

Mme. Lafarge: **Oui, ils sont dans le sac. Je vais bronzer. Amusez-vous bien!**
wee eel sohN dahN luh sahk zhuh veh brohnzay. ahmew-zay voo byaN.
Yes, they are in the sack. I'm going to work on my tan. Have fun!

Setting Up Camp

Camping is a great way to get away from it all. Traditionally in France, the months of July and August are when the French, especially the Parisians, head to the hills, so to speak. Highways are jammed with cars and campers escaping from the city. Along the French Riviera, traffic has been known to be stalled for hours as cars wind their way to the coast.

Camping along the coast is very well organized. Most campsites have showers and restaurants, as well as separate sites for bicycles and tent campers. Many are situated along the beaches. It is wise to make your reservations well in advance, especially during the months of July and August. Off-road camping is illegal. However, you may want to try asking a local farmer for permission to pitch your tent on his land. **Pouvons-nous camper ici, s'il vous plaît?** *(poo-vohN noo kahN-pay ee-see seel voo play)* (May we camp here, please?). He just may let you, provided that you leave the site as you found it and are not too noisy or destructive.

Camping and Caravaning is a free catalog that lists the addresses, telephone numbers, and dates of operation of campgrounds throughout France. It is available from the Departmental Office of Tourism 1, esplanade John-Fitzgerald-Kennedy, 06000 Nice or place Raimu, 83000 Toulon, France.

The Laurentian Mountains are about an hour's drive north of Montreal. First inhabited by the Algonquin Indians, it is an area of natural beauty. The long, narrow glacial lakes are fed by freezing cold streams coursing down wooded slopes of yellow birch, beech, pine, and maple trees. Camping along these river banks is one of the best ways to appreciate the rugged splendor of these mountains. Advance reservations are usually not required at park campgrounds operated by the Québec government.

For camping information in the Québec region, write to the Québec Department of Tourism, Fish, and Game, 150 Saint Boulevard East, Québec, Que. GIR 4YI, Canada.

Words to Know

monter la tente	mohN-tay lah tahNt	to pitch the tent
les allumettes	layz ahl-ewm-eht	matches
faire un feu de camp	fehr aN fuh duh kahN	start a campfire
un sac de couchage	aN sahk duh koosh-ahzh	sleeping bag
les douches	lay doosh	showers
les toilettes	lay twah-leht	toilets
les services	lay sehrv-ees	facilities
Nous sommes arrivés	noo sohmz ahr-ee-vay	We're here (We've arrived)
se lever	suh luh-vay	to get up

Talkin' the Talk

Ready for some practice? The following dialog is between Etienne *(ay-tee-ehn)* and Christine *(krees-teen),* who are going camping. Christine has been napping in the car.

Etienne: **Lève-toi! Nous sommes arrivés.**
lehv twah noo sohmz ahr-ee-vay
Get up! We're here.

Christine: **Oh! C'est très joli, n'est-ce pas!**
oh say tray zhoh-lee nehs-pah
Oh! How pretty!

Etienne: **Oui. Montons la tente.**
wee mohNt-ohN lah tahNt
Yes. Let's pitch the tent.

Christine:	**D'accord. Quels services y-a-til?**
	dah-kohr kehl sehr-vees ee-ah-teel
	Okay. What facilities do they have?

Etienne:	**Il y a des toilettes et des douches.**
	eel ee ah day twah-leht et day dewsh
	There are toilets and showers.

Christine:	**Voilà les sacs de couchage.**
	vwah-lah lay sahk duh koosh-ahzh
	Here are the sleeping bags.

Etienne:	**Merci. Trouves-tu les allumettes?**
	mehr-see trewv too layz ahl-ewm-eht
	Thanks. Have you found the matches?

Christine:	**Oui, les voilà.**
	wee lay vwah-lah
	Yes, here they are.

Etienne:	**Bon. Je vais faire un feu de camp.**
	bohN zhuh veh fehr aN fuh duh kahN
	Good. I'll start a campfire.

Because we're talking about going somewhere, this seems like a good place to discuss the use of the verb **aller** *(ahl-ay)* (to go). **Aller** is an irregular verb, so you must memorize its forms.

Conjugation	*Pronunciation*
je vais	zhuh vay
tu vas	too vah
il/elle va	eel vah
nous allons	noo ahlohN
vous allez	vooz ahlay
ils/elles vont	ehl vohN

You also can use **aller** with the infinitive of another verb to express something that will take place in the near future. Here are some examples.

- ✔ **Je vais nager.** *(zhuh vay nahzhay)* (I'm going to go swimming.)

- ✔ **Nous allons jouer au foot.** *(nooz ahlohN zhoo-ay o foot)* (We are going to play soccer.)

Words to Know

aller	ahl-ay	to go
pêcher	pehsh-ay	to go fishing
je n'aime pas	zhuh nehm pas	I don't like
lire	leer	to read
attrapper	aht-rah-pay	to catch
le poisson	luh pwah-sohN	fish
la canne à pêche	lah kahn ah pehsh	fishing pole
les vers	lay vehr	worms
dégoûtant	day-gewt-ahnt	disgusting

Talkin' the Talk

The following dialog is between Etienne and Christine, who are deciding what to do now that they've set up their campsite for the evening.

Etienne: **Christine, je vais pêcher.**
krees-teen zhuh vay pehsh-ay
Christine, I'm going fishing.

Christine: **Je n'aime pas pêcher. Je vais lire mon livre.**
zhuh nehm pas pehsh-ay zhuh vay leer mohN lee-vr
I don't like fishing. I'm going to read my book.

Etienne: **J'espère attraper des poissons pour le dîner.**
zhehs-pehr aht-rah-pay day pwah-sohN poor luh deenay
I hope to catch some fish for dinner.

Christine: **Tu as ta canne à pêche?**
tew ah tah kahn ah pehsh
Do you have your fishing pole?

Etienne: **Oui et des vers aussi.**
wee ay day vehr o-see
Yes, and some worms, too.

Christine: **Dégoûtant! Allez!**
day-gewt-ahnt ah-lay
Disgusting! Go away!

Fun & Games

Make the following sentences into commands, using the imperative form.

1. Nous écoutons la radio. (We listen to the radio.)

_____

2. Tu ne skies pas si vite. (You don't ski so fast.)

_____

3. Nous jouons au foot. (We play soccer.)

_____

4. Tu bois ton chocolat. (You drink your hot chocolate.)

_____

Answer Key:

4. Bois ton chocolat.

3. Jouons au foot.

2. Ne skie pas si vite.

1. Écoutons la radio

Chapter 9

Talking on the Phone

. . . .

. . . .

*W*hether you are visiting Canada, Belgium, or France, making phone calls is much easier than it used to be. Public pay phones in France, for example, used to work only with special tokens called **jetons** *(zheh-tohN)*, which you purchased at **la poste** *(lah pohst)* (the post office) or **le tabac** *(luh tah-bahk)* (the tobacco shop). Most French pay phones now will only take **la télécarte** *(lah tay-lay-kahrt)* (calling cards). In 1993, in fact, out of the 170,000 pay phones in France, 125,000 worked only with calling cards. Not only are these phones easier to use, but vandalism has also decreased as there is no money to steal!

In France, most families have one phone line and only one or two phones. The phone is usually in the living room, with an extension either in the den or master bedroom. Very rarely do you find a phone in the kitchen. Phone calls are infrequent and short because calls are charged by the minute. The French pay for each call separately and receive an itemized monthly phone bill.

France also has a unique machine called **Le Minitel** *(luh mee-nee-tehl)*. Towards the end of the 1970s, long before the advent of surfing the Web, **le Minitel** was making its way into homes across France. **Minitel** is a small terminal that allows you to access everything from **l'annuaire électronique** *(lahn-yoo-ahr ay-lehk-troh-neek)* (an electronic phone book), to transportation schedules, to the latest weather forecast, to movie showings and cultural events. **Le Minitel** even allows you to bank electronically. By 1993, France had 6,485,000 Minitels! Minitels are still used in France, even with the advent of the Internet.

Making a Phone Call

Making — or receiving — a phone call in French can be nerve wracking, and it certainly doesn't have to occur in a foreign country. One of the authors was surprised when the phone rang one day, and the caller was speaking French!

The call was for a job translating technical training manuals, and the company conducted an impromptu phone interview — entirely in French. Or, you may have a friend who feels more comfortable speaking French than English. These sorts of calls may be rare, but they do occur. The best thing to do is take a deep breath, and don't hesitate to ask the person on the other end to speak more slowly by saying, "**Parlez plus lentement, s'il vous plaît**" *(pahrlay ploo lahn-tuh-mahN, seel voo play).*

French has two words for hello. You use **"allô"** *(ah-loh)* when answering the telephone and **bonjour** *(bohN-zhoor)* when greeting people elsewhere. Also, in French, a telephone says "**drin, drin**" *(dreen, dreen)*, not "ring, ring."

Talkin' the Talk

The following dialogue is a telephone conversation where **Pierre** *(pee-ehr)* is calling to tell **Monique** *(moh-neek)* what time the movie starts. Her mother, **Mme. La Grange,** *(mah-dahm lah grahnzh)* answers the phone. (See Chapter 7 for more information on telling time and Chapter 8 for more information on leisure activities.)

Mme. La Grange: **Allô?**
ah-loh
Hello?

Pierre: **Allô, madame. C'est Pierre.**
ah-loh mah-dahm say pee-ehr
Hello Madame. It's Pierre.

Mme. La Grange: **Oui, Pierre. Ça va?**
wee pee-ehr sah vah
Yes, Pierre. How are you?

Pierre: **Ça va bien. Est-ce que Monique est là?**
Sah vah byaN ehs kuh moh-neek ay lah
I'm fine. Is Monique there?

Mme. La Grange: **Oui, un moment, s'il te plaît. Ne quitte pas.**
whee aN moh-mahN seel te play nuh keet pah
Yes, just a minute. Don't hang up.

Monique: **Allô, Pierre?**
ah-loh pee-ehr
Hello, Pierre?

Pierre:	**Monique, le film commence à 18h (heures).** *moh-neek luh feelm kohm-ahNs ah dees-weet uhr* Monique, the movie starts at 6:00 p.m.
Monique:	**C'est super! À bientôt.** *say soo-pehr ah byaN-toh* Super! I'll see you later.
Pierre:	**Au revoir. À bientôt.** *ohr-vwahr ah byaN-toh* Good-bye. See you later.

Words to Know

allô	ah-loh	hello
c'est Pierre.	seh pee-ehr	it's Pierre
ça va?	sah vah	how are you?
est-ce que Monique est là?	ehs kuh moh-neek eh lah?	is Monique there?
un moment, s'il vous plaît	aN moh-mahN seel voo play	one minute please
ne quitte pas	nuh keet pah	don't hang up
au revoir	ohr-vwahr	goodbye
à bientôt	ah byaN-toh	see you later

To your post!

La poste *(lah pohst)* (the post office) offers numerous services besides just mailing letters. You may purchase money orders, stamps, phone cards, use a pay phone, send a fax, open a bank account, take out a loan, or invest money!

Did you notice the informal tone of the preceding conversation? That's because it was between people who are well acquainted with each other. Here are two examples of how the conversation would have been different had Pierre and Monique been strangers:

- **Ça va?** *(sah vah)* This question literally means "It goes?" but is used to mean "How are you?" A more formal way to ask is **Comment-allez vous?** *(kohm-ahN tahlay voo)* (Literally: "How do you go?") **Va** *(vah)* and **allez** *(ahlay)* are both forms of the irregular verb **aller** *(ahlay)* (to go). In French, you do not use the verb **être** *(ehtruh)* (to be) to ask how some one is doing.

- **s'il te plaît** *(seel tuh play)* is Madame La Grange's informal way of saying, "please." The formal way to say the same thing is **s'il vous plaît**. The pronoun **te** refers to the informal subject you (**tu**), where the formal pronoun **vous** refers to the formal you (**vous**).

Leaving a Message

Many times the people we are trying to reach are not available. Whether you're leaving a message on **un répondeur** *(uhn ray-pohN-duhr)* (an answering machine) or leaving one in person, this section tells you what you need to know.

Talkin' the Talk

The following dialog is a telephone conversation where Pierre *(Pee-ehr)* is calling to talk to Marc *(Mahrk)*. Unfortunately, Marc is not home. Pierre leaves a message with Marc's sister Christine *(Krees-teen)*.

Christine:	**Âllo?**
	ah-loh
	Hello?

Pierre: **Âllo, Christine? C'est Pierre. Ça va?**
ah-loh krees-teen seh pee-ehr sah vah
Hello, Christine. It's Pierre. How are you?

Christine: **Ça va bien. Et toi?**
sah vah byaN ay twah
I am fine. And you?

Pierre: **Bien. Est-ce que Marc est là?**
byaN ehs kuh mark eh lah
Fine. Is Mark there?

Christine: **Non, il fait les courses.**
nohN eel fay lay koors
No, he's shopping.

Pierre: **Dommage! Dis-lui que j'ai téléphoné.**
dohm-ahzh deet lew-ee kuh zhay tay-lay-foh-nay
Darn! Tell him that I called.

Christine: **Bien sûr. Salut, Pierre.**
byaN sewr sah-lew pee-ehr
Sure. Bye, Pierre.

Pierre: **Salut, Christine.**
sah-lew krees-teen
Bye, Christine.

Words to Know

dîs-lui que j'ai téléphoné	dee lew-ee kuh zhay tay-lay-foh-nay	tell him that I called
il fait les courses	eel fay lay koors	he's shopping
salut	sah-lew	goodbye (slang)

Livin' in the past: Using the past tense

Based on the previous conversation, when Marc returns home, his sister will tell him that Pierre called while he was out. That phone call took place in the past.

In French, the past tense is formed by using a helping verb, either **avoir** _(ahv-wahr)_ (to have) or **être** _(eht-ruh)_ (to be) and a past participle. Most past participles use **avoir**; a small percentage use **être**.

Review the conjugation of **avoir** (to have) before continuing:

Conjugation	_Pronunciation_
j'ai	zhay
tu as	tew ah
il/elle a	eel/ehl ah
nous avons	noo zavohN
vous avez	voo zahvay
ils/elles ont	eel/ehl zohN

You make regular past participles by dropping the stem of the infinitive and adding the following endings:

✔ The past participle for **-er** verbs end in **é**:

   • **téléphoner** _(tay-lay-foh-nay)_ (to telephone or call):

   J'ai téléphoné à Monique. _(zhay tay-lay-foh-nay ah moh-neek)_ (I called [have called] Monique.)

   • **regarder** _(reh-gahr-day)_ (to watch)

   Nous avons regardé un film. _(noo zahvohN reh-gahr-day aN feelm)_ (We watched [have watched] a movie.)

✔ The past participle for **-ir** verbs end in **i**:

   • **choisir** _(shwah-zeer)_ (to choose): **Il a choisi une banane.** _(eel ah chwahzee ewn bahn-ahN)_ (He chose [has chosen] a banana.)

   • **finir** _(fee-neer)_ (to finish): **Elles ont fini leur conversation.** _(ehl zohN fee-nee luhr kohN-vehr-sah-see-ohN)_ (They finished [have finished] their conversation.)

✔ The past participle for **-re** verbs end in **u**:

   • **attendre** _(ah-tehn-druh)_ (to wait): **Tu as attendu le bus.** _(too ah ah-tehn-doo luh boos)_ (You waited [have waited] for the bus.)

   • **répondre** _(ray-pohN-druh)_ (to answer):

   Vous avez répondu à la question. _(voo zahvay ray-pohN-doo ah la kehs-tee-ohN)_ (You answered [have answered] the question.)

French also has several irregular past participles. The irregular verbs don't have a set pattern like the regular verbs do, so you just have to memorize them. Table 9-1 lists the most common irregular past participles.

Table 9-1	Common Irregular Past Participles	
Infinitive	*Past Participle*	*Translation*
être *(eh-truh)* (to be)	**été** *(ay-tay)*	been
avoir *(ahv-wahr)* (to have)	**eu** *(ew)*	had
faire *(fehr)* (to do/make)	**fait** *(fay)*	done/made
pouvoir *(poov-wahr)* (to be able to)	**pu** *(pew)*	could have
vouloir *(vool-wahr)* (to wish/want)	**voulu** *(voo-loo)*	wished/wanted

The following list gives some examples of how you use the past participles of irregular verbs in a sentence:

- ✔ **Nous avons été en retard.** *(nooz ahv-ohN ay-tay ehn reh-tahr)* (We were late.)

- ✔ **Il a eu un message.** *(eel ah euh uhn may-sazh)* (He had a message.)

- ✔ **Qu'est-ce que tu as fait**? *(kes kuh too ah fay)* (What did you do?)

- ✔ **Vous avez pu téléphoner à votre bureau.** *(vooz ahv-ay poo tay-lay-foh-nay vohtruh byoo-roh)* (You were able to call your office.)

- ✔ **J'ai voulu un sandwich.** *(zhay voo-loo uhn sahNd-veech)* (I wanted a sandwich.)

Using the past tense with être

Sixteen irregular verbs are conjugated with the helping verb **être** instead of **avoir**. Most of these verbs are verbs of motion.

The main difference in these 16 verbs is that the past participle must agree in number and gender with the subject. Luckily, most of the time the pronunciation doesn't change.

We can show you what we mean while reviewing the conjugation of **être** and using the past participle of **aller** *(ah-lay)* (to go):

- ✔ Suppose **Janine** *(zhah-neen)*, a girl, said that she'd gone to the post office. She would say:

    Je suis allée à la poste. *(zhuh sweez ah-lay ah ah pohst)*

    However, if John, a boy, said the same thing, it would sound the same, but be spelled differently:

    Je suis allé à la poste. *(zhuh weez ah-lay ah lah pohst)*

✔ Here's a mother telling her son, "You went to the post office": **Tu es allé à la poste.** *(tew ay ah-lay ah lah pohst)*

Now she tells her daughter the same thing:

Tu es allée à la poste. *(tew ay ah-lay ah lah pohst)*

Do you see the difference in spelling with the past participle? Here are some more:

✔ **Elle est allée à la poste.** *(ehl ayt ah-lay ah lah pohst)* (She [feminine, singular] went to the post office.)

✔ **Nous sommes allés à la poste.** *(noo sohmz ah-lay ah lah pohst)* (We [masculine, plural] went to the post office.)

✔ **Vous êtes allées à la poste.** *(vooz eht ah-lay ah lah pohst)* (You [feminine, plural] went to the post office.)

✔ **Ils sont allés à la poste.** *(eel sohNt ah-lay ah lah pohst)*(They [masculine, plural] went to the post office.)

The rules for making past participles agree with the number and gender of the subject are as follows:

✔ If the subject is masculine, singular, the past participle does not change. It will end in é, i, or u accordingly. The past participle changes spelling only in the following cases:

✔ If the subject is feminine, the past participle ends in an **-e.**

✔ If the subject is masculine plural, the past participle ends in **-s.**

✔ If the subject is feminine plural, the past participle ends in **-es.**

Here are some more examples of the most common **être** *(eh-truh)* verbs:

✔ **Nous sommes restés ici.** *(noo sohm rehs-tay ee-see)* (We stayed here.)

✔ **Il est tombé.** *(eel ay tohm-bay)* (He fell.)

✔ **Nous sommes descendus.** *(noo sohm day-sahN-doo)* (We went downstairs.)

✔ **Elle est entrée au supermarché.** *(ehl ayt ahN-tray oh sew-pehr-mahr-shay)* (She entered the supermarket.)

✔ **Vous êtes venus à la maison.** *(voo zeht veh-noo ah lah may-zohN)* (You came into the house.)

Fun & Games

Fill in the blanks with the correct form of the past participle.

1. **J'ai _____ le dîner. (finir)**

   I finished dinner.

2. **Est-ce qu'elles ont _____ au téléphone. (parler)**

   Weren't they talking on the phone?

3. **Il a _____ une nouvelle auto. (vouloir)**

   He wanted a new car.

4. **Nous avons _____ dans le Minitel. (chercher)**

   We looked in the Minitel.

5. **Qu'est-ce que vous avez _____? (faire)**

   What did you do?

6. **Il a _____ des téléphones. (vendre)**

   He sold telephones.

7. **J'ai _____ un Minitel. (avoir)**

   I had a Minitel.

Answer Key: 1. fini; 2. parlé; 3. voulu; 4. cherché; 5. fait; 6. vendu; 7. eu.

Chapter 10

At the Office and around the House

- -

In This Chapter

▶ Making an appointment

▶ Conducting business

▶ Using the Internet

▶ Visiting a private home

- -

*N*ot all foreign travel is purely for pleasure's sake. In this time of international trade and global marketing, businesspeople may travel extensively. If this is your first business trip to a French-speaking country, be assured that everyone wants to make your visit pleasant. Although some business practices may be different from your own, learning about and respecting these differences will not only impress your French-speaking counterparts but also bring you that much closer to closing your deal.

During the 1980s, French businesses experienced an entrepreneurial explosion. The state no longer had a monopoly on the radio and television stations or utilities. Privatization of media and public utilities changed the business relationships between France and the United States and Canada. Some of the newer and larger businesses have been reorganized by American management consultants. These businesses tend to be more flexible and have a less centralized decision-making process than the older, family-owned businesses. Still, you may not find the same teamwork atmosphere that prevails in the United States and Canada. Expect the **président-directeur général** *(pray-zee-dahN dee-rehk-tuhr zay-nay-rahl),* the head of the company who functions as C.E.O., chairman, and managing director, to make most decisions. Employees below the **P-DG** *(pay day zhay)* (président-directeur général) follow a strict chain of command, with the junior staff handing problems over to superiors. Foreign businesspersons should contact the P-DG, initially. American and Canadian companies should send their most senior official so as not to insult this chain of command. You may also notice a rather elitist atmosphere in business. Being from the "right" families and going to the "right" schools often lead to positions in management.

Women are generally holding more senior positions than they used to, especially in the fields of advertising, retail, and media. The south of France still has a more traditional mind-set, and you may still encounter some prejudice there against women in senior positions. Keep in mind that sexual harrassment is more of an American concept. Don't be surprised if French men seem to treat businesswomen more flirtatiously. When entertaining on business in Belgium, American businesswomen should make payment arrangements in advance or indicate that their company is paying. Belgian businessmen usually don't allow a woman to pay under any other circumstances.

Making an Appointment

It is considered polite in both France and Belgium to schedule appointments several weeks in advance. Be forewarned, however, that some French executives believe their prestige to be enhanced if they don't confirm an appointment until the last minute. Also, don't expect French secretaries to be able to schedule appointments. Most of them don't have access to their bosses' schedules or planners. Your best bet is to directly contact the person with whom you are trying to meet.

Business hours

Generally speaking, businesses are open 8:00 or 9:00 a.m. to noon, and 2:00 to 5:00 or 6:00 p.m., Monday through Friday. Many businesses open Monday at 2:00 p.m. and are open Saturday from 9:00 a.m.to noon or 1:00 p.m. Even though businesses may be open on Saturdays, don't try to schedule appointments then. It is usually a day reserved for sales meetings and conferences. It may also be difficult to schedule appointments in Belgium on **Bourse** *(boors)* days (Mondays in Antwerp and Wednesdays in Brussels) because this is when businesspeople meet professional colleagues for lunch.

Lunch hour

Europeans often take a longer lunch "hour" than their North American counterparts. **Le déjeuner** *(luh day-zhew-nay)*, or lunch, lasts anywhere from 1½ to 2 hours. This is extremely important when trying to set up appointments. Business lunches are also more common than business dinners. Lengthy lavish lunches are usually reserved for a first meeting, or for celebrating the closing of a deal. However, don't be the first to initiate business conversation at a meal. Let your host decide whether to discuss business right away or to wait until the after-meal coffee has been served.

Business around the holidays

Don't plan on doing business in France or Belgium during the two weeks before and after Christmas or Easter. Also avoid the months of July and August when stores, theaters, restaurants, and businesses often close for an annual vacation. (August is the vacation month for 80 percent of France.)

Talkin' the Talk

Dan Thompson, an American advertising executive, calls to set up an appointment to meet with Monsieur (M.) Jean-Michel Seiffert *(muh-syuh zhahN mee-shel see-fehr),* the CEO of a chain of French **supermarchés** *(sew-pehr-mahr-shay)* (supermarkets) in Nice. Monsieur Seiffert's secretary (**la secrétaire**) *(lah suh-kray-tehr)* answers initially.

La secrétaire:	**Companie France Supermarché, bonjour.** *kohN-pah-nyee frahNs sew-pehr-mahr-shay,* *bohN-zhoor* Hello, French Supermarket Company.
Dan:	**Bonjour. Dan Thompson à l'appareil.** **Passez-moi M. Seiffert, s'il vous plaît.** *bohN-zhoor Dan Thompson ah lah-pah-rehy* *Pah-say mwah muh-syuh see-fehr seel voo play* Hello. This is Dan Thompson calling. Please transfer me to Mr. Seiffert.
La secrétaire:	**Un instant. Ne quittez pas. Il est dans son** **bureau. Je vous le passe.** *aN aNs-tahN nuh kee-tay pah eel ay dahN sohN* *bew-roh Zhuh voo luh pahs* One moment. Don't hang up. He's in his office. I'll transfer you to him.
M. Seiffert:	**Allô, M. Thompson?** *ah-loh muh-syuh Thompson* Hello, Mr. Thompson?
Dan:	**Allô, M. Seiffert, bonjour. Je vais à Nice le 14** **juin. Je voudrais fixer un rendez-vous pour** **discuter votre stratégie de marketing.** *ah-loh muh-syuh seiffert bohN-zhoor zhuh vay* *ah nees luh kah-tohrz zhwaN zhuh voo-dray* *feek-say aN rahN-day voo poor dees-koo-tay* *voh-truh strah-tay-zhee du mahr-keh-teeng*

Hello Mr. Seiffert. I will be in Nice on the 14th of June. I would like to arrange a meeting to discuss your marketing strategy.

M. Seiffert: **Ah, bon. Un instant. Je consulte mon calendrier. Ça va, je suis libre le 14 juin à 15h30.**
ah bohN aN aNs-tahN zhuh kohN-sewlt mohN kahl-ahN-dree-ay sah vah zhuh swee lee-bruh luh kah-tohrz zhwaN ah kaNz uhr trahNt
Good. One minute. I'll consult my calendar. Yes, I'm free June 14th at 3:30 p.m.

Dan: **Très bien. Le 14 juin à 15h 30.**
tray byaN luh kah-tohrz zhwaN ah kaNz uhr trahNt
Very well. June 14th at 3:30 p.m.

M. Seifert: **Au revoir.**
ohr-vwahr
Good bye.

Words to Know

... à l'appareil	... ah lah-pah-rehy	This is ... calling.
Passez-moi ...	Pah-say mwah ...	Transfer me to ...
Un instant	aN aNs-tahN	One minute
Ne quittez pas.	nuh kee-tay pah	Don't hang up.
Il est/n'est pas dans son bureau.	eel ay/nay pah dahN sohn bew-ro	He's in/out of his office.
Je vous le/la passe.	zhuh voo luh/lah pahs	I'll transfer you to him/her
je consulte mon calendrier	zhuh kohN-sewlt mohN kah-lahN-dree-yay	I'll check my calendar
Je suis libre ...	zhuh swee lee-bruh	I'm free ...
un rendez-vous	aN rahN-day-roo	an appointment

Conducting Business

The first business meeting should be one where you become acquainted with one another. You should exchange business cards and answer questions about yourself. Both the French and Belgians like to feel that they can trust you as a person before trusting your company. You should also proceed cautiously until you have developed a sense for the company you're dealing with. You certainly don't want to appear overly aggressive in presenting an opinion or a solution to a problem.

Be punctual. Schedules are more adhered to in the north of France. Parisian traffic may make being punctual more difficult, so allow plenty of time to get to your appointment. Generally speaking, Parisians are accommodating and won't be upset if you are 10 to 15 minutes late. People are more relaxed about schedules in the south.

When traveling to Belgium, make sure that one side of your business cards is printed in English and the other side in either French or Dutch, depending on where you are conducting your business.

When you arrive, hand your business card to the receptionist or secretary. You can expect your initial contact to be in an office, as opposed to a restaurant or cafe. Unlike most other countries, you probably won't be offered any refreshments. Remember, in almost all aspects of life, the French are more formal than Americans. When you want to enter someone's office, be sure to knock and wait for an answer; don't just knock and walk in. When you leave an office, make sure to close the door behind you.

When presenting new ideas, don't be surprised if the French initially react negatively. The long history of French philosophy has spawned a nation that enjoys arguing and debating. The French can be won over by rational arguments supported by facts and figures. Sometimes the French want to understand why they should accept a proposal. They probably want to know the risks involved and possible alternative strategies. Be sure to avoid direct confrontations. The French dislike losing and prefer to work around problems.

Talkin' the Talk

The following dialog takes place during the meeting between Dan Thompson, the advertising executive, and Jean-Michel Seiffert, the **P-DG** of Companie France Supermarché.

M. Seiffert: **M. Thompson, bienvenue à Nice. Asseyez-vous.**
muh-syuh Thompson byaN-vuh-new ah nees ah-say-ay voo
Mr. Thompson, welcome to Nice. Have a seat.

Dan: **Merci, monsieur. Vous avez reçu mon message électronique?**
mehr-see muh-syuh vooz ahvay ruh-sew mohN mays-ahzh ay-lehk-troh-neek
Thank you, sir. Did you receive my e-mail?

M. Seiffert: **Oui, je l'ai reçu. Vouz pouvez l'expliquer, s'il vous plaît?**
Wee zhuh leh ruh-soo voo poo-vay layks-plee-kay seel voo play
Yes, I received it. Will you explain it, please?

Dan: **Bien sûr. Il y a un problème avec le zapping pendant vos spots, n'est-ce pas?**
byaN suhr eel ee ah aN proh-blehm ah-vehk luh zahp-een pahN-dahN voh spoht nehs pah
Of course. There's a problem with channel surfing during your commercials, right?

M. Seiffert: **Oui. Les consommateurs s'énervent et ils zappent constamment.**
wee lay kohn-sohm-ah-tuhr say-nehrv ay eel zahp kohN-stah-mahN
Yes, the consumers are annoyed and they surf constantly.

Dan: **J'ai une idée. Il vous faut un slogan émotionnel.**
zheh ewn ee-day eel voo fo aN sloh-gahN ay-moh-see-ohn-ehl
I have an idea. You need an emotional slogan.

M. Seiffet: **Intéressant. Mais, ils sont pratiques. Avez-vous des examples?**
aN-tay-ray-sahN meh eel sohN prah-teek ah-vay voo dayz ehks-ahN-pluh
Interesting. Now, they are practical. Do you have some examples?

Dan: **Les voilà. Ma sécretaire va télécopier notre contrat. Puis-je utiliser votre téléphone?**
lay vwah-lah mah suh-kray-tehr vah tay-lay-koh-pee-ay noh-truh kohN-trat pwee zhuh ew-teel-ee-zay voh-truh tay-lay-fohn
Here they are. My secretary will fax our contract. May I use your telephone?

M. Seiffert: **Mais certainement! Dans l'intervalle, ma sécretaire va faire des copies.**
may sehr-tehn-uh-mahN dahn laN-tehr-vahl mah suh-kray-tehr vah fayr day koh-pee
By all means. In the meantime, my secretary will make some copies.

Words to Know

Asseyez-vous	ah-say-ay voo	Have a seat
Vous avez reçu mon message électronique?	vooz ahvay ruh-sew mohN meh-sazh ay-lehk-troh-neek	You received my e-mail?
je l'ai reçu	zhuh lay ruh-sew	I received it
Vouz pouvez l'expliquer?	voo poo-vay layks-plee-kay	Will you explain it?
le zapping	luh zahp-een	channel surfing
pendant	pahn-dahN	during
vos spots	voh spoht	your commercials
une idée	ewn ee-day	an idea
pratique	prah-teek	practical
télécopier	tay-lay-koh-pee-ay	to fax
Puis-je utiliser votre téléphone?	Pwee zhuh oo-teel-ee-zay voh-truh tay-lay-fohn	May I use your phone?
faire les copies	fayr lay koh-pee	To make copies

Using the Internet

France was connected to the Internet in 1994. However, due to the fact that France already had access to the Minitel (see Chapter 9 for more details), the Internet was not as quick to flourish as it did in Great Britain and Germany. In French, the World Wide Web is sometimes called **la toile** *(lah twahl),* which literally means "the web." More often, French speaking people call it **Le Web** *(luh web)* or even **W3** *(doo-bluh-vay trwah* or *doo-blu-vay kewb).*

Many French businesses are convinced that the Internet will change their marketing strategies as well as their rapport with clients. Dozens of French businesses start up Web sites each week. Some of these sites are French or English only and some are bilingual.

Talkin' the Talk

After the copies are made, Dan and M. Seiffert continue their discussion of the new marketing strategy for Companie France Supermarché.

Dan:	**Il y a beaucoup de personnes qui surfent Le Web, n'est-ce pas?** *eel ee ah bo-koo duh pehr-sohn kee suhrf luh web nehs pah* There are lots of people who surf the Web, right?
M. Seiffert:	**Oui. Pourquoi?** *wee poor-kwah* Yes. Why?
Dan:	**Il vous faut un site pour Companie France Supermarché.** *eel voo fo aN seet poor kohN-pah-nyee frahNs sew-pehr-mahr-shay* You need a site for the French Supermarket Company.
M. Seiffert:	**Ça m'intéresse beaucoup. Continuez.** *sah maN-tehr-ehs bo-koo kohN-teen-ew-ay* That's very interesting. Continue.

Dan:	Chaque personne doit avoir un login. Vous pouvez envoyer un e-mail à chaque personne en annonçant ce qui est en solde.
	shahk pehr-sohn dwaht ah-vwahr aN lohg-in voo poo-vay ahN-vwa-yay aN ee-mehl ah shak pehr-sohn ehN ahN nohN-sahN suh kee eh-tahN sohld
	Each person will require a login. You can send an e-mail to each person, telling them what's on sale.

M. Seiffert:	Comment?
	koh-mahN
	How?

Dan:	Elles doivent s'abonner. Elles vont cliquer sur une icône pour recevoir vos publicités.
	ehl dwahv sah-bohn-ay ehl kleek sewr ewn eek-on poor ruh-suh-vwahr vos pewb-lee-see-tay
	They must subscribe. They will click on an icon to receive your advertisements.

M. Seiffert:	Excellent! Je crois que votre idée est indispensable. Nous avons reçu votre télécopie. Je vais lire votre contrat. Pouvez-vous dîner chez moi ce soir?
	ayk-say-lahN zhuh krwah kuh voh-tr ee-day ay aN-dees-pahN-sah-bluh nooz ah-vohN ruh-sew voh-truh tay-lay-koh-pee zhuh vay leer voh-truh kohN-traht poo-vay voo dee-nay shay mwah suh swahr
	Excellent! I think your idea is absolutely essential. We have received your fax. I will read through your contract. Will you come to my house for dinner tonight?

Dan:	Merci. À ce soir.
	mehr-see ah suh swahr
	Thank you. See you tonight.

Don't look for "dot com"

In Europe, each Internet address ends by the letters that identify the country that hosts that address. In France, these two letters are **.fr**. For example, if you want to connect to the French Yahoo! site, you would type **www.yahoo.fr**. Be forewarned! This site is entirely in French!

Words to Know

surfer le Web	suhr-fay luh web	to surf the Web
un site	aN seet	a (Web) site
un login	aN lohg-in	a login
envoyer des messages électroniques	ehN-voy-yay day may-sahzhay-lehk-trohN-eek	to send e-mail
en solde	ehN sohld	on sale
s'abonner	sah-bohn-ay	to subscribe
cliquer	klee-kay	to click
une icône	oon eek-ohn	an icon
les publicités	lay pewb-lee-see-tay	advertisements
une idée	oon ee-day	an idea
indispensable	aN-dees-pahN-sah-bluh	absolutely essential
recevoir une télécopie	ray-suh-vwahr ewn tay-lay-koh-pee	to receive a fax
dîner chez moi	dee-nay shay mwah	to dine at my house

Visiting a Private Home

The French keep their business and private lives separate. You can expect to be entertained in a restaurant rather than in a home, though outside Paris you may be invited home to a meal. And if a French business person invites you to a country house for the weekend, be sure to accept. This is a real sign that the person thinks of you as a friend!

You should never drop in unannounced in France or Belgium, no matter how well you know a person. You should always call ahead of time and don't call before 10:00 a.m. or after 10:00 p.m. It is acceptable to be late for a cocktail party, but not for dinner parties.

Even in their homes, the French are more formal than hosts are in the United States. You should not expect the "Grand Tour" of a French home. Guests are received in the living room and the doors to the other rooms are typically closed. It is considered rude to wander around both the inside and outside of the home. Always ask before making phone calls because it may be extremely expensive. Also, electricity is much more costly, so ask before using any electronic equipment.

In French, there's a difference between **la salle de bains** *(lah sahl duh baN)* and **les toilettes** *(lay twah-leht)*. **La salle de bains** literally means bathroom, or a place to bathe. It does not necessarily have a toilet. If you are looking for the restroom, be sure to ask for either **les toilettes** or the **W.C.** *(doo-bluh-vay say)* or "water closet."

If you are invited to a French or Belgian home for dinner, it is polite to take the host or hostess a gift. Candy, cookies, or an odd number of flowers is fine. Never bring carnations or chrysanthemums because those are flowers associated with funerals. Nor should you bring red roses, which express intimate affection and are also identified with the Socialist party. Do not bring wine or gifts of food because the French take great pride in choosing these themselves and often have excellent wine cellars.

Talkin' the Talk

 M. Seiffert has just called his wife, Élise, and informed her that he's bringing home his business associate for dinner. Madame Seiffert is talking to her two kids.

Elise:	**Charles! Joséphine! Vite! Vous devez m'aider à faire le ménage.** *shahrl zhoh-say-feen veet voo duh-vay may-day ah fehr luh may-nazh* Charles! Josephine! Quickly! You must help me clean the house.
Charles:	**Pourquoi, maman?** *poor-kwah mah-mahN* Why, mama?
Elise:	**Votre papa a invité un collègue à dîner.** *voh-truh pah-pah ah aN-vee-tay aN koh-lehgah dee-nay* Your father has invited an associate for dinner.
Joséphine:	**Je fais mon lit.** *zhuh fay mohN lee* I'll make my bed.
Charles:	**Je range ma chambre.** *zhuh rahNzh mah shahNbr* I'll clean up my room.
Elise:	**Charles, passe l'aspirateur dans la salle de séjour. Joséphine, nettoie la salle de bains et les toilettes.** *shahrl pahs lahs-peer-ah-tuhr dahn lah sahl duh say-zhoor zhoh-say-feen neht-wah lah sahl duh baN ay lay twah-leht* Charles, (you) vaccuum the living room. Josephine, (you) clean the bathroom and the toilet.
Joséphine:	**Et quoi d'autre, maman?** *ay kwah dohtruh mah-mahN* And what else, mama?
Élise:	**Mettez la table.** *meh-tay lah tah-bluh* (You two) Set the table.
Charles:	**Et toi maman, qu'est-ce que tu vas faire?** *ay mah-mahN kes-kuh tew vah fehr* And you, mama, what will you do?

Élise:	Moi? Je vais faire la cuisine, je vais faire un gâteau, et je vais faire la vaisselle!
	mwah zhuh veh fehr lah kwee-seen zhuh veh fehr aN gah-to ay zhuh veh fehr la veh-sehl
	Me? I'll cook, make a cake, and do the dishes!

Words to Know

faire le ménage	fayr luh may-nazh	clean the house
Je fais mon lit	zhuh fay mohN lee	I'll make my bed
Je range ma chambre	zhuh rahNzh mah shaNbr	I'll clean my room
passe l'aspirateur	pahs lahs-peer-ah-tuhr	vacuum
la salle de séjour	sahl duh say-zhoor	living room
nettoie la salle de bains et les toilettes	neht-wah lah sahl duh bihn ay lay twah-leht	clean the bathroom and the toilet
Mettez la table	meh-tay lay tah-bluh	(You two) Set the table
fais la cuisine	fay la kwee-zeen	make dinner
fais un gâteau	fay aN gah-to	make a cake
fais la vaisselle	fay lah veh-sehl	do the dishes

(For more on the future with "aller," see Chapter 8.)

Fun & Games

Name the rooms of the house that are illustrated in the following drawing.

A. _____

B. _____

C. _____

D. _____

E. _____

Part III
French on the Go

In this part . . .

*M*ost of the readers of this book are going to have to do some traveling in order to use French, and that's what this part is all about. We cover all aspects of travel, from exchanging money to using public transportation to reserving a hotel room.

Chapter 11

Money, Money, Money

. . . .

. . . .

Money (**l'argent**) *(lahr-zhahN)* makes the world go 'round, they say, and you need money to go 'round the world, so this chapter helps you express your needs clearly through several kinds of money transactions. In this chapter, I discuss the fun part of handling money: spending it. See Chapter 16 for coping with possible problems like losing it.

France, Belgium, Luxemburg and Switzerland all use francs, each one with a different exchange rate, of course. But fortunately there is hope on the horizon of the monetary world of Europe: The Euro is finally becoming reality!

So, pretty soon the French, the Belgian, and the Luxemburgian franc along with most other European currencies are going to be history because the Euro is coming in. Unified Europe is based on a common currency which means only one exchange rate for most European countries. Wonderful, right? And perfect for travelers. Well, almost perfect: Switzerland, along with Great Britain, Sweden, Denmark, Norway and Greece, are keeping, at least for a while, their own currencies. For the time being, however, the exchange "race" is still on and you still need several wallets when you travel to keep your moneys apart!

The Euro will become part of people's everyday lives from January 1, 2002 at the latest when Euro notes and coins will become available. However, the Euro has been legal currency from January 1, 1999, enabling it to be used in financial markets and for a range of company activities. Many transactions can be made and settled in Euro, but without Euro notes and coins.

When you travel to French-speaking Canada, you pay with Canadian dollars. No sweat — they are worth a little less than the U.S. dollar, so you have nothing much to figure. And then in Europe, you can use the Euro with its value also in the neighborhood of the U.S. dollar — yes, the math of traveling is going to be quite stressfree! If it only weren't for the language! But don't worry, this chapter explains how to conduct your business at a bank or a currency exchange smoothly.

At the Bank

One of the first places you may need to locate when you travel is a place to exchange your currency for the local currency. Following are the three convenient places to exchange money at a reasonable rate:

- ✔ **Banks** (**les banques**) *(lay bahNk)*. Banking hours (**heures d'ouverture et de fermeture**) *(uhr doo-vehr-tewr ay duh fehr-muh-tewr)* can range between 8 a.m. (8h00) and 9 a.m. (9h00) and between 3 p.m. (15h00) and 5 p.m. (17h00). Some banks close during lunch break, which can last up to two hours. Especially in smaller towns banks are often the most convenient since there might not be a specific currency exchange office.

- ✔ **Currency exchanges** (**un bureau de change**) *(aN bew-ro duh shahN-zh)*. These businesses are everywhere in big cities and where tourists hang out. However, check the rates and commissions first because they can vary greatly. A bank is often a good alternative.

- ✔ **Post offices** (**la poste**) *(lah pohst)*. In France, you can also change money in many post offices. They open at 8 a.m. and close at 6 p.m. (18h00), and even though this service is not offered in all post offices, they will always be able to send you to the nearest place where you can get money.

You may find other places, such as hotel lobbies, too, but their rates are usually less favorable. Likewise, although you may have to change a few dollars at the money exchange counter of the airport upon your arrival, remember that most likely you can get a better deal if you wait until you are in town to change money at a bank.

Entering a bank

When you enter a bank, someone there may ask you how he or she can help you. You may hear one of these phrases:

- ✔ **Vous désirez?** *(voo day-zee-ray)*
- ✔ **Je peux vous aider?** *(zhuh puh vooz ehday)*

Both mean: Can I help you?

But even if nobody asks you, just walk up to an employee and state what you want. The two most common things you want to accomplish in a French bank are changing money from one currency to another and cashing a check of some kind.

Start your request with

Je voudrais . . . *(zhuh voo-dray)* (I would like . . .)

and then add the specifics:

. . . **changer des dollars en francs français.** *(shan-zhay day doh-lahr ahN frahN frah-Nsay* like*)* (to change dollars into French francs.)

. . . **encaisser un chèque.** *(ahN-kehs-say aN shehk)* (to cash a check.)

Of course, since banks charge an additional fee (a flat rate that may vary from bank to bank), you usually want to know the exchange rate first, so simply ask for it very straightforwardly:

Quel est votre taux de change? *(kehl eh voh-tr to duh shahN-zh)* (What is your exchange rate?)

Talkin' the Talk

 Martin, a Canadian tourist, walks into a money exchange in Nice in order to exchange his Canadian dollars into French francs.

Employee:	**Bonjour, monsieur, vous désirez?**
	bohN-zhoor muh-syuh voo deh-zee-reh
	Hello, sir, what can I do for you?

Martin:	**Bonjour, madame. Je voudrais changer cent dollars canadiens.**
	bohN-zhoor muh-dahm zhuh voo-dreh shan-zhay sahN doh-lahr cah-nah-dyen
	Hello, ma'am. I would like to change one hundred Canadian dollars.

Employee:	**Tres bien, monsieur. Un moment, s'il vous plaît. . . . Bon ça fait FF 400. . . . Voilá, et votre reçu.**
	treh byaN muh-syuh aN moh-mahN seel voo play . . . bohn sah feh kah-truh-sahN frahN . . . vwah-lah ay voh-truh ruh-sew
	Very well, sir. One moment, please. . . . Well, it's 400 francs. . . . Here you are, and your receipt.

Martin:	**Merci, et au revoir.**
	mehr-see ay ohr-vwahr
	Thank you, and good-bye.

Employee:	**Au revoir, monsieur.**
	ohr-vwahr muh-syuh
	Good-bye, sir.

Words to Know

bonjour	bohn-zhoor	hello (during the day)
au revoir	ohr-vwahr	good-bye
vous désirez?	voo deh-zee-reh?	can I help you?
je voudrais ...	zhe voo-dray	I would like ...
changer	shahN-zay	to exchange
cent	sahN	one hundred
ça fait	sah-feh	it is (it makes)
voilà	vwa-lah	here you go
la banque	lah bahNk	bank
le bureau de change	luh bew-ro duh shahN-zh	currency exchange
la caisse	lah kehs	cash register
le caissier, la caissière	luh keh-syay, lah keh-syehr	teller
une carte de crédit	ewn kahrt duh kray-dee	credit card
un chèque de voyage	aN shehk duh vwah-yah-zh	traveler's check
le client, la cliente	luh klee-ahN, lah klee-ahNt	customer
le guichet (de change)	luh gee-sheh duh shahN-zh	cashier's window
une devise (étrangère)	ewn duh-veez ay-trahN-zhehr	foreign money
un distributeur (de billets)	uhn dees-tree-bew-tuhr	ATM (automated teller machine)
en argent liquide	ahN nahr-zahN lee-keed	in cash
le reçu	luh ruh-sew	receipt
la signature	lah seen-ya-tewr	signature

Cashing checks and checking your cash

If you take traveler's checks when you travel, you'll save yourself a lot of trouble getting them in the local currency of where you want to go. Cashing them should always be free of charge — **gratuit** *(grah-tew-ee)*. If it is not, go to another bank.

If your traveler's checks are **not** in the local currency, you are charged a fee when you go to exchange the checks into local money. Traveler's checks in U.S. dollars may be useful as a back-up source in case your plans change, you decide to stretch your visit to another country, or if it makes you just feel better to have a security blanket.

With local checks you can even pay in stores, just as if they were cash. However, sometimes (and this happens more frequently than in the United States) a store may not accept your local traveler's check, and that circumstance is why you want to have a credit card for the ATM or some extra cash when you go shopping.

Incidentally, you get your best rates by getting your funds out of an ATM with your credit card, but you need your PIN number for that.

Talkin' the Talk

Susan wants to cash traveler's checks in a bank.

Susan: **Bonjour, mademoiselle.**
            bohN-zhoor mahd-mwah-zehl
            Hello, miss.

            Je voudrais encaisser mes chèques de voyage.
            zhuh voo-ray en-keh-seh deh shehk duh vwa-yazh
            I would like to cash my traveler's checks.

Employee: **Ils sont en francs français?**
            eel sahN tahN frahN frahN-seh
            Are they in French francs?

Susan: **Oui, en francs français.**
            wee ahN frahN frahN-seh
            Yes, in French francs.

Employee: **Bon. J'ai besoin d'une pièce d'identité.**
            bohN zhay buh-zwaN dewn pyehs dee-dahN-tee-tay
            Very well. I need identification.

Susan:
J'ai mon passeport et une carte de crédit, c'est bon?
zhay mohN pahs-pohr ay ewn kahrt duh kray-dee seh bohN
I've got my passport and a credit card, will that do?

Employee:
Le passeport, c'est parfait . . . merci.
luh pahs-pohr seh pahr-feh . . . mehr-see
The passport, that's perfect . . . thank you.

Et votre sigature, s'il vous plaît.
eh voh-truh seen-ya-tewr seel voo play
And your signature, please.

Susan:
Ah oui, bien sûr, . . . voilà.
ah oo-ee byaN sewr . . . vwah-lah
Oh yes, certainly . . . here you go.

Words to Know

je voudrais encaisser . . .	zhuh voo-dray ahN-keh-say . . .	I would like to cash . . .
ils sont	eel sohN	they are
j'ai besoin de	zhay buh-zwaN duh	I need
une pièce d'identité	ewn pyehs dee-dahN-tee-tay	I.D.
c'est parfait	seh pahr-feh	that's perfect
votre signature	voh-truh seen-ya-tewr	your signature
bien sûr	byaN sewr	certainly

Expressing need

In English, you may say "I need something." The French have a slightly different way of expressing their needs. They say that they "have need of something," as follows:

- **j'ai besoin de (+ noun)** *(zhay buh-zwaN duh)* (I need [+ noun])
- **J'ai besoin d'une pièce d'identité.** *(zhay buh-zwaN dewn pyehs dee-dahN-tee-ta)* I need identification.

Therefore, to express a need, you pick the appropriate form of "to have":

avoir (j'ai, tu as, il a, nous avons, vous avez, ils ont)

ah-vwahr (zhay, tew ah, il ah, noo zah-vohN, voo zah-vay, eel zohN)

and add **besoin de** plus whatever you need. For example:

- ✔ **Christine a besoin d'argent.** *(krees-teen uh be-swuhn dahr-zhahN)* (Christine needs money.)
- ✔ **Avez-vous besoin d'un distributeur?** *(ah-vay voo buh-swuhn duhn dees-tree-bew tuhr?)* (Do you need an ATM?)

Dealing with possessive adjectives

Possessive adjectives — my, your, his, and so on — change to "agree" with the gender and number (singular or plural) of the noun, just as the articles (**le, la, les**) *(luh, lah, leh)* do.

Masculine noun in the singular:

mon, ton, son chèque *(mohN, tohN, sohN shek)*: my, your, his/her check

notre, votre, leur chèque *(nohtr, vohtr, lewr shek)*: our, your, their check

Feminine noun in the singular:

ma, ta, sa carte *(mah, tah, sah kart)*: my, your, his/her card

notre, votre, leur carte *(nohtr, vohtr, lewr kahrt)*: our, your, their card

Masculine or feminine noun in the plural:

mes, tes, ses dollars *(meh, teh, ses dohlahr)*: my, your, his/her dollars

nos, vos, leurs dollars *(no, vo, lewr dohlar)*: our, your, their dollars

Making change

The equivalent for the English expression "I need change" (small coins) is **J'ai besoin de monnaie** *(zheh buh-swaN duh mo-nay)* in French.

Be wary not to accidentally translate the English word "money" to **monnaie,** just because "money" and **monnaie** look and sound so much alike. The word "money" corresponds with **argent** *(ahr-zhahN)* in French.

In France (in a coffee bar for example, when the employee wants you to pay in a smaller denomination than a 20-franc bill) you may be asked:

Avez-vous de la (petite) monnaie! *(ah-vay voo duh lah puh-teet moh-nay)* (Do you have (small) change?)

In Québec, however, you may be asked in the same situation:

> **Avez-vous du p'tit change?** *(ah-vay voo dew p'tee shahNzh)* meaning exactly the same thing.

Or you may hear in Québec:

> **Je voudrais faire du change** *(zhuh voo-dray fehr dew shahNzh):* I would like to get some change.

which in France would be:

> **Je voudrais faire de la monnaie** *(zhuh voo-dray fehr duh moh-nay),* again meaning exactly the same thing.

Staying Current with French Currency

In this section, I discuss the currencies used in France and other French-speaking countries.

The franc (Le franc) (luh frahN)

Besides French francs, there are also Swiss, Belgian, and Luxemburgian ones, and their values are quite different from one another. When these units are listed in the exchange bureau, or in the newspapers, you can differentiate them by the following abbreviations:

- ✔ The French franc: FRF
- ✔ The Swiss franc: CHF
- ✔ The Belgian franc: BEF
- ✔ The Luxemburgian franc: LUF
- ✔ The Euro: EUR

By the way, these abbreviations are the official ones that you find listed in banks and currency exchanges. Throughout the respective countries, however — for example in stores or restaurants — you may see other notations, such as FF for the French franc and SFR, BFR, LFR for Swiss, Belgian, and Luxemburgian francs.

Remember when you do your banking or shopping that the French separate francs and centimes with a comma, not with a period. For example, you request FRF 100,00 if you want one hundred francs.

French money (L'argent français) (lahr-zhahN frahN-seh)

The French franc like all other monetary units comes in the form of coins and bills in several denominations. You may see any of the following:

- **Coins:** 5, 10, 20, 50 centimes; 1, 2, 5, 10, 20 francs
- **Bills:** 20, 50, 100, 200, 500 francs. Unlike U.S. dollar bills, which all have the same size and color, French bills grow in size with the denomination, are very colorful, and depict famous French people such as writers, painters, and musicians. The coins vary in size, but, just like U.S. coins, they don't necessarily grow in proportion to the denomination.

The new Euro bills, very symbolically, sport European bridges.

Using Credit Cards and ATMs

Credit cards are widely accepted in French-speaking countries. However, you cannot necessarily count on being able to use them outside big cities, and if you can, you may just happen to be carrying the wrong kind. Also, places that take credit cards are often pricier than the ones that don't.

Using your credit card at an ATM

ATMs have become quite the rage ever since they appeared. You find them in big and small towns, usually at a bank, in a shopping area, at train stations, at post offices. You can access them all day and night . . . unless, of course, they are temporarily out of order. But nothing is perfect, right?

The exchange rate you get is definitely the most favorable because it's a direct bank exchange between the ATM's bank and your bank if you use your ATM card, or between the ATM's bank and your credit card if you are using your credit card. Most credit cards charge a nominal fee for cash advance (around 1 percent), but your bank doesn't — at least most of the banks don't.

Machines basically work the same way they do at home. Usually you can choose your prompts to be in English; if not, the following section, "Getting to know ATM language," should help you get through the ordeal of accessing your money.

Getting to know ATM language

Just in case the machine doesn't give you a language choice, here are the French phrases you need to know to use an ATM:

- **Insérez votre carte svp.** *(aN-seh-ray vohtr kahrt seel voo play)* (Insert your card, please.)

- **Tapez votre code svp.** *(tah-pay vohtr kohd seel voo play)* (Type your PIN, please.)

- **Retrait d'espèces.** *(ruh-tray dehs-pehs)* Cash withdrawal.

- **Voulez-vous un reçu?** *(voo-lay-voo aN ruh-sew)* (Would you like a receipt?)

- **Carte en cours de vérification.** *(kahrt ahN koor duh veh-ree-fee-ka-syohN)* (Checking your balance.)

- **Patientez svp.** *(pa-syahN-tay, seel voo play)* (Wait, please.)

- **Reprenez votre carte svp.** *(ruh-pruh-nay vohtr kahrt, seel voo play)* (Take your card, please.)

- **Prenez votre argent.** *(pruh-nay votr ahr zhahN, seel voo play)* (Take your money, please.)

- **N'oubliez pas votre reçu.** *(noo-blee-ay pah vohtr ruh-sew)* (Don't forget your receipt.)

- **Au revoir.** *(ohr-vwahr)* Good-bye.

Talkin' the Talk

Marc and his French friend Claire are at an ATM trying to withdraw money. Marc is experiencing difficulties with the prompts.

Marc: **Zut! C'est tout en français.**
sewt seh too tahN frahN-seh
Oh no! This is all in French.

Tu peux traduire pour moi?
tew puh trah-dew-eer poor mwah
Can you translate for me?

Claire: **Mais oui, avec plaisir.**
meh wee ah-vehk pleh-seer
Certainly, with pleasure.

Marc: **Okay, insérez votre carte . . . pas de problème.**
oh-kay aN-seh-ray votr kahrt . . . pahd pro-blehm
Okay, insert your card . . . no problem.

Tapez votre code? C'est le *PIN*, correct?
ta-pay vohtr kohd seh luh PIN koh-rehkt
Key in your code? That's the PIN number, right?

Claire: **Correct. Et puis, tu as le choix:**
koh-rehkt ay pew-ee tew ah luh shwah
Right. And then you have a choice:

Tu choisis "retrait d'espèces" . . . cash.
tew shwah-zee ruh-tray dehs-pehs . . . kahsh
You choose cash.

Tu veux un reçu . . . a receipt?
tew vuh uhn ruh-sew
Do you want a receipt?

Marc: **Oui. Et puis, on attend? Patience, patience . . .**
oo-ee ay pew-ee oh-na-tahN pah-see-ahNs pah-see-ahNs . . .
Yes. And then we wait? Patience, patience . . .

Voilà ma carte . . . mon argent . . . mon reçu.
vwahlah mah kahrt . . . moh-nar-zhahN . . . mahN ruh-sew
Here comes my card . . . my money . . . my receipt.

Fantastique, merci pour ton aide.
fahN-tahs-teek mehr-see poor tohN nehd
Fantastic, thank you for your help.

Words to Know

tout	too	everything
tu peux traduire	tew puh trah-dew-eer	you can translate
pour moi	poor mwah	for me
avec plaisir	ah-vek pleh-zeer	with pleasure
pas de problème	pahd proh-blehm	no problem
et puis	ay pew-ee	and then
tu as le choix	tew ah luh shwah	you have a choice
tu choisis	tew shwah-zee	you choose
on attend	oh-nah-tahN	one waits
une aide	ewn ehd	help

Verbs such as can, want, and need

Verbs such as can, want, or need require a verb after them in the infinitive form, as in these examples:

- **Tu peux traduire** *(tew puh trah-dew-eer)* (You can translate.)
- **Vous pouvez choisir** *(voo poo-vay shwah-zeer)* (You can choose.)
- **Pouvez-vous signer ici?** *(poo-vay voo see-nyay ee-see)* (Can you sign here?)
- **Je veux changer de l'argent** *(zhuh vuh shahN-zhay duh lar-zhahN)* (I want to change money.)
- **Il doit attendre un peu** *(eel dwah-tah-tahN-draN puh)* (He has to wait a little.)

Objects of prepositions

After a preposition such as "for, with, without," and so on, me, you, him, us, you (plural), or them become **moi, toi,** or **lui/elle, nous, vous, eux/elles** *(mwah, twah, lew-ee/ehl, noo, voo, uh/ehl).* Here are the personal pronouns after prepositions:

✔ **pour moi** *(poor mwah)* (for me)

✔ **avec moi** *(ah-vek mwah)* (with me)

✔ **sans toi** *(sahN twah)* (without you)

✔ **pour lui/elle** *(poor lew-ee/ehl)* (for him/her)

✔ **avec nous** *(ah-vek noo)* (with us)

✔ **sans vous** *(sahN voo)* (without you)

✔ **pour eux/elles** *(poor uh/ehl)* (for them)

We/one

When speaking generally, the French use a fairly simple construction with an impersonal subject. That is, instead of saying "we paid cash," they usually prefer to say "one (impersonal) paid cash." The French word for one is **on** *(ohN).* For example,

> **Nous avons besoin d'argent liquide.** *(noo zah-vohN buh-zwaN dahr-zhahN lee-keed)*

becomes

> **On a besoin d'argent liquide.** *(ohN-na buh-zwaN dahr-zhahN lee-keed)* (We need cash.)

Similarly, the French prefer:

> **On peut payer ici.** *(ohN puh peh-yay ee-see)* (We can pay here.)

On peut sounds a lot better to French ears than the good old **nous pouvons** *(noo poo-vohN)* (we can) form. **On** *(ohN)* (one, in the impersonal meaning) is what you usually hear, and sometimes it also replaces the "they" form, maybe just to be more casual:

> **Ah, ils ouvrent!** *(ah, eel-soo-vruh)*

becomes

> **Ah, on ouvre!** *(ah, ohN-noovruh)* (Ah, they are opening.)

Talkin' the Talk

 Julie bought a couple of travel guides and wants to pay with her credit card. Unfortunately, the store does not accept credit cards.

Julie:
Bonjour, monsieur, vous acceptez les cartes de crédit?
bohN-zhoor muh-syuh voo-zahk-sehp-tay leh kahrt duh kray-dee
Hello, sir do you accept credit cards?

Salesperson:
Ah, non, désolé.
ahnohN day-soh-lay
Oh no, sorry.

Julie:
Zut! Alors, où est-ce qu'il y a un distributeur près d'ici?
zewt ah-lohr oo ehs-kee-lee-yah aN dees-tree-bew-tuhr preh dee-see
Oh no! Then, where is an ATM close to here?

Salesperson:
Il y en a un en face.
ee-lee ahN nah aN ahN fahs
There is one across the street.

Julie:
Je reviens tout de suite.
zhuh ruh-vyaN toot sweet
I'll be back right away.

Pouvez-vous garder mes guides?
poo-vay voo gahr-day meh geed
Can you hold my guides?

Salesperson:
Avec plaisir. Ne vous inquiétez pas.
ah-vehk pleh-zeer nuh voo zaN-kee-ay-tay pah
Gladly. Don't worry.

Julie:
Merci, à tout de suite.
mehr-see ah toot sweet
Thank you, I'll be right back.

Words to Know

vous acceptez	voo-zahk-sehp-tay	you accept
désolé	day-soh-lay	sorry
alors	ah-lohr	then, so then
où	oo?	where?
je dois aller	zhuh dwah-zah-lay	I have to go
il y en a un	ee-lee-ahN nah aN	there is one
en face	ahN fahs	across the street
je reviens	zhuh ruh-vyaN	I'll come back
tout de suite	toot sweet	right away
à tout de suite	ah toot sweet	see you in a minute
ne vous inquiétez pas	nuh voo-zaN-kee-ay-tay pah	don't worry

Negative commands

For negative commands you need to "wrap" the **ne . . . pas** (*nuh pah*) (not) that you use for straightforward negations around the verb, including any pronoun, such as **vous,** that goes with the verb. Check out these examples:

> ✔ **N'attendez pas Paul.** (*nah-tahn-day pah pohl*) (Don't wait for Paul.)
>
> ✔ **Ne vous inquiétez pas.** (*nuh voo-zaN-kee-ay-tay pah*) (Don't worry.)

And just like in English, never use a subject in a command, be it negative or positive.

The little preposition **à** translates in a great many different ways. Whereas in English we say "see you" in combination with time notions, in the following phrases it means "until:"

> ✔ **à tout de suite** (*ah toot sweet*) (see you in a minute)
>
> ✔ **à demain** (*ah duh-maN*) (see you tomorrow)
>
> ✔ **à ce soir** (*ah suh swahr*) (see you tonight)
>
> ✔ **à samedi** (*ah sahm-dee*) (see you on Saturday)

Currency Wisdom

You may want to practice your French in some other interesting country, so we have listed below the countries where French is the official language. There are many more places where much French is spoken, such as many regions of Africa, although not as the official language.

The countries outside of Europe that use the French currency form part of the French motherland and are called **la France d'outremer** *(lah frahNs doo-tr-mehr)*. Corsica belongs to France just like Normandy or Brittany.

Europe:

- France*: French francs (FRF)
- Monaco*: French francs
- Andorra*: French Francs
- Belgium* (Walloon part): Belgian francs (BEF)
- Luxemburg*: Luxemburgian Francs (LUF)
- French Switzerland: Swiss francs (CHF)
- Corsica*: French francs

Americas:

- Québec, Canada: Canadian dollars (CAN$)
- St Pierre and Miquelon: French francs
- French Guiana: French francs

North Atlantic Ocean (Caribbean):

- Guadeloupe with St Martin: French francs
- Martinique: French francs
- Haiti: Gourdes (Gde)

Indian Ocean:

- Madagascar: Malagasy francs (MGF)
- Mayotte: French francs
- La Réunion: French francs

French Polynesia:

- ✔ Tahiti: CFP francs (XPF)
- ✔ New Caledonia: CFP francs
- ✔ Vanuatu: CFP francs
- ✔ Wallis-et-Futuna: CFP francs

*Remember, these countries are in the process of converting to the new Euro. In many places, you will already encounter two prices on price tags in order to allow people to develop a sense of the new currency.

If you want to find current exchange rates of any of these countries, you can look them up at www.finance.yahoo.com on the Internet.

Fun & Games

Find the French equivalents and fill out the lines:

_ _ _ i _ i _une banque

avec _ _ _ i _ i _

carte _ _ _ _ _ _ _ i _

vous _ _ _ i _ _ _ _

_ _ _ _ i _ _ _ _ un chèque

_ _ _ i _ _ _ _ _ _, s'il vous plaît

_ i _ _ _ i _ _ _ _ _ _ de billets

Here are the English equivalents (not in order) of the words that you are looking for:

cash a check – credit card – ATM machine – with pleasure – to choose a bank –
wait, please – can I help you

Chapter 12

Where Is the Louvre? Asking Directions

*W*hen you set out for a trip, you probably have a pretty good idea of all the things you want to do and the places you want to see. You figure out beforehand how you'll manage to get there, what type of transportation you need, and how to arrange for it. But once you are there, you'll always be confronted with questions such as where the nearest bus stop or bank is, or how to find the restroom or telephone. You may have to change plans, or you may decide to try something completely different. Whatever the reason, rarely will there be a trip without your having to ask for directions.

Asking "Where" Questions

Where questions are made the same way in French as they are in English. The verb most often connected with the question word **où** *(oo)* is the verb to be: **être** *(ehtr).*

> ✔ **Où <u>est</u> le Louvre?** *(oo eh luh loovr)* (Where is the Louvre?)
>
> ✔ **Où <u>est</u> la place Victor Hugo?** *(oo eh lah plahs veek-tohr ew-go)* (Where is the Victor Hugo Square?)
>
> ✔ **Où <u>sont</u> les toilettes?** *(oo sohN leh twah-leht)* (Where is the bathroom?)

There is, however, another verb, **se trouver** *suh troo-vay* (to be located), that is very frequently used in this context:

✔ **Où <u>se trouve</u> le Louvre?** *(oo suh troov luh loovr)* (Where is the Louvre [located])?

✔ **Où <u>se trouve</u> la place Victor Hugo?** *(oo suh troov lah plahs veek-tohr ew-go)* (Where is the Victor Hugo Square?)

✔ **Où <u>se trouvent</u> les toilettes?** *(oo suh troov lay twah-leht)* (Where is the bathroom?)

You see in either case that **où** is followed by the verb which is followed by the subject.

This sentence structure is used for all other verbs you choose to connect **où** with:

✔ **Où va ce bus?** *(oo vah suh bews)* (Where is this bus going?)

✔ **Où mène cette rue?** *(oo mehn seht rew)* (Where does this road lead to?)

Answering "Where" Questions

Asking questions is always easy — answering them, only sometimes. As a rule, you can use the preposition **à** *(ah)* meaning "to," "in," or "at" when you want to say that you are going to or staying *in a city.* For example:

✔ **Je vais à Lille.** *(zhuh vay ah leel)* (I am going to Lille.)

✔ **Ils sont à Montréal.** *(eels son tah mohN-reh-ahl)* (They are staying in Montreal.)

However, when you want to talk about going to or staying at places in general, such as museums, cathedrals, or churches, you need to add an article after **à.** This can seem tricky, because **à** contracts with the masculine, and only with the masculine **le** *(luh)* and the plural **les** *(leh).* The following examples show how **à** combines with each of the articles:

✔ **Sylvie va <u>au</u>** (à + le = au) **musée.** *(seel-vee vah oh mew-say)* (Sylvie is going to the museum.)

✔ **Guy veut aller <u>à la</u> cathédrale.** *(gee vuh tah-lay ah lah kah-tay-drahl)* (Guy wants to go to the cathedral.)

✔ **Les Martin vont <u>à l'église</u> St. Paul.** *(lay mahr-tahN vohN tah lay-glees sahn pohl)* (The Martins go to St. Paul's church.)

✔ **Allez aux** (à + les = aux) **feux!** *(ah-lay oh fuh)* (Go to the traffic lights!)

Sometimes you can get a really quick answer, especially when the place you are asking about is right in front of you. (With all the noise and confusion around, one loses perspective at times . . . and how about that: You are already where you want to be.) So, you may ask for the post office or something, and someone may tell you:

- ✔ **Voici la poste . . . le musée . . . l'université!** *(vwah-see lah pohst luh mew-zay lew-nee-vehr-see-tay)* (Here is the post office . . . the museum . . . the university!)
- ✔ **Voilà les bureaux!** *(vwah-lah lay bew-roh)* (There are the offices!)

But even more likely, you get one of these simple phrases for an answer:

- ✔ **Le voici!** (=**le musée**) *(luh vwah-see)* (Here it is.)
- ✔ **La voilà!** (=**l'université** f.) *(lah vwah-lah)* (There it is.)
- ✔ **Les voilà!** (=**les bureaux**) *(lay vwah-lah)* (There they are.)

The **la, le,** or **les** replaces the noun that was mentioned in the question, but remember to put them in front of the **voici** or **voilà**.

Words to Know

ils restent	eel rehst	they stay
elle mène à	ehl meh-nah	it leads to
ce bus	suh bews	this bus
cette rue	seht rew	this street
il se trouve	eel suh troov	it is (located)
la place	lah plahs	square
les toilettes	leh twah-leht	bathroom
le musée	luh mew-zay	museum
la cathédrale	lah kah-tay-drahl	cathedral
l'église (f.)	lay-gleez	church
les feux	leh fuh	traffic light

Getting Direction about Directions

Whenever and wherever you travel, you are bound to need directions at some point. It's often difficult enough to catch everything you're told upon inquiring in your own language, let alone in French. However, understanding a few basic expessions can enable you to get the general idea or direction of where to go.

But what if you don't understand the directions just because the person to whom you are speaking is talking too fast or mumbling or has a strong accent? Well, don't give up! Before you find out how to get directions in more detail, think about what you are going to say if this happens: You finally mustered up enough courage to ask, but you just don't get it. You need to be able to say that you didn't understand the first time and ask the person to repeat the information more slowly. That's when the following phrases can help you:

- **Excusez-moi!** *(ehx-kew-say mwah)* (Excuse me.)

- **pardon** *(pahr-dohN)* (pardon)

- **Je ne comprends pas.** *(zhuh nuh kohN-prahN pah)* (I don't understand.)

- **Est-ce que vous pouvez répéter, s'il vous plaît?** *(ehs-kuh voo poo-vay ray-pay-tay, seel voo play)* (Can you repeat that, please?)

- **(Parlez) plus lentement.** *([pahr-lay] plew lahN-tuh-mahN)* ([Speak] more slowly.)

- **Qu'est-ce que vous avez dit?** *(kes-kuh voo zah-vay dee)* (What did you say?)

Of course, it's always handy to know how to say "thank you," or "thank you very much," which in French is **merci** *(mehr-see)* or **merci beaucoup** *(mehr-see bo-koo)*. In reply, you may hear **de rien** *(duh ryaN)* or **Je vous en prie** *(zhuh voo zaN pree)* which mean respectively "not at all" or "you are welcome."

Words to Know

le centre-ville	luh sahNtr veel	downtown
près/loin (de)	preh/lwahN duh	close to/far (from)
allez!	ah-lay	go!
la gare	lah gahr	train station
là-bas	lah bah	over there
prenez . . . !	pruh-nay	take...!
la station de métro	lah stas-yohN duh may-troh	subway station
à deux minutes	ah duh mee-newt	only two minutes away
il y a	eel yah	there is/are
la station-service	lah stas-yohN sehr-vees	gas station
à gauche	ah gosh	left
suivez!	swee-vay	follow!
la rue	lah rew	street
à droite	ah drwaht	right
j'ai besoin de	zhay buh-zwaN duh	I need
le croisement	luh crwah-zuh-mahN	intersection
tout droit	too drwah	straight ahead
au bout (de)	o boo duh	at the end (of)

Talkin' the Talk

 John and Ann are in their hotel lobby inquiring about directions to go to Notre Dame cathedral.

Desk Clerk: **Bonjour, monsieur. Vous désirez?**
bohN-zhoor muh-syuh voo day-zee-ray
Hello, sir. Can I help you?

John: **Nous voulons aller à pied à Notre Dame. Est-ce que c'est loin?**
noo voo-lohn zah-lay ah pyeh ah nohtr dahm ehs-kuh seh lwahN
We want to walk to Notre Dame. Is it far?

Desk Clerk: **Non, c'est à 15 minutes peut-être. Vous sortez de l'hôtel, tournez à gauche et continuez tout droit.**
nohn seh tah kahNz mee-newt puh-tehtr voo sohr-tay duh loh-tel toor-nay ah gosh eh kohN-tee-new-ay too drwah
No, it's 15 minutes maybe. You leave the hotel, turn left, and keep going straight ahead.

John: **Et ensuite?**
eh ahN-sweet
And then?

Desk Clerk: **Vous allez voir la cathédrale après le Pont Neuf.**
voo zah-lay vwahr lah kah-teh-drahl ah-preh luh pohN nuhf
You'll see the cathedral after the Pont Neuf.

John: **Merci beaucoup.**
mehr-see bo-koo
Thank you very much.

Desk Clerk: **Je vous en prie.**
zhuh voo zahN pree
You are welcome.

Words to Know

nous voulons	noo voo-lohN	we want
à pied	ah pyeh	by foot
peut-être	puh-tehtr	maybe
vous sortez	voo sohr-tay	you leave
vous tournez	voo toor-nay	you turn
vous continuez	voo kohN-tee-new-ay	you continue
ensuite	ahN-sweet	then
vous allez voir	voo zah-lay vwahr	you'll see
après	ah-pray	after

Using commands

When someone directs you to a location, that person is giving you a command. It is understood that *you* are being adressed, but because there are two ways of saying *you* in French (the familiar **tu** and the polite **vous**) there are two different command forms.

As discussed in Chapter 8, to form the command, you just omit the **tu** or the **vous** in front of the verb form (as you drop the "you" in English, actually):

- **Va au centre!** *(vah o sahNtr)* (Go to the center!)
- **Allez tout droit!** *(ah-lay too drwah)* (Go straight ahead!)

For **-er** verbs only, drop the final -s from the tu form in all commands, as in these examples:

Infinitive (-er)	Tu form	Command form
aller *(ah-lay)* (to go)	**tu vas** *(tew vah)*	**va!** *(vah)* (go!)
continuer *(kohN-tee-new-ay)* (to go on)	**tu continues** *(tew kohN-tee-new)*	**continue!** *(kohN-tee-new)* (go on!)

Expressing distances (time and space)

As explained in Chapter 11, you can use the **à** for time expressions such as "see you *in* 15 minutes, tomorrow, next week," but you can also use it for distance away from you, as in the following:

- **à deux minutes** *(ah dew mee-newt)* (it takes only two minutes)
- **à cent mètres** *(ah sahN mehtr)* (only 100 meters farther)
- **C'est à cent mètres (d'ici).** *(seh tah sahn mehtr dee-see)* (It's 100 meters [from here].)
- **C'est à deux kilomètres.** *(seh-ah duh kee-loh-mehtr)* (It's 2 kilometers away.)

Discovering ordinal numbers

If you're going to follow directions, you need to know your ordinal numbers, so that you know where to turn: at the first, second or third street or traffic light. A couple of simple rules can help you recognize ordinal numbers:

- Except for **premier** *(pruhm-yay)* (first), they all have **-ième** after the number (just like the *-th* ending in English).
- If the cardinal number ends in an **-e**, the **-e** is dropped: For example, **quatre** *(kahtr)* (four) becomes **quatrième** *(kat-ree-ehm)* (fourth).

Un *(aN)* (one), **cinq** *(saNk)* (five), and **neuf** *(nuhf)* (nine) have special forms, as you can see in Table 12-1.

Table 12-1	Ordinal Numbers
Word (Numeral)	**Pronunciation**
premier (1e)	(pruhm-yeh)
deuxième (2e)	(duh-zyehm)
troisième (3e)	(trwah-zyehm)

Word (Numeral)	Pronunciation
quatrième (4e)	(kah tryehm)
cinquième (5e)	(sahN-kyehm)
sixième (6e)	(see-zyehm)
septième (7e)	(seh-tyehm)
huitième (8e)	(wee-tyehm)
neuvième (9e)	(nuh-vyehm)
dixième (10e)	(dee-zyehm)
onzième (11e)	(ohN-zyehm)
douzième (12e)	(doo-zyehm)
treizième (13e)	(treh-zyehm)
quatorzième (14e)	(kah-tohr-zyehm)
quinzième (15e)	(kahN-zyehm)
seizième (16e)	(seh-zyehm)
dix-septième (17e)	(dee-seh-tyehm)
dix-huitième (18e)	(dee-zweet-yehm)
dix-neuvième (19e)	(deez nuhvyehm)
vingtième (20e)	(vahN-tyehm)
vingt et unième (21e)	(vahN-teh-ewn-yehm)
vingt-deuxième (22e)	(vahN-duh-zyehm)
trentième (30e)	(trahN-tyehm)
quatre-vingtième (80e)	(kahtr vahN-tyehm)
quatre-vingt-deuxième (82e)	(katr-vahN duh-zyehm)
centième (100e)	(sahN-tyehm)
deux centième (200e)	(duh sahN-tyehm)

To say that you live on a particular floor of a building, you can use an ordinal number by itself, without saying **étage** *(ay-tahzh)* (floor) after it:

> **L'appartement est au troisième** *(lah-pahr-tuh-mahN eh to trwah-zyehm)* (The apartment is on the third floor.)

When you speak with people who live in Paris, you often hear them use ordinal numbers to tell what section of the city a restaurant is in, for example. There are 20 districts called **arrondissements** *(ah-rohN-dees-mahN)*. They may say:

> **Dans quel arrondissement est le restaurant?** *(dahn kehl ah-rohN-dees-mahN eh luh reh-stoh-rahN)* (In which district is the restaurant?)

> **Il est dans le deuxième.** *(eel eh dahN luh duh-zyehm)* (It is in the second district.)

When you talk about kings, queens, and other rulers, French uses cardinal numbers, rather than ordinal numbers like English does, except for **premier/première** (the first). For example:

🖊 **Charles Ier** is called **Charles premier** *(sharl pruhm-yeh)*

🖊 **Henri VIII** is called **Henri huit** *(ahN-ri weet)*

🖊 **Louis XIV** is called **Louis quatorze** *(loo-ee kah-tohrz)*

In French buildings, floors are counted differently: Because the ground floor is called **le rez-de-chaussée** *(luh reht-shoh-say)* (street level), the first floor **(le premier)** is then what Americans consider to be the second floor of any building. So, if they tell you in the hotel that your room is **au deuxième** (on the second floor), it is probably on the third.

Talkin' the Talk

Vivian is looking for place Rodin. She asks a police officer for directions.

Vivian: **Excusez-moi, s'il vous plaît. Pour aller place Rodin?**
ehx-kew-zay mwah seel voo play poor ah-lay plahs roh-dahN
Excuse me, please. How do I get to Rodin square?

Policeman: **Prenez la troisième rue à droite, et c'est tout droit.**
pruhnay lah trwah-zyehm rew ah drwaht ay seh too drwah
Take the third street on the right, and it's straight ahead.

Vivian: **Bon. La troisième à droite. Elle s'appelle comment, cette rue?**
bohn lah trwah-zyehm ah drwaht ehl sah-pehl koh-mahn seht rew
Okay. The third on the right. What's the name of that street?

Policeman:	**C'est la rue Mottes. Il y a la poste au coin.**
	seh lah rew moht eel yah lah pohst o kwahN
	It's Mottes Street. There is a post office on the corner.
Vivian:	**Merci beaucoup.**
	mehr-see bo-koo
	Thank you very much.

Going north, south, east, and west

If you decide to go exploring a French-speaking country by car, this section gives you some pointers on how to ask for directions or get out of a jam if you get lost.

First, you may need to know the cardinal points of the compass:

- ✔ **nord** *(nohr)*
- ✔ **nord-est** *(nor-ehst)*
- ✔ **est** *(ehst)*
- ✔ **sud-est** *(sew-dehst)*
- ✔ **sud** *(sewd)*
- ✔ **sud-ouest** *(sew-dwehst)*
- ✔ **ouest** *(oo-ehst)*
- ✔ **nord-ouest** *(nor-wehst)*

When you ask or give directions, always add <u>**au**</u> or <u>**à l'**</u> *(o or ahl)* (to the) in front of the cardinal point, as in the following examples:

- ✔ **Paris est <u>au</u> nord de Nice.** *(pah-ree eh to nohr duh nees)* (Paris is north of Nice.)
- ✔ **New York est <u>au</u> sud de Montréal.** *(noo york eh to sewd duh mohn-rey-ahl)* (New York is south of Montreal.)
- ✔ **Madagascar est <u>au</u> sud-est de l'Afrique.** *(mah-dah-gahs-kahr eh to sew dest duh lah-freek)* (Madagascar is southeast of Africa.)
- ✔ **La Belgique est <u>à l'</u>est de la France.** *(lah behl-zheek eh tah lehst duh lah frahNs)* (Belgium is east of France.)

  Since **ouest** begins with an o, which is a vowel, you use **à l'** instead of the contracted **au** (**à**+**le**=**au**).

Talkin' the Talk

Julie asks her French friend Cécile about the location of the Versailles castle.

Julie: **Cécile, où est le château de Versailles?**
say-seel oo eh luh shah-toh duh vehr-sahy
Cécile, where is the castle of Versailles?

Cécile: **Il se trouve au sud-ouest de Paris.**
eel suh troov o sew dwest duh pah-ree
It's southwest of Paris.

Julie: **C'est loin?**
seh lwahN
Is it far?

Cécile: **Ton hôtel est à l'est, n'est-ce pas? C'est à une heure en voiture, à peu près. Nous pouvons aller ensemble samedi, peut-être.**
tonoh-tehl eh-tah lehst nehs pah seh tah ewn uhr ahN vwah-tewr ah puh preh noo poo-vohN ah-lay ahN-sahN-bluh sahm-dee puh tehtr
Your hotel is in the east, right? It's one hour by car, roughly. We can go together on Saturday, maybe.

Julie: **Très bonne idée!**
treh bohn ee-day
That's a very good idea.

Cécile: **OK. On va se téléphoner avant samedi.**
oh-kay ohN vah suh tay-lay-foh-nay ah-vahN sahm-dee
Okay. We'll telephone before Saturday.

Julie: **Très bien. Adieu, Cécile.**
treh byaN ah-dyuh say-seel
Great. Bye-bye, Cécile.

Words to Know

le château	luh shah-toh	castle
n'est-ce pas?	nehs pah?	isn't that so?
une heure	ewn uhr	hour
en voiture	ahN vwah-tewr	by car
à peu près	ah puh preh	roughly
nous pouvons	noo poo-vohN	we can
on va se téléphoner	ohN vah suh tay-lay-foh-nay	we'll telephone
avant	ah-vahN	before
adieu!	ah-dyuh	bye-bye (casual)

In French, most adjectives are placed after the noun that they describe, which is the opposite from English: **un voyage intéressant** *(aN vwah-yazh ahn-tay-reh-sahN)* means "an interesting trip."

However, this rule changes when the adjectives relate to

- ✔ Beauty: **beau/belle** *(boh/behl)* (beautiful), **joli** *(zhoh-lee)* (pretty), and so on

- ✔ Age: **jeune** *(zhuhn)* (young), **vieux/vieille** *(vyuh/vyehy)* (old), and so on

- ✔ Goodness, or lack of it: **bon/bonne** *(bohN/bon)* (good), **mauvais** *(moh-vay)* (bad), and so on

- ✔ Size: **grand** *(grahN)* big, **petit** *(puh-tee)*, and so on

Adjectives like these generally precede the noun (think of **B-A-G-S** to help you remember).

✔ **Est-ce que c'est la bonne route pour Versailles?** *(ehs-kuh seh lah bohn root poor vehr-sahy)* (Is this the right way to Versailles?)

✔ **Où va cette rue?** *(oo va seht rew)* (Where does this street go?)

✔ **Comment s'appelle cette ville?** *(koh-mahN sah-pehl seht veel)* (What's the name of this town?)

And here are some answers you can expect:

✔ **Allez au rond-point.** *(ah-lay o rohN pwahN)* (Go to the traffic circle.)

✔ **Passez les feux.** *(pah-say lay fuh)* (Go through the traffic lights.)

✔ **Après le bois, prenez à gauche.** *(ah-preh luh bwah, pruh-nay ah gosh)* (After the woods, turn left.)

It's Necessary to Know about "Il Faut"

It always seems so absolute to say "you have to, he has to, they have to," doesn't it? So in French, you have a way out of this impoliteness: You can use just one form for everybody — **il faut** *(eel foh)* (one has to). This form never changes; simply put the infinitive of any verb after it, as in the following examples:

✔ **Il faut retourner à l'hôtel.** *(eel foh ruh-toor-nay ah loh-tehl)* (I, you, we [depending on context] have to go back to the hotel.)

✔ **Alors, il faut aller au centre-ville.** *(ah-lohr eel foh ah-lay oh sahnNtr veel)* (I, you, we [depending on context] have to go downtown.)

✔ **Il faut prendre un taxi.** *(eel foh prahNdre aN tah-xee)* (I, you, we [depending on context] have to take a cab.)

Fun and Games

A guest in a hotel lobby asks you, "**Excusez-moi. Où est la gare? C'est loin?**" Tell her it's only ten minutes away and give her directions:

Follow this street straight ahead.

At the fourth traffic light, turn left.

Go to the traffic circle.

Take the first street on the right.

Only 100 meters farther,

you'll see the subway station on the corner.

You continue to the west. There it is!

The train station is at the second intersection.

Your fellow guest nods, says "**Merci,**" and then gets on a bus outside the hotel.

La gare se trouve au deuxième croisement.

Vous continuez a l'ouest. La voilà!

À cent metres, vous allez voir la station de métro au coin.

Prenez la première rue à droite.

Allez au rond-point.

Aux les quatrième feux, tournez à gauche.

Suivez cette rue tout droit.

Answers:

Chapter 13

Staying at a Hotel

. . . .

. . . .

Sometimes hotels are your home away from home, so it's good to know how to secure the kind of lodging you prefer. Bear in mind that it's not always the price that makes a wonderful place to stay. This chapter can help you understand the French terms for the various types of accommodations, as well as walk you through the basics of checking over a hotel, checking in, and checking out.

Hôtels (o-tehl) or **hôtels de tourisme** (o-tehl duh too-reez-muh) range from basic one-star accommodations to luxury four-star establishments. Room prices, fixed according to amenities, size, and rating, must be posted visibly at the reception desk or in the window and behind each room door. Most hotels offer breakfast, but not all have a restaurant. The names for different types of hotels may vary a little throughout the French-speaking countries. **Hôtel garni** (o-tehl gahr-nee) means bed and breakfast, and the **maison de logement** (meh-sohN duh lohzh-mahN) in French-speaking Canada is a smaller hotel or tourist home which in other countries is sometimes also called a **pension (de famille)** (pahN-syohN duh fah-meey), a **logis** (loh-zhee), or **auberge** (o-behrzh).

And then, in France, there are also those exquisite **châteaux-hôtels** (shah-to o-tehl). Sure, they tend to be on the more expensive side, but the ambiance and the high-quality service are hard to surpass if you're looking for something special.

In recent years, alternatives to traditional hotels have become increasingly popular, such as the **gîtes ruraux** (zheet rew-ro) in France which are furnished holiday cottages or flats, farmhouse arrangements in Belgium, chalets in Switzerland, or even former monasteries.

Finally, for the young and young at heart, there are about 200 youth hostels in France alone, well scattered throughout the country, with varying facilities. Your national youth hostel association can give you details or else you can go on the Internet. The address for Canadian youth hostels, for example, is `www.hostellingmontreal.com`.

Of course when planning a trip to Europe, you can always get more information by browsing the Internet, particularly at `www.hotels.fr`, `www.hotels.be`, `switzerlandvacation.ch`, and `www.relaischateaux.fr`.

It's time now to check out some of these wonderful places.

Arriving at the Hotel

After a long trip, arriving at a hotel is probably your first highlight . . . and perhaps your first interaction with French. You may wonder how to address the hotel staff, especially when you arrive to inquire about a room. The titles **Monsieur** *(muh-syuh)*, **Madame** *(mah-dahm)*, and **Mademoiselle** *(mah-duh-mwah-zehl)* are used in French much more than in English and do not sound as formal. In fact, it is polite to add them after **bonjour** *(bohN-zhoor),* especially when addressing someone you don't know.

Male members of hotel staff are called **Monsieur**, female members **Madame** or **Mademoiselle**. This applies to waiters and waitresses as well. Many people nowadays regard the word **garçon** *(gahr-sohN)* (boy) as old-fashioned and improper.

Talkin' the Talk

Peter and Janet have just arrived in Lausanne in Switzerland. Janet goes to inquire about a room while Peter waits in the car.

Janet: **Bonjour. Je voudrais une chambre pour deux personnes.**
bohN-zhoor zhuh voo-dreh ewn shahNbr poor duh pehr-sohn
Hello. I would like a room for two people.

Receptionist: **Je regrette. L'hôtel est complet.**
zhuh ruh-greht lo-tehl est kohN-pleh
I am sorry. The hotel is booked.

Janet: **Oh. Est-ce qu'il y a un autre hôtel près d'ici?**
o ehs-keel-yah an-notr o-tehl preh dee-see
Oh. Is there another hotel nearby?

Receptionist: **Oui, madame. L'hôtel Royal est au bout de la rue.**
*wee mah-dahm lo-tehl rwa-yahl eh to boo duh
lah rew*
Yes, ma'm. The Hotel Royal is at the end of the street.

Words to Know

la chambre	lah shahNbr	room
pour	poor	for
la personne	lah pehr-sohn	person
je regrette	zhuh ruh-greht	I am sorry
complet	kohN-pleh	booked
il y a	ee lee ah	there is/are
près d'ici	preh dee-see	near here
un autre	an notr	another
au bout de	o boo duh	at the end of
la rue	lah rew	street

Talkin' the Talk

Peter and Janet are now approaching the Hotel Royal, which they've heard has vacancies. It looks so promising to Peter and Janet that both of them go in this time to ask for a room.

Peter: **Bonsoir. Est-ce que vous avez une chambre libre?**
bohN-swahr ehs-kuh voo-zah-vay ewn shahNbr leebr
Good evening. Do you have vacancies?

Attendant: **Oui. Pour combien de nuits?**
wee poor kohN-byaN duh nwee
Yes. For how many nights?

Janet: **Pour deux ou trois. C'est combien par nuit?**
poor duh oo trwah seh kohN-byaN pahr nwee
For two or three. How much is it a night?

Attendant: **Ça dépend . . . une chambre double avec douche —
150,00 francs. . . avec baignoire 200,00 francs.**
*sah day-pahN . . . ewn shahNbr doobl ah-vehk doosh
sahN sahN-kahNt frahN ... ah-vehk behn-ywahr duh
sahN frahN*
That depends . . . a double room with shower —
150 francs . . . with a bathtub 200 francs.

Peter: **Est-ce qu'on peut voir la chambre?**
ehs kohN puh vwahr lah shahNbr
Can we see the room?

Attendant: **Mais oui. Suivez-moi.**
meh wee swee-vay mwah
Certainly. Follow me.

Words to Know

une chambre libre	ewn shahNbr leebr	vacant room, vacancy
combien de . . . ?	kohN-byaN duh	how many/much . . . ?
par nuit	pahr nwee	per/night
c'est combien?	seh kohN-byaN?	how much is it?
ça dépend	sah day-pahN	it depends
une chambre double	ewn shahNbr doobl	double room
avec	ah-vehk	with
la douche	lah doosh	shower
la baignoire	lah behn-ywahr	bathtub
on peut voir	ohN pew vwahr	we can see
mais oui!	meh wee	certainly
suivez-moi!	swee-vay mwah	follow me!

For commands, you drop the personal pronoun before the verb (for example, **vous suivez** becomes **suivez**), and then you add **-moi** *(mwah)* (<u>not</u> **me** *[muh]*!) after the verb, as in **Suivez-moi!** *(swee-vay mwah)* (Follow me!)

In many countries, the sink and bathtub/shower are separate from the toilet and the bidet, an arrangement which is wonderful, of course. However, showers are often hand-held in the bathtub with no curtain around it, and that method takes a bit getting used to, but works fine, too.

Talkin' the Talk

Mr. and Mrs. Dalton are tired from driving and decide to call it a day in Annecy, a beautiful, small, French town close to the Swiss border. They stop at a pretty country inn.

Mr. Dalton:	**Bonjour! Nous voulons une chambre avec des lits jumeaux.** *bohN-zhoor noo voo-lohN zewn shahNbr ah-vek deh lee zhew-moh* Hello! We want a room with twin beds.
Concierge:	**Côté cour ou côté rue?** *koh-tay koor oo koh-tay rew* Looking out on the yard or the street?
Mrs. Dalton:	**Côté cour. Et avec salle de bains, s'il vous plaît. Quel est le prix?** *koh-tay koor ay ah-vehk sahl duh baN seel voo play kehl eh luh pree* To the yard. And with a bathroom, please? What is the price?
Concierge:	**Je vérifie . . . au rez-de-chaussée ça coûte 410,00 francs.** *zhuh vay-ree-fee . . . o rayt-sho-say sah koot kaht sahN dee frahN* I am checking . . . on the ground floor that'll cost 410 francs.
Mrs. Dalton:	**Et au premier étage?** *ay o pruhm-yay ray-tahzh* And on the second floor?
Concierge:	**Je regrette. Le premier étage est complet.** *zhuh ruh-greht luh pruhm-yay ray-tahzh eh kohN-pleh* I'm sorry. The second floor is booked.
Mr. Dalton:	**Pas de problème. Le rez-de-chaussée nous convient.** *paht proh-blehm luh rayt-sho-say noo kohN-vyaN* No problem. The ground floor suits us fine.

Words to Know

un lit	aN lee	bed
des lits jumeaux	deh lee zhew-mo	twin beds
côté cour	koh-tay koor	facing the yard
côté rue	koh-tay rew	facing the street
je vérifie	zhuh vay-ree-fee	I am checking
le rez-de-chaussée	luh reht-sho-say	ground floor [lit: street level]
ça coûte	sah coot	that costs
au premier étage	oh pruhm-yeh ray-tahzh	on the second floor
il nous convient	eel noo kohN-vyaN	it suits us

Pas de problème! *(paht proh-blehm)* (No problem!) is used as often in French as it is in English. It is a short form of the underlying: **Je n'ai pas de problème avec ça** *(zhuh nay paht proh-blehm ah-vehk sah)* (I don't have a problem with that.)

Since the ground floor in French buildings is called **rez-de-chaussée** *(reht-sho-say)* (street level), buildings only start numbering from the first floor up. Check out the elevator pad in your hotel or in any other multistory building and you usually see this:

3

2

1

rez-de-chaussée

Asking inverted questions

Aside from asking questions with **est-ce que** (which is explained in Chapter 13 and which you can always stick to doing), you have the option of making "inverted" questions, just as in English (have you? are you? can you? must you? will you?), by simply turning around (inverting) the subject and the verb.

> ✔ **Avez-vous une chambre libre?** *(ah-vay voo/ewn shahNbr leebr)* (Do you have a vacancy?)
>
> ✔ **Êtes-vous/es-tu français?** *(eht voo/eh tew frahN-seh)* (Are you French?)
>
> ✔ **Pouvez-vous/Voulez-vous remplir ça?** *(poo-vay voo/voo-lay voo rahN-pleer sah)* or
>
> **Peux-tu/Veux-tu remplir ça?** *(puh tew/vuh tew rahN-pleer sah)* (Can you/do you want to fill this out?)

You hear this kind of question mostly for the **tu** and **vous** forms. It is easiest for you if you do not invert any other forms.

Losing your objection to object pronouns

In a conversation, you wouldn't sound very natural if you kept repeating the same words: "I would like <u>a room</u>. Can I see <u>the room</u>? Let's go and see <u>the room</u>."

Saying "I would like <u>a room</u>. Can I see <u>it</u>? Let's go and see <u>it</u>" sounds a lot better, doesn't it?

So, drop your object and replace it with **le, la , l',** or **les**, depending on whether it is feminine or masculine, singular or plural, but be careful: You must put it in *front* of the verb. Check out these examples:

Il voit le guide/l'hôtel.	*Il le voit.*
(eel vwah luh geed/lo-tehl)	*(eel luh vwah)*
He sees the guide/the hotel.	He sees it.
Nous suivons la réceptionniste.	*Nous la suivons.*
(noo swee-vohN lah ray-sehp-syoh-neest)	*(noo lah swee-vohN)*
We are following the receptionist.	We are following her.
Elle vérifie les dates.	*Elle les vérifie.*
(ehl vay-ree-fee leh daht)	*(ehl leh vay-ree-fee)*
She is checking the dates.	She's checking them.

The other object pronouns are even easier because there is only one form for masculine and feminine. Here are a few examples:

- ✔ **Elle <u>me</u> regarde.** *(ehl muh ruh-gahrd)* (She looks at me.)

- ✔ **Je <u>te</u> vois.** *(zhuh tuh vwah)* (I see you.)

- ✔ **Il <u>nous</u> suit.** *(eel noo swee)* (He follows us.)

- ✔ **La réceptionniste <u>vous</u> écoute.** *(lah ray-sehp-syho-neest voo zay koot)* The receptionist listens to you.

Naturally, there is an exception to the preceding rule: When you have a helping verb plus the infinitive in your sentence, you need to put the object pronoun in front of the infinitive form.

Il veut voir la chambre.	*Il veut la voir.*
(eel vvuh vwahr lah shahNbr)	*(eel vuh lah vwahr)*
He wants to see <u>the room</u>.	He wants to see <u>it</u>.

Checking In to a Hotel

When you arrive at a hotel, chances are, you have to fill out the registration form, which will ask you for these items:

- ✔ **nom/prénom** *(nohN/pray-nohN)* (name/first name)

- ✔ **lieu de résidence** *(lyuh duh ray-zee-sahNs)* (address)

- ✔ **rue/numéro** *(rew/new-may-roo)* (street/number)

- ✔ **ville/code postal/** *(veel/kohd pohs-tahl)* (city/zip code)

- ✔ **état/pays** *(ay-tah/peh-ee)* (state/country)

- ✔ **numéro de téléphone** *(new-may-ro duh tay -lay-fohn)* (telephone number)

- ✔ **nationalité** *(nasyoh-nah-lee-tay)* (nationality)

- ✔ **date/lieu de naissance** *(daht/lyuh duh neh-sahNs)* (date/place of birth)

- ✔ **numéro de passeport** *(new-may-ro duh pahs pohr)* (passport number)

- ✔ **signature** *(seen-yah-tewr)* (signature)

- ✔ **numéro d'immatriculation de la voiture** *(new-may-roh dee-mah-tree-kew-las-yohN duh lah vwa-tewr)* (license plate number)

- ✔ **pays** *(peh-ee)* (country)

Should you tip hotel staff such as bellboys and maids? A service charge is generally included in hotel and restaurant bills. However, if the service has been particularly good, you may want to leave an extra tip. The following chart is a guide:

Service	France	Belgium	Switzerland
Porter	5 FRF	30 BEF	1-2 CHF
Maid, per week	50–100	100–150	10
Waiter	optional	optional	optional

Talkin' the Talk

Carol is checking in at the reception desk while Max brings in the luggage with the doorman's help.

Carol: **Nous prenons la belle chambre au troisième étage.**
noo pruh-nohN lah behl shahNbr o trwah-zyehm ay-tahzh
We'll take the beautiful room on the fourth floor.

Hotel clerk: **Bon. Veuillez remplir cette fiche, s'il vous plaît, et j'ai besoin de vos passeports.**
bohN vuh-yay rahN-pleer seht feesh seel voo pleh ay zhay buh zwaN duh vo pahs-pohr
Good. Would you please fill out this form, and I need your passports.

Carol: **Les voilà . . . et la fiche . . . C'est fait.**
leh vwah-lah . . . ay lah feesh . . . seh feh
Here they are . . . and the (registration) form.

Hotel clerk: **Merci, madame. L'ascenseur est à gauche. Je vous souhaite une bonne soirée.**
mehr-see mah-dahm lah-sahN-suhr eh tah gosh zhuh voo soo-eht ewn bohn swah-ray
Thank you, ma'm. The elevator is on the left. I wish you a nice evening.

Carol: **Merci. À quelle heure fermez-vous la porte principale?**
mehr-see ah keh luhr fehr-may voo lah pohrt praN-see-pahl
Thank you. What time do you close the main door?

Hotel clerk: **À minuit, mais vous pouvez toujours sonner.**
ah mee-nwee meh voo poovay too-zhoor soh-nay
At midnight, but you can always ring.

Words to Know

veuillez remplir	vuh-yay rahN-pleer	would you please fill out
la fiche	lah feesh	registration form
j'ai besoin de	zhay buh-zwaN duh	I need
c'est fait	seh feh	it's done
l'ascenseur	lah-sahN-suhr	the elevator
à gauche	ah gosh	on the left
je vous souhaite	zhuh voo soo-eht	I wish you
une bonne soirée	ewn bohN swah-ray	a nice evening
à quelle heure?	ah kehl uhr?	at what time?
vous fermez	voo fehr-may	you close
la porte principale	lah pohrt praN-see-pahl	main door
à minuit	ah mee-nwee	at midnight
toujours	too-zhoor	always
vous pouvez sonner	voo poo-vay soh-nay	you can ring

Checking Out of a Hotel

For whatever reason, the checkout time is hardly ever convenient, but you probably realize that rooms have to be cleaned before the next guest arrives, and you may have to remove your belongings from a room before you're ready to depart from your location. The hotel will usually allow you to leave your luggage in the lobby, or some such place, until you leave.

Talkin' the Talk

 Judy Cole's plane is leaving in the evening. So she wants to spend her last day in town and get the luggage later.

Judy: **À quelle heure faut-il libérer la chambre?**
ah keh luhr fo teel lee-bay-ray lah shahNbr
At what time do we have to vacate the room?

Clerk: **Avant midi, madame.**
ah-vahN mee-dee mah-dahm
Before noon, ma'am.

Judy: **Je peux laisser mes bagages ici jusqu'à seize heures?**
zhuh puh leh-say meh bah-gahzh ee-see zhews-kah seh-zuhr
Can I leave my luggage here until 4:00 p.m.?

Clerk: **Oui, vous pouvez les laisser ici. Voulez-vous la note maintenant?**
wee voo poo-vay leh leh-say ee-see voo-lay voo lah noht maN-tuh-nahN
Certainly, you can leave them here. Would you like the bill now?

Judy: **Oui, s'il vous plaît. Voyons, les coups de téléphone . . . le minibar . . . Très bien. Vous acceptez les cartes de crédit, n'est-ce pas?**
wee seel voo play vwah-yohN leh koo duh tay-lay-fohn luh mee-nee-bar treh byaN voo-zahk-sehp-tay leh kahrt duh kray-dee nehs-pas
Yes, please. Let's see, the phone calls . . . the minibar . . . Very well. You accept credit cards, don't you?

Clerk: **Oui, Visa ou Mastercard . . . merci . . . et voici votre reçu.**
wee vee-sah oo mah-stehr-kahrd . . . mehr-see . . . ay vwah-see vohtr ruh-sew
Yes, Visa or Mastercard . . . thank you . . . and here is your receipt.

Judy: **Merci. Pouvez-vous m'appeler un taxi, s'il vous plaît?**
mehr-see poo-vay voo mah-puh-lay uhN tah-ksee seel voo play
Thank you. Can you call a taxi for me, please?

Clerk: **Bien sûr.**
byaN sewr
Of course.

CULTURAL WISDOM

Keep current on electrical currents

The 220 volt, 50 cycle AC is now almost universal in France, Belgium and Switzerland, although 110 volt may still be encountered, especially in older buildings.

If you bring your own electrical appliances, buy a continental adapter plug (round pins, not square) before leaving home. You may also need a transformer appropriate to the wattage of the appliance.

Words to Know

il faut libérer la chambre	eel faut lee-bay-ray lah shahNbr	we have to vacate the room
avant midi	ah-vahN mee-dee	before noon
je peux laisser	zhu puh leh-say	I can leave (behind)
le bagage	luh bah-gahzh	baggage
ici	ee-see	here
bien sûr	byaN sûr	certainly
jusqu'à	zhews-kah	until
là-bas	lah bah	over there
au coin	o kwaN	in the corner
la note	lah noht	bill
maintenant	maN-tuh-nahN	now
un coup de téléphone	uhN koo duh tay-lay-fohn	telephone call
la carte de crédit	lah kahrt duh kray-dee	credit card
vous acceptez	voo zahk-sehp-tay	you accept
le reçu	luh ruh-sew	receipt
vous pouvez appeler	voo poo-vay ah-puh-lay	you can call

Fun and Games

• •

There seems to be a mistake on your hotel bill, so you are going over the details with the desk clerk. You had a room for two with twin beds and a bathtub, on the second floor, facing the street, for two nights. Correct him as needed by circling the correct response and clarifying any answers as needed.

Clerk: Je vérifie. Un chambre double?

A You: Oui/Non. _____

Clerk: Avec douche?

B You: Oui/Non. _____

Clerk: Au rez-de-chaussée?

C You: Oui/Non. _____

Clerk: Côté rue?

D You: Oui/Non. _____

Clerk: Pour trois nuits?

E You: Oui/Non. _____

Answers: A. Oui, une chambre avec des lits jumeaux; B. Non. Avec salle de bain/avec baignoire; C. Non, au deuxième; D. Oui; E. Non. Pour deux nuits.

• •

Chapter 14

Transportation

· ·

In This Chapter

▶ Getting through the airport

▶ Getting a taxi

▶ Navigating public transportation

▶ Renting a car and getting gas

· ·

*Y*our first concern may be getting to your destination country, but as soon as you are there, you want to get around. After all, that's why you came in the first place, right? This chapter can help you navigate your way through the airport, train station, or subway system as well as rent a car or flag down a taxi, to get where you're going on time.

When you arrive in any French-speaking country, you're instantly surrounded by a flood of French language: The porter, the taxi driver, and the customs people all address you in French. The customs officials ask you your name, want to know where you came from, and inquire what your plans are. Don't worry — you have this book handy, (maybe you even went through some of it as you were planning your trip or you've been listening to the tapes on the plane) and even if this is the moment when you are opening the book for the first time, this chapter can help you walk through customs and on to the exciting travel experiences ahead.

Getting Through the Airport

You just flew in, and now you have to get through this brief moment of bureaucratic business. The airport personnel are usually very helpful, and they usually speak some English, too. But you want to make it on your own, don't you? While you're standing in line, you can read the following dialogue to get an idea of what they may ask and how to reply.

It's best not to joke around with an immigration or customs officer. He also has to control his sense of humor. He's there for serious business.

Talkin' the Talk

The immigration officer is the first person Nicola Pranter encounters in the French airport. She hands him her passport and her customs slip, and he starts right in with his questions:

Customs Officer: **Nicola Pranter . . . Bonjour. Bienvenue en France. Allez-vous rester en France pendant votre séjour?**
bohN-zhoor byaN-vuh-new ahN frahNs ah-lay voo reh-stay ahN frahNs pahN-dahN vohtr say-zhoor
Hello. Welcome to France. Are you going to stay in France during your stay?

Nicola: **Non, je vais aussi à Bruxelles et en Suisse.**
nohN zhuh veh zoh-see ah brew-zehl ay ahN swees
No, I am also going to Brussels and to Switzerland.

Customs Officer: **Et la raison de votre voyage?**
ay lah reh-zohN duh vohtr vwah-yazh
And the reason for your trip?

Nicola: **C'est pour les affaires et le plaisir.**
seh poor leh zah-fehr ay luh pleh-zeer
It's for business and pleasure.

Customs Officer: **Combien de temps restez-vous en tout?**
kohn-byaN duh tahN rehs-tay voo ahN too
How much time are you staying altogether?

Nicola: **Deux semaines.**
duh suh-mehn
Two weeks.

Customs Officer: **Je vous souhaite un bon séjour!**
zhuh voo soo-eht aN bohN say-zhoor
I wish you a nice stay.

Nicola: **Merci, monsieur. Au revoir.**
mehr-see muh-syuh ohr-vwahr
Thank you, sir. Good-bye.

When you are talking about staying in a city, you use **à** *(ah)* to express the English "in." For countries, it's usually **en** *(ahN)* because most countries are feminine (such as **la France** *(lah frahNs)*, **la Suisse** *(lah swees)*, **l'Italie** *(lee-tah-lee)*, and so on). For the few that are not (such as **le Canada** *(luh kah-nah-dah)*, **le Portugal** *(luh pohr-tew-gahl)*, **les États-Unis** *(leh-zay-tah-zew-nee)*, and so on) you use **au(x)** *(o)* to mean "in." For example, you may say:

- *Je vais en France, en Suisse, en Italie. (zhuh vay zahN frahNs ahN swees, ahN-nee-tah-lee)* (I'm going to France, to Switzerland, to Italy.)

- *Je vais au Canada, au Portugal, aux États-Unis. (zhuh vay zo kah-nah-dah o pohr-tew-guhl o zay-tah-zew-nee)* (I'm going to Canada, to Portugal, to the United States.)

For more details, also see Chapter 3.

Words to Know

contrôle des passeports	kohN-trohl duh pahs-poh	passport control
douane	doo-ahn	customs
rien à déclarer	ryaN nah day-klah-ray	nothing to declare
marchandises à déclarer	mahr-shahN-dee zah day-klah-ray	goods to declare
marchandises hors taxe	mahr-shahN-deez ohr tahk	duty-free goods

Talkin' the Talk

Most likely, you won't even get stopped by the customs officer, except to hand him your customs slip, but in case he or she does pick you out for further questioning, here is what you might expect:

Customs officer: **Avez-vous quelque chose à déclarer?**
ah-vay voo kehl-kuh sho zah day-klah-ray
Do you have something to declare?

Tourist:	**Non, rien.**
	nohN ryaN
	No, nothing.
Customs officer:	**Avez-vous des appareils électroniques?**
	ah-vay voo deh zah-pah-rehy ay-lehk-tro-neek
	Do you have electronic items?
Tourist:	**Seulement pour mon usage personnel.**
	suhl-mahN poor moh new-zazh pehr-soh-nehl
	Only for my personal use.
Customs officer:	**Pouvez-vous ouvrir votre sac?**
	poo-vay voo zoo-vreer vohtr sahk
	Can you open your bag?
Tourist:	**Oui, monsieur . . . voilà.**
	wee muh-syuh vwah-lah
	Yes, sir . . . here you go.
Customs officer:	**Qu'est-ce que c'est que ça?**
	kes-kuh seh kuh sah
	What is this?
Tourist:	**C'est mon ordinateur portable.**
	she mohn ohr-dee-nah-tuhr pohr-tahbl
	That's my laptop.
Customs officer:	**Branchez-le là-bas, s'il vous plaît.**
	brahN-shay luh lah bah seel voo play
	Plug it in over there, please.

Leaving the Airport: Finding a Taxi

Now you've collected your baggage, and you want to get out of this place. If you need a porter or a cart for your bags or assistance in finding the taxis, the following dialogue may help you get oriented.

Talkin' the Talk

 Derek and Karen have decided to take a taxi into town, but they need to find out where the taxi stands are.

Derek:
Où sont les taxis, s'il vous plaît?
oo sohn lay tak-see seel voo play
Where are the taxis, please?

Airport attendant:
Vous sortez porte 5 et ils sont sur votre droite.
voo sor-tay pohrt saNk ay eel sohN sewr votr drwaht
You exit through door 5, and they are on your right.

Karen:
Merci beaucoup. Vous voyez un porteur ou un chariot?
mehr-see bo-koo voo vwah-yay aN por-tuhr oo aN shar-yo
Thank you very much. Do you see a porter or a cart?

Airport attendant:
Les chariots sont dehors mais je peux appeler un porteur.
leh shar-yo sohN duh-ohr meh zhuh puh ah-puh-lay aN por-tuhr
The carts are outside, but I can call a porter.

Karen:
Merci . . . c'est gentil!
mehr-see seh zhahN-tee
Thank you . . . that's nice.

Getting a Taxi

Convenient and quick, taxis are reasonably priced in Paris. In Brussels, they double the rates once you leave the city limits and charge an extra BEF 75 at night. Inquire about flat rates for the airport. Tipping suggestions: Tips are optional in Belgium, but you may expect to pay 10 to 15 percent in France and Switzerland.

Talkin' the Talk

Fortunately for Karen and Derek, the Brussels airport is only a few miles out of town, and they were lucky enough to get the attention of a taxi driver right away.

Karen: **Bruxelles, hôtel Gillon, s'il vous plaît.**
brew-sehl o-tehl zhee-lohn seel voo play
Brussels, hotel Gillon, please.

Taxi driver: **Avec plaisir. C'est dans quelle rue?**
ah-vehk pleh-zeer seh dahN kehl rew
With pleasure. On which street is that?

Derek: **Voyons . . . c'est 22 rue Albert. C'est combien?**
vwah-yohN seh vaNt duh rew ahl-behr seh kohn-byaN
Let's see . . . it's 22 Albert Street. How much is it?

Taxi driver: **600 francs. C'est le tarif normal. Je mets les valises dans le coffre?**
see sahn frahn seh luh tah-reef nor-mahl zhuh meh leh vah-leez dahN luh kohfr
600 francs. That's the normal rate. I put the suitcases in the trunk?

Karen: **Très bien, mais je garde mon sac à dos avec moi.**
treh byaN meh zhuh gahrd mohN sah-kah do ah-vehk mwah
Very well, but I am keeping my backpack with me.

Words to Know

le séjour	luh say-zhoor	stay
les affaires (f)	leh zah-fehr	business
la semaine	lah suh-mehn	week
vous sortez	voo sor-tay	you exit
vous voyez	voo vwah-yeh	you see
la porte	lah pohrt	door
le chariot	luh shar-yo	cart
la rue	lah rew	street
je mets	zhuh meh	I put
la valise	lah vah-leez	suitcase
le coffre	luh kohfr	trunk
le sac à dos	luh sah kah do	backpack

Getting Around in Major Cities

The public transportation system in most major cities of Europe and Canada is excellent. This chapter gives general information. The respective Web pages on the Internet can help you find out more details about traveling and public transportation in these places:

- ✔ **Canada:** www.canadatourism.com and www.tourismMontreal.org under "transportation"
- ✔ **Switzerland:** www. switzerlandvacation.ch, www.geneva.ch, and www.tpg.ch
- ✔ **Belgium:** www.b-rail.be, and www.planitram.ibelgique.com, and www.brussel.irisnet.be
- ✔ **France:** www.sncf.fr (trains) and www.ratp.fr (bus, metro, RER)

The following list may give you an idea of the range of choices available for getting around in various cities:

- ✔ **Montreal:** bus, subway (four lines), STCUM (urban train system), Amtrak, VIA Rail (national train system)

- ✔ **Brussels:** subway, bus, tramway, SNCB (national train system)

- ✔ **Geneva:** tramway, bus, trolleybus, trains

- ✔ **Nice:** bus, SNCF (national train system), tramway (being built, first phase to be completed in 2001)

- ✔ **Paris:** subway and RER (express trains into larger Paris), bus, SNCF (national train system), tourist boats

In addition, for long-distance traveling between France, Belgium, and the Netherlands, you may want to try the **TGV**, an extra-high-speed train which you can use only with reservations. It is very fast and efficient, can take you across France in no time, and is truly worth the experience. The **TGV Thalys** runs Paris to Bruxelles to Amsterdam and back.

Also convenient, the **Eurostar/Le Shuttle** is a passenger Channel Tunnel (Chunnel) link from London's Waterloo train station to Paris and Brussels with no reservations necessary. Cars cross from Folkstone and Calais. They are shuttled on the train along with the people.

Buying a Train Ticket

Train stations around the world are always busy, noisy, and confusing, but you can usually find helpful people around, such as the police and station employees, that you can turn to for direction. Here are some useful phrases to know:

- ✔ **Pardon, où sont** *(pahr-dohN, oo sohn)* (Pardon, where are . . .)

  - **les guichets** *(leh gee-sheh)* (the ticket windows?)

  - **les quais** *(leh keh)* (the platforms?)

  - **les renseignements** *(leh rahN-sehn-yuh-mahN)* (information desks?)

- ✔ **Excusez-moi, où est** *(eks-kew-say mwah, oo eh)* (Excuse me, where is . . .)

  - **la consigne** *(lah kohN-seenyuh)* (baggage room?)

  - **la salle d'attente** *(sahl dah-tahN)* (waiting room?)

  - **le bureau des objets trouvés?** *(leh bew-ro day-zohb-zheh troo-vay)* (the lost-and-found?)

Talkin' the Talk

Susan wants to meet her old friend Julie in Versailles. So she takes a day off from her group and is trying her luck on her own.

Susan:	**Je voudrais un billet pour Versailles, s'il vous plaît.** *zhuh voo-dreh aN bee-yeh poor vehr-sahy seel voo play* I would like a ticket to Versailles, please.
Employee:	**Aller-simple ou aller-retour?** *ah-lay saNpl oo ah-lay ruh-toor* One way or round trip?
Susan:	**Aller-retour, s'il vous plaît. Deuxième classe.** *ah-lay ruh-toor seel voo play duh-zyehm klahs* Round trip, please. Second class.
Employee:	**Ça fait soixante francs.** *sah feh swah-sahNt frahN* That'll be 60 francs.
Susan:	**Est-ce que je dois changer de train?** *ehs-kuh zhuh dwah shahN-zhay duh traN* Do I have to change trains?
Employee:	**Oui, vous avez une correspondance à Issy.** *wee voo zah-vay ewn koh-rehs-pohN-dahN-sah ee-see* Yes, you have a connecting train in Issy.
Susan:	**Et de quel quai part le train?** *ay duh kehl keh pahr luh traN* And from which platform does the train leave?
Employee:	**Quai 12A.** *keh dooz ah* Platform 12A.
Susan:	**Merci. Au revoir.** *mehr-see ohr-vwahr* Thank you. Good-bye.

This little unobtrusive **y** *(ee)* meaning "there," is used just like an object pronoun (refer to Chapter 4 for more on object pronouns). Normally, you stick it in front of the verb **j'y vais** *(zhee vay)* (I'm going there), and if there are two verbs in a sentence, the **y** goes in front of the infinitive **je peux y aller** *(zhuh puh zee ah-lay)* (I can go there).

There is an exception, however, to placing "y" or an object pronoun in front of the verb: In the case of positive commands only (perhaps to make them a bit more forceful), the little pronouns are attached at the end of the verb. For example:

- ✔ **Vas-y!** *(va-zee)* (Go there!)

- ✔ **Prends-le/la!** *(prahN luh/lah)* (Take it!)

- ✔ **Regarde-les!** *(ruh-gahrd leh)* (Look at them!)

Notice how such constructions work in the negative:

- ✔ **N'y va pas!** *(nee vah pah)* (Don't go there!)

- ✔ **Ne le prends pas!** *(nuh luh prahN pah)* (Don't take it!)

- ✔ **Ne la regarde pas!** *(nuh luh ruh-gahrd pah)* (Don't look at her!)

When asking questions involving the words *which* or *what,* you use the word **quel(s)** or **quelle(s)** *(kehl),* depending on whether the noun referred to is masculine or feminine. Here are some examples:

- ✔ **Il arrive par quel train?** *(eel ah-reev pahr kehl trahn)* (Which train is he arriving on?)

- ✔ **De quelle ville es-tu?** *(duh kehl veel eh tew)* (Which town are you from?)

- ✔ **Quelles places avez-vous?** *(kehl plahs ah-vay voo)* (Which seats do you have?)

Words to Know

le train (pour)	luh trahn poor	train (to)
la gare	lah gahr	train station
la ville	lah veel	town
il prend	eel prahN	he takes
le billet	luh bee-yeh	ticket
un aller-simple	aN nah-lay sahNpl	one-way (ticket)
un aller-retour	aN nah-lay ruh-toor	round trip
la correspondance	lah koh-rehs-pohn-dahNs	connection (train/bus)
la place	lah plahs	seat
la fenêtre	lah fuh-nehtr	window

Taking the Bus

If you have time, the bus is probably the most wonderful way not only to get an impression of the different **quartiers** *(kahr-tyay)* (neighborhoods) of a city, but also to experience that city's people a bit.

Tickets can normally be bought from the driver, but remember that large bills are not welcome; it's best to have the correct change. However, in many cities, the subway system is connected with the bus system, so you can use the same tickets. Generally, it is cheaper to buy tickets in a book of ten **(carnet)** *(kahr-nay)*.

By the way, you must always validate your ticket **(composter le billet)** *(kohN-pohs-tay luh bee-yeh)* in a machine that is installed for that purpose on the bus. It gets awfully expensive when a **contrôleur** *(kohN-troh-luhr)* gets on and checks everybody. And they do!

Talkin' The Talk

Mr. and Mrs. Meyer are standing at a bus stop. They are reading the bus schedule, but are not really sure if they have read it correctly. Bus number 82 is arriving. Mr. Meyer turns to a young woman next to him.

Mr. Meyer:
Excusez-moi, mademoiselle. C'est bien le bus pour l'hôtel de ville?
eks-kew-say mwah mahd-mwah-zehl seh byaN luh bews poor loh-tehl duh veel
Excuse me. Is that the correct bus to City Hall?

Young woman:
Non, il faut prendre le bus numéro 67.
nohN eel foh prahNdr luh bews new-may-roh swah-sahN seht
No, you have to take bus number 67.

Mr. Meyer:
À quelle heure est-ce qu'il arrive?
ah keh luhr ehs keel ah-reev
What time does it come?

Young woman:
Il passe tous les quarts d'heure, mais il est souvent en retard.
eel pahs too leh kahr duhr meh eel eh soo-vahN ahN ruh-tahr
It comes every 15 minutes, but it is often late.

Mr. Meyer:
Et c'est à combien d'arrêts d'ici?
ay seh tah kohN-byaN dah-reh dee-see
And how many stops is it from here?

Young woman:
Ce n'est pas très loin, c'est le prochain arrêt. Ah, le voilà! Il est à l'heure!
suh neh pah treh lwaN seh luh proh sheh-nah-reh ah luh vwah-lah eel eh-tah luhr
It's not very far. It's the next stop. Ah, there he is! It is on time.

Mr. Meyer:
Merci beaucoup. Au revoir.
mehr-see bo-koo ohr-vwahr
Thank you. Good-bye.

The little word **tout (toute, tous, toutes)** is used in many different combinations. It adjusts its ending to the noun it gets connected with. It means "every" when it is connected with a time definition in the plural, such as:

✔ **tous les quarts d'heure** *(too leh kahr duhr)* (every quarter of an hour)

✔ **tous les jours** *(too leh zhoor)* (every day)

✔ **toutes les vingt minutes** *(toot leh vahN mee-newt)* (every 20 minutes)

However, when it is connected with time definitions in the singular, it takes on a different meaning:

✔ **toute la matinée** *(toot lah mah-tee-nay)* (all morning long)

✔ **toute la journée** *(toot lah zhoor-nay)* (all day long)

✔ **toute la vie** *(toot lah vee)* (the entire life)

Taking the Subway

Paris, Brussels, Lille, and Lyon, as well as Montreal, all have subway systems. Big maps in each station make the systems easy to use. In these cities, the fare is standard, irrespective of the distance you travel.

The Paris métro closes from 12:50 a.m. to 5:30 a.m. So if you are out on the town later than Cinderella, you have to find another way home.

Talkin' the Talk

Mr. Meyer and Mrs. Meyer split up for the morning to see different museums. Now it's time to meet for lunch. Mr. Meyer wants to try out the subway, but he thinks he needs a map and stops at a kiosk.

Mr. Meyer: **Bonjour. Est-ce que vous avez un plan de métro?**
bohn-zhoor ehs-kuh voo zah-vay aN plahN duh may-troh
Hello. Do you have a metro map?

Employee: **Le voici. . . . Est-ce que je peux vous aider?**
Luh vwah-see ehs-kuh zhuh puh voo zeh-day
Here it is. . . . Can I help you?

Mr. Meyer: **Oui, pour la Grande Place, c'est quelle ligne?**
wee poor lah grahN plahs seh kehl leen-yuh
Yes, to Grande Place, which line is it?

Employee:	**C'est direct avec la ligne 3.**
	seh dee-rehkt ah-vehk lah leen-yuh trwah
	You can go directly with line 3.

Mr. Meyer:	**Combien de temps est-ce qu'il faut?**
	kohn-byaN duh tahN ehs-keel foh
	How long does it take?

Employee:	**Disons . . . 20 minutes.**
	dee-zohN vaN mee-newt
	Let's say . . . 20 minutes.

Mr. Meyer:	**Merci beaucoup, madame.**
	mehr-see bo-koo mah-dahm
	Thank you very much, ma'am.

Employee:	**Je vous en prie.**
	zhuh voo zahN-pree
	You're welcome.

Pas de quoi *(paht kwah)* is also casual. You can be more formal when you don't abbreviate it, but rather say the entire thing: **Il n'y a pas de quoi.** *(eel nya paht kwah).*

Voici *(vwah-see)* means "here is," and **voilà** *(vwah-lah)* means "there is."

You can put all the other direct object pronouns in front of **voici** and **voilà**, too. Table 14-1 shows how it works:

Table 14-1	Using Pronouns with Voici and Voilà	
Word	*Pronunciation*	*Meaning*
Me voici/me voilà!	muh vwah-see, muh vwah-lah	Here I am/There I am!
Te voici/te voilà!	tuh vwah-see, tuh vwah-lah	Here/There you are!
Le voici/le voilà!	luh vwah-see, luh vwah-lah	Here/There he/it is!
La voici/la voilà!	lah vwah-see, lah vwah-lah	Here she/it is!
Nous voici/nous voilà!	noo vwah-see, noo vwah-lah	Here/There we are!
Vous voici/vous voilà!	voo vwah-see, voo vwah-lah	Here/There you are!
Les voici/les voilà!	leh vwah-see, leh vwah-lah	Here/There they are!

Renting a Car

Depending on the kind of trip you are planning, if you like driving and have an inquisitive nature, renting a car seems to be the ultimate pleasure. You can stop wherever you want, change plans according to the weather or your mood, and not worry about interfering with anyone else's plans. Sure, there may be pitfalls, such as an occasional flat tire or traffic jam, but what's a little pitfall compared to all this freedom? And besides, you'll be confronted with another chance to practice your French.

Here are a few car rental tips:

- ✔ It is generally cheaper to reserve your car when you book your flight than to rent it when you get there.

- ✔ In most countries all you need is your normal, valid driver's license. In others, they may ask you for your International Drivers' License. I have made it a habit to always have both on me, just in case. The American and Canadian automobile drivers' associations will be glad to help you, whether you are a member or not.

Many of the French **autoroutes** *(o-to-root)* (highways) require tolls, and they are not cheap. Always have coins handy, although most of the time you pick up a ticket at the point of entry and pay at the exit. In France, tollbooths usually accept credit cards, and it's truly a fantastic convenience: Insert your ticket into a machine at the tollbooth, then your credit card, wait, get your receipt, and make sure you pull your card out again. On you go.

To avoid an unnecessary rise in blood pressure, make sure that you are in the correct lane where credit cards will be accepted. Otherwise, fellow drivers are sure to express their outrage by honking violently while you try to back up into the proper lane.

Talkin' the Talk

George and Gina arrived in Lyon. They are now picking up the car that they ordered from back home because they want to take day trips into the surrounding **Rhône-Alpes** and visit castles and cathedrals. Gina does all the talking.

Gina:	**Bonjour. Nous avons une réservation pour une voiture sous le nom de "Sheldon."**
	bohN-zhoor noo zah-vohN zewn ray-zehr-vas-yohN poor ewn vwah-tewr soo luh nohN duh shehl-dohn
	Hello. We have a reservation for a car under the name of "Sheldon."

Employee: **Bienvenue, messieurs-dames. Un instant, je vérifie. . . . Voilà, une Renault Espace. C'est pour dix jours?**
byaN-vuh-new mes-yuh dahm aN naN-stahN zhuh vay-ree-fee vwah-lah ewn ruh-no ehs-pahs seh poor dee zhoor
Welcome, Mr. and Mrs. Sheldon. One moment please, I am checking. . . . Here we go, a Renault Espace. It's for ten days?

Gina: **Oui, c'est ça. Nous n'avons pas besoin d'assurance tous risques. C'est couvert avec la carte de crédit.**
wee seh sah noo nah-vohN pah buh-zwaN dah-sew-rahns too reesk seh koo-vehr ah-vek lah kahrt duh cray-dee
Yes, that's it. We don't need full insurance. That's covered with the credit card.

Employee: **Très bien. Dans quels pays allez-vous conduire?**
treh byaN daN kehl peh-ee ah-lay voo kohN-dweer
Very well. In what countries are you going to drive?

Gina: **En France et en Suisse. On met quoi comme carburant?**
ahN frahNs ay ahN swees ohN meh kwah kohm kahr-bew-rahN
In France and in Switzerland. What do we use for fuel?

Employee: **Du sans-plomb. Voulez-vous rendre la voiture remplie ou vide?**
dew sahN plohN voo-lay voo rahNdr lah vwah-tewr rahN-plee oo veed
Unleaded. Do you want to return the car full or empty?

Gina: **Vide. Et nous rendons la voiture où?**
veed ay noo rahN-dohN lah vwah-tewr oo
Empty. And we return the car where?

Employee: **Ici, chez nous, avant dix heures, le vingt-neuf. Voilà vos papiers et les clés. Vous sortez, tournez à gauche, et c'est le numéro 11 dans le parking. Bon voyage!**
ee-see shay noo ah-vahN dee zuhr luh vaNt nuhf vwah-lah voh pah-pyeh ay leh klay voo sohr-tay toor-nay ah gosh ay seh luh new-may-roh ohNz dahN luh pahr-keeng bohN vwah-yazh

Here, with us, before 10:00 a.m., on the 29th. Here are your papers and the keys. You exit, turn left, and it's number 11 in the parking lot. Have a nice trip!

Gina: **Merci. Au revoir.**
          mehr-see ohr-vwahr
          Thank you. Good-bye.

Words to Know

il arrive	eel ah-reev	he/it arrives
il passe	eel pahs	he/it comes by
à l'heure	ah luhr	on time
en retard	ahN ruh-tahr	late
un arrêt	aN-nah-reh	a stop
la ligne	lah leen-yuh	line
il aide	eel ehd	he/it helps
le jour	luh zhoor	day
une assurance tous risques	ewn ah-sew-rahNs too reesk	full insurance
le pays	luh peh-ee	country
conduire	kohN-dweer	to drive
rendre	rahNdr	to return (something)

When talking about unspecified quantities, French uses an article that we don't have in English. It's called the **partitif** *(pahr-tee-teef)* because it describes a "part" of a quantity. You construct it by combining the preposition **de** (of) + the definite article **le, la, les:**

✔ **de+le=du** *(dew)*

✔ **de+la =de la** *(duh lah)*

✔ **de+les =des** *(deh)*

✔ **de+l' =de l'** *(duhl)*

You can translate these constructions as "some," as in this example:

> **Je voudrais *du* carburant** *(zhuh voo-dray duh kahr-bew-rahN)* (I would like <u>some</u> gas.)

Getting Gas

Most gas stations seem to be self-service in Europe, but then, of course, some are not. The following little phrases can help you out in case of the unexpected:

✔ **Où est-ce qu'il y a une station service?** *(oo ehs keel-yah ewn stas-yohN sehr-vees)* (Where is there a gas station?)

✔ **Est-ce qu'il y a une station-service près d'ici?** *(ehs keel-yah ewn stas-yohN sehr-vees preh dee-see)* (Is there a gas station near here?)

✔ **Le plein, s'il vous plaît.** *(luh plaN seel voo pleh)* (Fill it up, please.)

✔ **du super/de l'ordinaire/du sans plomb/du diesel** *(dew sew-pehr/duh lohr-dee-nehr/dew sahN plohn/dew dy-ay-zehl)* (super/regular/unleaded/diesel)

✔ **Où est le compresseur pour l'air?** *(oo eh luh kohN-preh-suhr poor lehr)* (Where is the air compressor?)

Fun & Games

• •

The following puzzle contains seven hidden French words. And they really are hidden: Up or down, diagonally from the right or from the left, anything is possible.

Here are the English equivalents of those elusive words:

train, backpack, suitcase, train station, trunk, town, trip

P.S. Ignore any accents.

```
A   S   B   V   C   D   X   L
C   V   A   L   I   S   E   G
Y   O   Z   C   E   L   T   A
S   Y   F   X   A   R   L   R
I   A   P   F   A   D   G   E
E   G   N   I   R   E   O   H
G   E   N   K   M   E   U   S
E   N   A   R   Z   W   L   P
```

• •

Chapter 15

Travel Abroad

• •

In This Chapter

▶ Planning ahead for your trip

▶ Dealing with passports, visas, and other travel necessities

▶ Understanding dates and times

▶ Deciding where to stay

▶ Packing everything you need

• •

*T*raveling is one way to relax, to get away, and to seek the new. Planning your travels in advance is the first step to set the switches for a rewarding, fulfilling time. Maybe you are looking for adventure or maybe just for beach time? Or are you looking for cultural enlightenment?

France has it all.

Would you like a more or less rough ocean? Do you want to see olive trees and vineyards, rolling green meadows bounded by straggling hedgerows, dazzling expanses of naked rock and arid ruddy soil? Or would you prefer to view former homes or playgrounds of kings, counts, and feudal lords, romanesque village churches, and spectacular Gothic cathedrals? How about ruins of Roman architecture and medieval monasteries?

France has it all.

✔ The Alps — **les Alpes** *(lay zahlp)* — in the east and

✔ The Pyrenees — **les Pyrenées** *(lay pee-ray-nay)* — in the southwest,

✔ The sundrenched **Côte d'Azur** *(koht dah-zuhr)* along the Mediterranean coast — **la Méditerranée** *(lah may-dee-teh-rah-nay)*, and

✔ The blue-green **Jura** *(zhew-rah)* and

✔ **Vosges** *(vohzh)* mountains in the east and

✔ The rugged, dry mountains of the **Massif Central** *(mah-seef sahN-trahl)* in Central France.

✔ Sandy Atlantic beaches in the west, but

✔ The rocky coasts of Brittany — **la Bretagne** *(lah bruh-tahny)* —

✔ Normandy — **la Normandie** *(lah nohr-mahN-dee)* in the northwest.

It's even possible to tour the country by water, by way of its four major rivers — **la Seine** *(lah sehn)*, **la Loire** *(lah lwahr)*, **la Garonne** *(lah gah-rohn)*, **le Rhône** *(luh ron)* — and many others that crisscross the entire country.

France has it all.

On top of all this variety, if you want your trip to be more exotic, you can choose to visit an overseas state of France **Départements d'outremer (DOM)** *(day-pahrt-mahN dootr-mehr)* such as **la Réunion** *(ray-ew-nyohN)* in the Indian Ocean, or an overseas territory **Territoire d'outremer (TOM)** *(teh-ree-twahr dootr-mehr)* such as **Tahiti** *(ta-ee-tee)* in French Polynesia.

If you want to stay fairly close to home, but want to experience a country where they speak French, **Québec** *(kay-behk)* and **Montréal** *(mohN-ray-ahl)* are all you can ask for, and they are within reach; you may even be able to drive there.

After you decide where you want to go, you need to make the appropriate travel plans, and the following sections in this chapter can help.

Where Do You Want to Go?

What do you like to do? Answer that question and you will come a long way in deciding where to travel. But asking yourself what you like to do just leads to more questions that you need to answer:

✔ **Qu'est-ce que vous préférez en hiver? La plage ou le ski?** *(kes-kuh voo pray-fay-ray ahN nee-vehr lah plahzh oo luh skee)* (What do you prefer in the winter? The beach or skiing?)

✔ **Et en été? La mer ou la montagne?** *(ay ahN nay-tay lah mehr oo lah mohN-tah-nyuh)* (And in the summer? The ocean or the mountains?)

✔ **Au printemps? la campagne ou les grandes villes?** *(o praN-tahN lah kahN-pan-yuh oo lay grahNd veel)* (In the spring? the country or the cities?)

✔ **En automne? Les musées ou les monuments?** *(ahN noh-tohn lay mew-say oo lay moh-new-mahN)* (In the fall? museums or monuments?)

With seasons, to express "in the" use **au** before a consonant sound and use **en** before a vowel sound. So you say **au printemps** *(oh praN-tahN)* (in the spring), **en été** *(ahN nay-tay)* (in the summer), **en automne** *(ahN noh-tohn n)* (in the fall), and **en hiver** *(ahN nee-vehr)* (in the winter).

Talkin' the Talk

Lynne is on the phone with her friend Anne in Paris. Anne and her husband Michel want Lynne and her husband David to join them during the holidays.

Anne: **Écoute, Lynne. J'ai une proposition.**
ay-koo leen zhay ewn pro-po-zees-yohN
Listen, Lynne. I have a proposition.

Que faites-vous pendant les fêtes?
kuh feht voo pahN-dahN lay feht
What are you doing during the holidays?

Lynne: **Nous? Pas grand-chose.**
noo pah grahN shoz
Us? Not much.

Nous allons beaucoup dormir et nous détendre.
noo zah-lohN bo-koo dohr-meer ay noo day-tahNdr
We are going to sleep a lot and relax.

Anne: **Nous aussi. Mais voilà ma proposition:**
noo zoh-see meh vwah-lah mah proh-po-sees-yohN
Us too. But here is my proposition:

Venez à Nice avec nous!
vuh-nay ah nees ah-vehk noo
Come to Nice with us!

Lynne: **À Nice? Comment ça?**
ah nees koh-mahN sah
To Nice? How come?

Anne: **Nous avons loué une petite maison. Pour vous et pour nous.**
noo zah-vohN loo-ay ewn puh-teet meh-zohN poor voo ay poor noo
We rented a little house. For you and for us.

Lynne: **Oh là là, Anne. C'est fantastique!**
oh lah lah ahn seh fahN-tahs-teek
Oh wow, Anne! That's fantastic!

Je vais l'annoncer à David.
zhuh veh lah-nohN-say ah dah-veed
I'm going to announce it to David.

Nice! Mon rêve! Je te rappelle.
Nees mohN rehv zhuh tuh rah-pehl
Nice! My dream! I'll call you back.

To brush up on the past tense, see Chapter 9, and on the future, see Chapter 8.

Words to Know

vous faites	voo feht	you do
les fêtes [f]	lay feht	holidays
pas grand-chose	pah grahN shohz	not much
dormir	dor-meer	to sleep
se détendre	suh day-tahNdr (reflexive)	to relax
nous avons loué	noo zah-vohN loo-ay	we rented
je te rappelle	zhuh tuh rah-pehl	I call you back
la plage	lah plahzh	beach
la mer	lah mehr	the ocean
la montagne	lah mohn-tahn-yuh	the mountains
la campagne	la cahN-pahn-yuh	the country
les grandes villes [f]	lay gahNd veel	cities

Passports and Visas

The requirements to enter different countries can vary. A travel agent should be able to help you. The consulates of the country or countries where you are going should also be able to help. If you're a U.S. citizen, you need a valid passport, except for Canada where a driver's license or a birth certificate suffices. It is important to check the expiration date on your passport early because it takes weeks to get it renewed. Don't even dream of getting it renewed overnight! If you need to get a brand new passport because you haven't ever had one, make sure you start procedures at least six weeks before you want to leave.

There are no visa requirements for Europe if you plan to stay less than five or six months.

Once you are in Europe, you can hop from country to country to your heart's desire. In most cases, you are not even asked to show your passports. If you want to find out more about entry requirements anywhere in the world (Tahiti? Martinique? Madagascar?), you can browse on the Internet at `http://travel.state.gov/foreignentrysreqs.html`.

Talkin' the Talk

David wants to make sure that he doesn't need a visa, so he calls the French Consulate. He chooses to speak French to the employee just to get into the spirit.

David:	**Bonjour. C'est le consulat français?** *bohN-zhoor seh luh kohN-sew-lah frahN-seh* Hello. Is this the French consulate?
Employee:	**Oui, est-ce que je peux vous aider?** *wee ehs-kuh zhuh puh voo zeh-day* Yes, can I help you?
David:	**Est-ce qu'il faut un visa pour aller en France?** *ehs-keel foh-taN vee-zah poor-ah-lay ahN frahNs* Do you need a visa to go to France?
Employee:	**Vous êtes américain?** *voo zeht ah-may-ree-kaN* Are you American?
David:	**Oui, madame. Et je veux rester trois semaines en France.** *wee mah-dahm ay zhuh vuh rehs-tay trwah suh-mehn ahN frahNs* Yes, ma'am. And I want to stay three weeks in France.

Employee:	**Il faut un passeport valide et c'est tout. Bon voyage!**
	eel foh taN pahs-pohr vah-leed ay seh too bohN
	vwah-yazh
	You need a valid passport and that's all. Have a nice
	trip!
David:	**Merci. Au revoir.**
	mehr-see ohr-vwahr
	Thank you. Good-bye.

Buying Tickets

Whether you hook up with an agency or buy your tickets via the Internet, you want to have your facts straight.

- When can you leave? (month, day)
- When must you be back? (month, day)
- Is there any room to play with those dates?
- Are you interested in a package tour?
- Do you want hotel accommodations?
- How much are you willing to spend?

Getting Your Dates Straight

Since we're talking about the whens and wheres of travel, it may help for you to know the months of the year in French:

- **janvier** *(zhan-vyay)* January
- **février** *(fay-vree-ay)* February
- **mars** *(mahrs)* March
- **avril** *(ah-vreel)* April
- **mai** *(meh)* May
- **juin** *(zhwaN)* June
- **juillet** *(zhwee-yeh)* July

- ✔ **août** *(oot)* August
- ✔ **septembre** *(sehp-tahNbr)* September
- ✔ **octobre** *(ok-tohbr)* October
- ✔ **novembre** *(noh-vahNbr)* November
- ✔ **décembre** *(day-sahNbr)* December

Specific dates

When expressing a more specific date, you use the following construction:

> Le + cardinal number + month + year

Here is an example

C'est	*le*	*six*	*avril*	*2000*
seh	luh	see	zah-vreel	duh meel
It's	the	sixth of	April	2000

Use this formula to express all dates, except for the first of the month:

> **C'est le premier mai.** *(seh luh pruhm-yay meh)* It's the first of May.

The following are some important dates:

- ✔ **La fête nationale française est le 14 juillet.** *(lah feht nas-yoh-nahl frahN-sehz eh luh kah-tohrz zhwee-yeh)* (The French national holiday is on the 14th of July.)
- ✔ **La fête nationale américaine est le 4 juillet.** *(lah feht nas-yoh-nahl ah-may-ree-kehn eh luh kahtr zhwee-yeh)* (The American national holiday is on the 4th of July.)
- ✔ **La fête nationale suisse est le premier août.** *(lah feht nas-yoh-nahl swees eh luh pruhm-yay root)* (The Swiss national holiday is on the first of August.)
- ✔ **La fête nationale belge est le 17 juillet.** *(lah feht nas-yoh-nahl behlzh eh luh dee seht zhwee-yeh)* (The Belgian national holiday is on the 17th of July.)

Less specific dates

Use **en** *(ahN)* with months to express "in":

✔ **En janvier, je pars pour la Martinique.** *(ahN zhaN-vyay zhuh pahr poor lah mahr-tee-neek)* (In January, I leave for Martinique.)

✔ **Je reviens en avril.** *(zhuh ruh-vyaN ahN nah-vreel)* (I am coming back in April.)

(See Chapter 4 for seasons.)

Here are a few question-and-answer sequences using this scheduling vocabulary:

Quel jour est-ce aujourd'hui?	**Aujourd'hui, c'est lundi.**
(kehl zhoor ehs oh-zhoor-dwee)	*(oh-zhoor-dwee seh laN-dee)*
What day is today?	Today is Monday.
Quelle est la date?	**C'est le onze juillet.**
(kehl eh lah daht)	*(seh luh ohNz zhwee-yeh)*
What is the date?	It's the 11th of July.
Quand voulez-vous partir?	**Le quinze mai.**
(kahN voo-lay voo pahr-teer)	*(luh kaNz meh)*
When do you want to leave?	On the 15th of May.
J'aime voyager au printemps.	**Moi aussi: en avril ou en mai.**
(zhehm vwah-yah-zhay o praN-tahN)	*(mwah oh-see ahN ah-vreel oo ahN meh)*
I like to travel in the spring.	Me too: in April or in May.
Mon ami arrive en septembre.	**Il reste jusqu'à la fin du mois?**
(moh nah-mee ah-reev ahN sehp-tahNbr)	*(eel rehst zhews-kah lah faN dew mwah)*
My friend arrives in September.	Does he stay until the end of the month?

Timing phrases

Here are some timing phrases that may come in handy when making travel plans, meeting friends, making appointments, and more:

✔ **demain matin** *(duh-maN mah-taN)* (tomorrow morning)

✔ **tôt le matin** *(toh luh mah-taN)* (early in the morning)

✔ **demain après-midi** *(duh-maN ah-preh mee-dee)* (tomorrow afternoon)

- **après-demain** *(ah-preh duh-maN)* (the day after tomorrow)
- **samedi prochain** *(sahm-dee proh-shaN)* (next Saturday)
- **la semaine prochaine** *(lah suh-mehn proh-shehn)* (next week)
- **il est (trop) tôt** *(eel eh tro to)* (it is (too) early)
- **il est (trop) tard** *(eel eh tro tahr)* (it is (too) late)
- **pour combien de personnes?** *(poor kohN-byaN duh pehr-sohn)* (For how many people?)
- **à quelle heure?** *(ah kehl uhr)* (At what time?)
- **un moment/un instant** *(aN moh-mahN aN naN-stahN)* (one moment)

Talkin' the Talk

While their friends are making their travel arrangements in New York, Anne is at the travel agency to book her and her husband's flight to Nice.

Anne:
Bonjour, monsieur.
bohN-zhoor muh-syuh
Good morning, sir.

Agent:
Bonjour, madame. Vous désirez?
bohN-zhoor mah-dahm voo day-zee-ray
Good morning, ma'am. Can I help you?

Anne:
Nous voudrions prendre l'avion pour Nice en décembre.
noo voo-dree-ohN prahNdr lah-vee-oN poor nees ahN day-sahNbr
We would like to take a plane to Nice in December.

Agent:
C'est pour combien de personnes?
seh poor kohN-byaN duh pehr-sohn
For how many people?

Anne:
Pour deux personnes, monsieur.
poor duh pehr-sohn muh-syuh
For two people, sir.

Agent:
Et pour quelle date? Vous voulez rester pour combien de jours?
ay poor kehl daht voo voo-lay rehs-stay poor kohN-byaN duh zhoor
And for which date is this? How many days do you want to stay?

Anne:	**Dix jours: du 22 décembre au 2 janvier** *dee zhoor dew vahNt duh day-sahNbr o duh zhahN-vyay* Ten days: from the 22nd of December to the 2nd of January.
Agent:	**Vous avez de la chance. J'ai encore deux places. Votre nom?** *voo zah-vay duh lah shahNs zhay ahN-kohr duh plahs vohtr nohN* You're lucky. I still have two seats. Your name?
Anne:	**Anne et Michel Brasse: B-R-A-S-S-E.** *ah-nay mee-shehl brahs bay ehr ah doobl ehs uh* Anne and Michel Brasse: B-R-A-S-S-E.
Agent:	**C'est le vol Air France 7702 qui part à 10 heures de Charles de Gaulle.** *seh luh vohl ehr frahNs swah-sahNt zay-roh duh kee pahr duh shahrl duh gohl* It's the Air France flight # 7702 which leaves at 10 a.m. from Charles de Gaulle.
	Ça vous convient? *sah voo kohN-vyahN* Does that suit you?
Anne:	**Oui, c'est parfait. À quelle heure est-ce qu'il arrive?** *wee seh pahr-feh ah kehl uhr ehs keel ah-reev* Yes, that's perfect. At what time does it arrive?
Agent:	**Il arrive à Nice à 11h30.** *eel ah-reev ah nees ah ohNz uhr trahNt* It arrives in Nice at 11:30 a.m.
Anne:	**Bon. Pouvez-vous réserver deux sièges pour nous?** *bohN poo-vay voo ray-sehr-vay duh syehzh poor noo* Good. Can you reserve two seats for us?
Agent:	**Mais oui, bien sûr.** *meh wee byaN sewr* Yes, of course.

There are idioms in every language — expressions that can't be translated literally. **Vous avez de la chance** (*voo zah-vay duh lah shahNs*) (you are lucky) is one of them.

Words to Know

rester	rehs-tay	to stay
la semaine	lah suh-mehn	week
je reviens	zhuh ruh-vyaN	I am coming back
aujourd'hui	oh-joor-dwee	today
partir	pahr-teer	to leave
voyager	vwah-yazhay	to travel
jusqu'à	zhews-kah	until
la fin du mois	lah faN dew mwah	end of the month
le vol	luh vohl	flight
le siège	luh syehzh	seat
à quelle heure?	ah kehl uhr	at what time?
le lendemain	luh lahN-duh-mahN	next day

In the preceding dialog, you came across this phrase: **Ça vous convient?** *(sa voo kohN-vyaN)* (Does that suit you?; Is that convenient for you?) You can replace the indirect object pronoun (replaces an object with **à**) with others, depending on what you want to express, as in the following examples:

- ✔ **Ça me convient.** *(sa muh kohN-vyaN)* (That suits me.)
- ✔ **Ça te convient?** *(sa tuh kohN-vyaN)* (That suits you.)
- ✔ **Ça lui convient.** *(sa lwee kohN-vyaN)* (That suits him/her.)
- ✔ **Ça nous convient.** *(sa noo kohN-vyaN)* (That suits us.)
- ✔ **Ça leur convient.** *(sa voo kohN-vyaN)* (That suits them.)

By the way, only **lui** and **leur** differ from the direct object pronouns (which are **le, la, les**); the others coincide. (See Chapter 14 for information on direct object pronouns.)

These are indirect object pronouns, replacing an indirect object with **à**:

✔ **Ça convient à M./Mme Paulet; Ça lui convient.** *(sa kohN-vyaN ah muhs-yuh mahdahm poh-leh sah lwee kohN-vyaN)* (It suits Mr./Mrs. Paulet. It suits him/her.)

✔ **Ça convient à M. et Mme Paulet; Ça leur convient.** *(sa kohN-vyaN ah muhs-yuh ay mahdahm poh-leh; sah luhr kohN-vyaN)* (It suits Mr. and Mrs. Paulet. It suits them.)

Choosing Accommodations

Not everybody is so lucky as to have good friends abroad. Most likely, you'll fly to your destination, book a hotel from back home, and compose some sort of itinerary to help you take in the sights, the people, and the food.

Many people prefer a planned group trip. There are advantages to this, too. You don't have to worry about too many things, and you won't find yourself alone or not taken care of. This sort of trip is for the gregarious spirit that likes to live experiences with others.

Either way, whether you travel individually or as a group, you get to choose the type of accommodation you want as you book. Chapter 13 talks extensively about the different types of hotels that you can choose from.

You may find signs with these expressions in your hotel. They tell you more about the accomodations.

✔ **hôtel 4 étoiles** *(ho-tel kahtr ay-twahl)* (4-star hotel)

✔ **hôtel 2 étoiles** *(ho-tel duh zay-twahl)* (2-star hotel)

✔ **hôtel 1 étoile** *(ho-tel ewn ay-twahl)* (1-star hotel)

✔ **air conditionné** *(ehr kohN-dee-syoh-nay)* (air conditioning)

✔ **recommandé dans** *(ruh-koh-mahN-day dahN)* (recommended in)

✔ **piscine** *(pee-seen)* (swimming pool)

✔ **salle de gym** *(sahl duh zheem)* (fitness room)

✔ **site historique** *(seet hees-toh-reek)* (historic site)

Oh, and you can't live without your laptop? Fine, so bring it, but be fore-warned about three things:

✔ You may be asked at customs to turn it on, so be sure to have a loaded battery.

✔ You won't be able to use e-mail unless you bring an access number from your ISP with you for the area you are vacationing in. Plus, of course, you need a telephone jack that you can use.

✔ You also need to bring along an adapter for the telephone jack. Plus an adapter for the electric outlet so you can recharge your battery.

Talkin' the Talk

You're happily writing on your laptop in your wonderful hotel room when the battery goes dry. You are rummaging in your bag, but you can't find an adapter to plug the computer in with. You are now at the reception desk for help.

Touriste: **Bonsoir, monsieur.**
bohN-swahr muh-syuh
Good evening, sir.

L'employée: **Bonsoir, madame. Est-ce que je peux vous aider?**
bohN-swahr mah-dahm ehs-kuh zhuh puh voo zeh-day
Good evening, ma'm. Can I help you?

Touriste: **Je l'espère. Où est-ce que je peux acheter un adaptateur pour brancher mon ordinateur?**
zhuh lehs-pehr oo ehs-kuh zhuh puh ash-tay aN ah-dahp-tah-tuhr poor brahN-shay mohn ohr-dee-nah-tuhr
I hope so. Where can I buy an adapter in order to plug in my computer?

L'employée: **Vous avez de la chance, la boutique de l'hôtel vend des adaptateurs.**
voo zah-vay duh lah shahNs lah boo-teek duh loh-tehl vahN deh zah-dahp-tah-tuhr
You are lucky, the hotel shop sells adapters.

Touriste: **Excellent. J'y vais tout de suite. Merci, monsieur.**
ehk-seh-lahN zhee veh toot sweet mehr-see muh-syuh
Great. I'll go there right away. Thank you, sir.

L'employée: **Je vous en prie.**
zhuh voo zahN pree
You are welcome.

The preceding dialog contains this statement: **j'y vais** (*zhee veh*) (I am going there). This harmless little one-letter-word, **y** *(ee)* (there), is used just like an object pronoun and should always be in front of the verb.

Finally, one more hot tip for those among you who feel just so much more secure with a cellular phone close by. You can order one to be delivered to you upon your arrival at the airport. They are expensive to rent, but what can you do if you need it, right? Check out this service on the Internet at www.ellinas.com.

Words to Know

vous êtes prêts?	voo zeht preh	are you ready?
les vacances [f]	leh vah-kahNs	vacation
vous venez	voo vuh-nay	you are coming
le billet	luh bee-yeh	ticket
rentrer	rahN-tray	to go home
la météo	lah may-tay-oh	weather report
vous venez nous chercher	voo vuh-nay noo shehr-shay	you are coming to pick us up
j'espère	zhehs-pehr	I hope
un ordinateur	aN ohr-dee-nah-tuhr	computer
acheter	ash-tay	to buy
brancher	brahN-shay	to plug in
il vend	eel vahN	he sells

Packing Your Suitcases

What should you take with you? Generally less than you think. Take things that are easy to wash, easy to handle, and easy to wear.

When you visit historical monuments in France, such as cathedrals and churches, you never see locals wearing shorts, tank tops and the like, and you shouldn't either. It's very much a question of respect and reverence for religious grounds.

Talkin' the Talk

Lynne has never been to the south of France, so she calls up Anne about what type of clothes to take.

Lynne: **Anne, je fais les valises.**
zhuh feh leh vah-leez
Anne, I am packing.

Qu'est-ce que tu me conseilles comme vêtements?
kehs kuh tew muh kohN-sehy kohm veht-mahN
What do you advise me about clothes?

Anne: **C'est facile. Des choses légères mais un pull pour le soir.**
seh fah-seel deh shohz lay-zhehr meh aN pewl poor luh swahr
That's easy. Light things, but a sweater for the evening.

Lynne: **Okay. Alors, je prends des shorts et des t-shirts pour nous deux.**
okeh ah-lohr zhuh prahN deh short ay deh tee shirt poor noo duh
Okay. So, I take shorts and t-shirts for both of us.

Anne: **Et peut-être une robe et une jupe pour sortir.**
ay puh tehtr ewn rohb ay ewn zhewp poor sohr-teer
And maybe a dress and a skirt in order to go out.

Plus une cravate, des pantalons, une ou deux chemises pour David.
plews ewn krah-vaht deh pahN-tah-lohN ewn oo duh shuh-meez poor dah-veed
Plus a tie, pants, one or two shirts for David.

Lynne: **Ah oui, et une veste pour lui.**
ah wee ay ewn vehst poor lwee
Oh yes, and a jacket for him.

Anne: **Voilà. Mais ne prenez pas trop de choses.**
vwah-lah meh nuh pruh nay pah trohd shohz
That's it. But don't take too many things.

Il y a une machine à laver.
eel yah ewn mah-sheen ah lah-vay
There is a washing machine.

Lynne: **Génial. Et des sandales et des baskets, ça suffit?**
zhay-nyahl ay deh sahN-dahl ay deh bahs-keht sah sew-fee
Great. I am going to take sandals and sneakers, is that enough?

Anne: **Moi, j'aime des chaussures pour les promenades, mais tu fais comme tu veux.**
mwah zhehme deh choh-sewr poor leh proh-muh-nahd meh tew feh kohm tew vuh
Me, I like shoes for walking, but you do as you like.

Lynne: **Chez nous, c'est David qui aime les chaussures. Merci, Anne.**
shay noo seh dah-veed kee ehm leh shoh-sewr mehr-see ahn
With us, it's David who likes shoes. Thanks, Anne.

Anne: **Et n'oublie pas les lunettes de soleil!**
ay noo-blee pah lay lew-neht duh soh-leh-y
And don't forget the sunglasses!

For more clothes vocabulary, see Chapter 6.

Fun & Games

Provide the French equivalents for as many items as possible in the following scene:

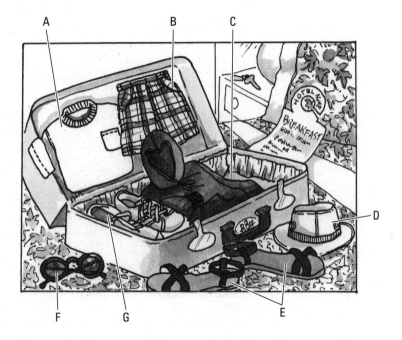

A. _____

B._____

C. _____

D. _____

E. _____

F. _____

G. _____

Chapter 16

Handling Emergencies

. . . .

In This Chapter

▶ Getting medical help

▶ Talking with a doctor

▶ Asking for help from the police

. . . .

I sincerely wish you didn't have to read this chapter, but I strongly suggest that you do. Emergencies are not fun situations, especially in foreign environments. This chapter is divided into two main sections: First, the health section deals with health problems; then the legal section deals with legal matters.

Getting Medical Help

No matter where you go as a tourist and foreigner, you will find that people, in a case of emergency, tend to be helpful and caring. They usually do their best to get you help and try to activate whatever English they know or rush to find someone who does.

Following are some key French phrases you need to know in an emergency:

✔ **Est-ce qu'il y a quelqu'un qui parle anglais?** *(ehs keel yah kehl kaN kee pahrl ahN-gleh)* (Is there someone who speaks English?)

✔ **Est-ce qu'il y a un docteur/une infirmière qui parle anglais?** *(ehs keel yah aN dohk-tuhr/ewn ahn-feer-myehr kee pahrl ahn-gleh)* (Is there a doctor/nurse who speaks English?)

✔ **À l'aide! Vite!** *(ah lehd veet)* (Help! Fast!)

✔ **Au secours!** *(oh suh-koor)* (Help!)

✔ **Au feu!** *(oh fuh)* (Fire!)

Talkin' the Talk

 There has been a car accident. A tourist attempts to get help for an injured man.

Tourist: **Pouvez-vous nous aider, s'il vous plaît?**
              poo-vay voo noo zeh-day seel voo play
              Can you help us, please?

              Appelez un docteur!
              ah-puh-lay uhn dohk-tuhr
              Call a doctor!

              Cet homme est blessé.
              suh tohm eh bleh-say
              This man is hurt.

              Il saigne et il a perdu connaissance.
              eel sehn-yuh ay eel ah pehr-dew koh-neh-sahNs
              He is bleeding, and he is unconscious.

Doctor: **Je suis médecin. Qu'est-ce qui s'est passé?**
              zhuh swee mayd-saN kes kee seh pah-say
              I am a doctor. What happened?

Tourist: **Il y a eu une collision. Il s'est évanoui.**
              eel yah ew ewn kohl-lee-syohN eel seh tay-vah-noo-ee
              There was a collision. He fainted.

Doctor: **Ah, il ouvre les yeux.**
              ah eel oovr lay zyuh
              Ah, he is opening his eyes.

              Monsieur! Où avez-vous mal?
              muhs-yuh oo ah-vay voo mahl
              Sir! Where does it hurt?

Tourist: **J'ai mal à la jambe.**
              zhay mahl ah lah zhahNb
              My leg hurts.

Doctor: **Ne bougez pas. Je vais examiner votre jambe.**
              nuh boo-zhay pah zhuh veh ehk-zah-mee-nay
              voh-truh zhahNb
              Don't move. I am going to examine your leg.

Est-ce que ça fait mal?
ehs-kuh sah feh mahl
Does that hurt?

Tourist: **Oui, ça fait très mal.**
wee sah feh treh mahl
Yes, it hurts a lot.

Doctor: **Il s'est cassé la jambe. Et il a une coupure.**
eel seh kah-say lah zhahNb ay eel ah ewn coo-pewr
He broke his leg. And he has a cut.

Je vais appeler une ambulance.
zhuh veh ah-puh-lay ewn ahN-bew-lahNs
I'll call an ambulance.

Here are a few extra pieces of vocabulary for your reading pleasure:

✔ **un hôpital** *(uhn oh-pee-tahl)* (hospital)

✔ **les urgences** (f) *(leh zewr-zhahns)* (emergency room)

✔ **le/la secouriste** *(luh/lah suh-koo-reest)* (paramedic)

Qu'est-ce qui s'est passé? *(kehs kee seh pah-say)* (What happened?) is an idiomatic expression that you probably want to memorize because it is so frequently used. **Ça fait mal!** *(sah feh mahl)* (That hurts!) is another expression you may want to memorize because it comes in quite handy at times.

In French you use the definite article **(le, la, les)** in front of body parts, contrary to English, where you use possessives. For example:

✔ **Il ouvre les yeux** *(ee loovr lay zyuh)* (He is opening his eyes.)

✔ **Il s'est cassé la jambe** *(eel seh kah-say lah zhahNb)* (He broke his leg.)

When you want to say that a body part hurts, you can use this construction: **j'ai mal à/au/aux** *(zheh mahl ah/oh/oh)* + any body part. You are using the verb **avoir** *(ah-vwahr)* (to have) plus the preposition **à** *(ah)*. Here are some examples:

✔ **j'ai mal à la jambe** *(zheh mahl ah lah zhahNb)* (my leg hurts)

✔ **il/elle/a mal aux yeux** *(eel/ehl ah mahl oh zyuh)* (his/her eyes hurt)

Talkin' the Talk

Fortunately, the ambulance came pretty quickly, and now a doctor is examining the tourist's leg at the hospital.

Doctor: **La coupure n'est pas grave, mais nous allons faire une radio de la jambe.**
lah koo-pewr neh pah grahv meh noo zah-lohN fehr ewn rah-dyo duh lah zhahNb
The cut is not serious, but we'll take an X-ray of your leg.

On vous met sur cette table . . . voilà. . . .et ne bougez pas . . . merci.
ohn voo meh sewr set tahbl . . . vwah-lah. . . . ay nuh boo-zhay pah . . . mehr-see
We are putting you on this table . . . there. . . . and don't move . . . thank you.

Doctor: **La radio est prête.**
lah rah-dyo eh preht
The X-ray is ready.

Voilà la fracture. Oui, vous vous êtes cassé la jambe.
vwah-lah lah frahk-tewr wee voo voo zeht kah-say lah zhahNb
Here is the fracture. Yes, your leg is broken.

Tourist: **C'est une fracture avec complications?**
seh tewn frahk-tewr ah-vehk kohN-plee-kahs-yohN
Is it a complicated fracture?

Doctor: **Non, mais il vous faut un plâtre.**
nohn meh eel voo fo taN plahtr
No, but you need a cast.

Be sure to tell attending medics and doctors if there are complicating factors in your or your companion's medical history, such as:

✔ **Je suis cardiaque.** *(zhuh swee kahr-dyahk)* (I have a heart condition.)

✔ **J'ai eu une crise cardiaque il y a (deux) ans.** *(zheh uh ew kreez kahr-dyahk eel-yah duh zahN)* (I had a heart attack two years ago.)

✔ **J'ai de l'hypertension.** *(zhay duh lee-pehr-tahn-syohn)* (I have high blood pressure.)

✔ **Je suis diabétique/allergique à . . .** *(zhuh swee dee-ah-bay-teek/ah-lehr-zheek ah)* (I am diabetic/allergic to . . .)

France has a socialized medical system, but private insurance also exists. You should always, before you leave on a trip, call your insurance company and ask what you should do in case an emergency occurs in the countries you are planning to visit.

Over there, as a tourist, if you need emergency services of any kind or an operation, show them proof of your insurance in the United States, call your insurance company back home, and explain what's happening. Usually you will have to pay your bill (with your credit card) there, but your insurance company will reimburse you when you present the detailed bill . . . unless you forgot to notify them when it happened.

In any case, be sure to get this info before you leave home.

When someone gives you instructions, you may hear a command with a personal pronoun, as in, **Il vous faut un plâtre** *(el voo foh tuhn plahtr)* (You need to have a cast). This structure is a step beyond the impersonal **il faut+article+noun** (one has to . . .) which is explained in Chapter 12.

Although the impersonal format is handy in many circumstances, sometimes (especially in an emergency) you want to be more specific. Here is a way to personalize that structure by adding an indirect object pronoun of your choice in front of the verb:

✔ **il me faut un docteur** *(eel muh foh tuhn dohk-tuhr)* (I need a doctor)

✔ **il te faut un docteur** *(eel tuh foh tuhn dohk-tuhr)* (you need a doctor)

✔ **il lui faut un docteur** *(eel lwee foh tuhn dohk-tuhr)* (he/she needs a doctor)

✔ **il nous faut un docteur** *(eel noo foh tuhn dohk-tuhr)* (we need a doctor)

✔ **il vous faut un docteur** *(eel voo foh tuhn dohk-tuhr)* (you need a doctor)

✔ **il leur faut un docteur** *(eel luhr foh tuhn dohk-tuhr)* (they need a doctor)

The following list provides words for some other body parts that one can break (or would rather not break . . .):

Words to Know

le bras	luh brah	arm
la main	lah mahN	hand
le doigt	luh dwah	finger
le nez	luh nay	nose
les côtes (f.)	lay koht	ribs
le pied	luh pyeh	foot
un bleu	aN bluh	bruise
une égratignure	ewn ay-grah-teen-yewr	scrape
une brûlure	ewn brew-lewr	burn
une coupure	ewn koo-pewr	cut
la figure	lah fee-gewr	face
un œil, les yeux	aN nuhy, leh zyuh	eye, eyes
une oreille	ewn oh-rehy	ear
le cou	luh koo	neck
une épaule	ewn ay-pohl	shoulder
la poitrine	lah pwah-treen	chest
le genou	luh zhuh-noo	knee
un orteil	aN ohr-teh-y	toe

Talking with Doctors

Okay, enough of these highly unpleasant situations covered in the preceding sections. Suppose you just want to make an appointment with a doctor in a nonemergency situation?

For a cold, a cough, indigestion, or diarrhea, go talk first to a pharmacist. In France, pharmacists are allowed to suggest medication for you. When you go there, you can say any of these things:

- **Pourriez-vous me donner un conseil?** *(poo-ree-ay voo muh doh-nay uhN kohN-sehy)* (Could you give me some advice?)

- **J'ai très mal à la tête.** *(zhay treh mahl ah lah teht)* (I have very bad headache.)

- **J'ai le nez bouché.** *(zhay luh nay boo-shay)* (I have a stuffed nose.)

- **J'ai un gros rhume.** *(zhay aN groh rewm)* (I have an awful cold.)

- **J'ai la diarrhée.** *(zhay lah dee-ah-ray)* (I have diarrhea.)

- **Je suis constipé(e).** *(zhuh swee kohN-stee-pay)* (I am constipated.)

Also, if you need to see a doctor, pharmacists can gladly give you the address of one or call a doctor's office for you, if you like. Of course, the hotel receptionist can do the same thing.

Doctors usually have consultation hours for patients who do not have an appointment. You may have to wait a long time, so it's better to try to call ahead. In Paris, you can call **Prompt Secours** (18) or the **Police** (17) and even ask for an English-speaking doctor. In the provinces, all the emergency numbers are on one page of the telephone book. The local paper carries a list of pharmacies that remain open all night and during the weekend. In case of a toothache, the procedure is the same.

Talkin' the Talk

Going to a doctor's office may not be a fun prospect, but it's probably better than having been involved in an accident. Julia has not been feeling well, so she calls an office in order to make an appointment.

Julia: **Bonjour. C'est Julia Mills au téléphone.**
bohn-zhoor seh zhew-lyah meels oh tay-lay-fohn
Hello. This is Julia Mills speaking.

Est-ce que je pourrais prendre rendez-vous le plus tôt possible?
ehs-kuh zhuh poo-reh prahndr rahn-day voo luh plew toh poh-seebl
Could I have an appointment as soon as possible?

Receptionist: **De quoi souffrez-vous?**
duh kwah soo-fray voo
What are you suffering from?

Julia: **Je suis tombée et maintenant j'ai très mal à la tête.**
zhuh swee tohN-bay ay maN-tuh-nahN zhay treh mal ah lah teht
I fell and now I have a bad headache.

Receptionist: **Avez-vous mal au cœur?**
ah-vay voo mahl oh kuhr
Do you feel nauseous?

Julia: **Oui, je ne me sens pas très bien.**
wee zhuh muh nuh sahN pah treh byahN
Yes, I don't feel very well.

Receptionist: **Pouvez-vous venir tout de suite?**
poo-vay voo vuh-neer toot sweet
Can you come in right away?

Julia: **Oui, merci. À tout à l'heure.**
wee mehr-see ah too tah luhr
Yes, thank you. See you shortly.

Chapter 9 covers the past tense. You need the verb **avoir** to make it, as in **j'ai eu** *(zheh ew)* (I had). However, 16 verbs of coming and going take **être** instead, as with **tomber** *(tohn-bay)* (to fall):

Past Tense	*Pronunciation*
je <u>suis</u> tombé(e)	zhuh swee tohN-bay
tu <u>es</u> tombé(e)	tew eh tohN-bay
il <u>est</u> tombé; elle <u>est</u> tombée	eel eh tohN-bay; ehl eh tohN-bay
nous <u>sommes</u> tombé(e)s	noo sohm tohN-bay
vous <u>êtes</u> tombé(e)s	voo zeht tohN-bay
ils <u>sont</u> tombés, elles <u>sont</u> tombées	eel sohN tohN-bay, ehl sohN tohN-bay

If the subject is feminine and/or plural, you need to add an extra **–e** or **–s** or **–es** to the past participle. You can only hear the difference if the last letter of the past participle was a consonant to begin with.

Table 16-1 shows the 16 participles that make their past tense with **être**:

Table 16-1	Participles That Make Their Past Tense with *être*		
Participle	*Pronunciation*	*Infinitive*	*Translation*
Verbs of coming			
allé	ah-lay	aller	to go
arrivé	ah-ree-vay	arriver	to arrive
entré	ahN-tray	entrer	to enter
venu	vuh-new	venir	to come
Up and down verbs			
descendu	deh-sahN-dew	descendre	to go down
monté	mohN-tay	monter	to go up
resté	rehs-tay	rester	to stay
tombé	tohN-bay	tomber	to fall
Verbs of leaving			
parti	pahr-tee	partir	to leave
passé	pah-say	passer	to pass by
sorti	sohr-tee	sortir	to go out
rentré	rahN-tray	rentrer	to come back home
Verbs for in and out of life			
né	nay	naître	to be born
mort	mohr	mourir	to die
décédé	day-say-day	décéder	to decease
devenu	duh-vuh-new	devenir	to become

Talkin' the Talk

 Julie arrives at the doctor's office for an examination:

Doctor: **Depuis quand vous sentez-vous comme ça?**
            duh-puis kahN voo sahN-tay voo kohm sah
            How long have you been feeling like this?

Julia: **Depuis hier, quand je suis tombée.**
            duh-pwee yehr kahN zhuh swee tohN-bay
            Since yesterday, when I fell.

Doctor: **Avez-vous perdu l'appétit?**
            ah-vay voo pehr-dew lah-pay-tee
            Have you lost your appetite?

Julia: **Oui, et j'ai mal au cœur.**
            wee ay zhay mahl oh kuhr
            Yes, and I feel nauseous.

Doctor: **Vous avez une légère commotion cérébrale.**
            voo zah-vay ewn lay-zhehr koh-moh-syohN say-
            ray-brahl
            You have a light concussion.

            Reposez-vous bien pendant quelques jours.
            ruh-poh-zay voo byaN pahN-dahN kehl-kuh zhoor
            Take it very easy for a few days.

            Est-ce que vous prenez des médicaments?
            ehs-kuh voo pruh-nay deh may-dee-kah-mahN
            Do you take any medication?

Julia: **Non. Mais je suis allergique à l'aspirine.**
            nohn meh zhuh swee zah-lehr-zheek ah lahs-pee-reen
            No. But I am allergic to aspirin.

Doctor: **Bon. Voilà une ordonnance . . . en cas de douleurs.**
            bohn vwah-lah ewn ohr-doh-nahNs . . . ahN kaht
            doo-luhr
            Good. Here is a prescription . . . in case of pain.

            Prenez un comprimé toutes les quatre heures et
            revenez dans trois jours.
            pruh-nay uhn kohN-pree-may toot lay kaht ruhr ay
            ruh-vuh-nay dahN trwah zhoor
            Take one pill every four hours and come back in three
            days.

Julia: **Merci, docteur. Au revoir.**
            mehr-see dohk-tuhr ohr-vwahr
            Thank you, doctor. Good-bye.

Words to Know

une maladie	ewn mah-lah-dee	illness
la grippe	lah greep	flu
les amygdales (f.)	zah-mee-dahl	tonsils
une appendicite	ewn ah-paN-dee-seet	appendicitis
une intoxication alimentaire	ewn aN-toh-ksee-kahs-yohN ah-lee-mahN-tehr	food poisoning
s'étouffer	say-too-fay	to choke
la rougeole	lah roo-zhohl	measles
une apoplexie	ewn ah-poh-plek-see	seizure
une sciatique	ewn see-ah-teek	sciatica
une insolation	ewn aN-soh-lahs-yohN	sunstroke
l'asthme m.	lahsm	asthma
l'arthrite f.	lahr-treet	arthritis
un torticolis	tohr-tee-koh-lee	a stiff neck
une rage de dents	ewn razh duh dahN	violent toothpain
une ordonnance	ewn ohr-doh-nahNs	a prescription
un comprimé	aN kohN-pree-may	a pill
un généraliste	aN zhay-nay-rah-leest	a general practitioner
un dentiste	aN dahN-teest	a dentist
une piqûre	ewn pee-kewr	an injection
un calmant	aN kahl-mahN	sedative
une de mes lentilles de contact	ewn duh may lahN-teey duh kohN-takt	one of my contact lenses
les lunettes f.	lay lew-neht	glasses
un verre	aN vehr	a lens

In French, you don't excuse yourself when you sneeze. Quite to the contrary, your sneezing causes others to wish you fulfillment of your wishes, and someone may immediately say:

À vos/tes souhaits! *(ah voh/tay soo-eh)* (To your wishes!)

Talkin' the Talk

Peter Hayden developed a terrible toothache on the second day of his trip and couldn't even begin to enjoy this marvelous French food. So he went to the dentist in a rush.

Mr. Hayden: **Cette dent me fait mal.**
seht dahN muh feh mahl
This tooth hurts.

Dentist: **Oui, sans doute. Le plombage est tombé.**
wee sahN doot luh plohN-bazh eh tohN-bay
Yes, undoubtedly. The filling fell out.

Mr. Hayden: **Pourriez-vous le remplacer tout de suite?**
poo-ree-ay voo luh rahN-plah-say toot sweet
Could you replace it right away?

Dentist: **Je peux seulement vous donner un traitement provisoire.**
zhuh puh suhl-mahN voo doh-nay uhn treht-mahN proh-vee-zwahr
I can give only you a temporary treatment.

Mr. Hayden: **Bon. Mais faites-moi une anesthésie locale, s'il vous plaît.**
bohN meh feht mwah ewn ah-nehs-tay-zee loh-kahl seel voo play
Okay. But give me a local anesthetic, please.

Dentist: **Voilà . . . vous pouvez vous rinser, s'il vous plaît.**
vwah-lah . . . voo poo-vay vous raN-say seel voo play
Here we go . . . you can rinse, please.

Ne mangez pas pendant quatre heures.
nuh mahN-zhay pah pahN-dahN kahtr uhr
Don't eat anything for four hours.

Mr. Hayden: **Merci bien et au revoir.**
mehr-see byaN ay ohr-vwahr
Thank you very much and good-bye.

Words to Know

vous souffrez	voo soo-fray	you are suffering
je me sens bien	zhuh muh sahN byaN	I feel well
tout de suite	toot sweet	immediately
depuis hier	duh-pwee yehr	since yesterday
une commotion cérébrale	ewn koh-moh-sohN say-ray-brahl	concussion
quelques jours	kehl-kuh zhoor	several days
la douleur	lah doo-luhr	pain
prenez un comprimé	pruh-nay uhn kohN-pree-may	take a pill/tablet
sans doute	sahN doot	undoubtedly
provisoire	proh-vee-zwahr	temporary
ne mangez pas!	nuh mahN-zhay pah	don't eat!

Getting Legal Help

Most likely, you'll never have a need for your consul, but it is important to know this: While you are in a country that's not your own, the laws of that country override the laws of your own. And it's your consul who is really on your side, more so than any local lawyer or police.

If you are planning to stay several months, you should even register at your consulate. In case of an emergency, your consul is the most appropriate person to help you.

When planning a trip to France, you should find out ahead of time where the American or Canadian consulates are located. You can find this information on the Internet at www.amb-usa.fr/. Other French-speaking countries may have similar Web sites for locating your country's consulate.

Accidents

In the event of an accident, report the accident to the police (compulsory if there is personal injury). Here is what you need to report to whom:

- ✔ give your name, address, and insurance company to the other party;
- ✔ report to the appropriate insurance bureau of the other party and your own company;
- ✔ don't make any statement, certainly not written, without advice of a lawyer or an automobile club official;
- ✔ note all relevant details of the other party (such as name, address, vehicle registration, insurance agent, and so on) and independent witnesses of the accident;
- ✔ in France, get a police officer (**agent de police** *[ah-zhahN duh poh-lees]*) to make a report of major accidents in towns; on country roads, send for a **gendarme** *(zhahN-dahrm)* (police officer).

Most likely, you'll never have a need for this list, but it can be quite helpful for you to have all these phrases handy that you can pick from in the event of an accident.

- ✔ **Il y a eu un accident. . . .** *(eel yah ew aN nak-see-dahN)* (There has been an accident. . . .)
- ✔ **sur l'autoroute** *(sewr loh-toh-root)* (on the highway)
- ✔ **la route** *(lah root)* (road)
- ✔ **près de** *(preh duh)* (near)
- ✔ **Appelez . . . !** *(ah-puh-lay)* (Call . . . !)

    une ambulance *(ewn ahN-bew-lahNs)* (an ambulance)

    un docteur *(aN dohk-tuhr)* (a doctor)

    les pompiers *(lay pohN-pyeh)* (the fire brigade)

    la police *(lah poh-lees)* (the police)

When the police arrive, they usually ask a great many questions, such as:

- ✔ **Est-ce que je peux voir votre . . . ?** *(ehs-kuh zhuh puh vwahr vohtr)* (Can I see your . . . ?)

    permis de conduire (m.) *(pehr-meet kohN-dweer)* (driver's license)

    certificat d'assurance (m.) *(sehr-tee-fee-kah dah-sew rahNs)* (insurance certificate)

    carte grise (f.) *(kahrt greez)* (vehicle registration document)

✔ **Quel est votre nom et adresse?** *(kehl eh vohtr nohN ay ah-drehs)* (What is your name and address?)

✔ **À quelle heure est-ce que ça s'est passé?** *(ah keh luhr ehs kuh sah seh pah-say)* (At what time did this happen?)

✔ **Est-ce qu'il y a des témoins?** *(ehs keel ee ah day tay-mwaN)* (Are there any witnesses?)

They may also say phrases such as the following that you will want to understand:

✔ **Vos feux ne marchent pas.** *(voh fuh nuh mahrsh pah)* (Your lights are not working.)

✔ **Vous devez payer une amende.** *(voo duh-vay peh-yay ewn amahNd)* (You have to pay a fine.)

✔ **Vous devez venir au commissariat pour faire une déposition.** *(voo duh-vay vuh-neer oh koh-mee-sah-ree-ah poor fehr ewn dees-poh-zees-yohN)* (You need to make a statement at the station.)

And then, maybe you want to say a few things, too? Some of the following phrases may help you explain:

✔ **Il m'est rentré dedans.** *(eel meh rahN-tray duh-dahn)* (He ran into me.)

✔ **Elle a conduit trop vite/près.** *(ehl ah kohN-dwee troh veet/preh)* (She drove too fast/close.)

✔ **J'ai fait . . . kilomètres à l'heure.** *(zhay feh . . . kee-loh-mehtr ah luhr)* (I was doing . . . kilometers per hour.)

✔ **Je voudrais un interprète/un avocat.** *(zhuh voo-dray aN nahN-tehr-preht/aN-nah-voh-kah)* (I would like an interpreter/a lawyer.)

Robbery, theft, aggression

Here are words to cry out to get just anyone's attention:

✔ **À l'aide!** *(ah lehd)* Help!

✔ **Au secours!** *(oh suh-koor)* Help!

✔ **Arrêtez-le/la!** *(ah-reh-tay luh/lah)* Stop him/her!

✔ **Au voleur!** *(oh voh-luhr)* Catch the thief!

✔ **Police!** *(poh-lees)* Police!

You should report to the **commissariat de police** *(koh-mee-sah-ree-aht poh-lees)* in major cities or to the **gendarmerie nationale** *(zhahn-dahr-muh-ree nahs-yoh-nahl)* in smaller towns. To get the police in an emergency, dial **17** in France, **101** in Belgium, and **117** in Switzerland.

You may need to ask this question of a stranger:

> ✔ **Où est le commissariat de police le plus proche?** *(oo eh luh koh-mee-sah-ree-aht poh-lees luh plew prosh)* (Where is the closest police station?)

When you get to the police station, you may need some of these phrases:

> ✔ **Est-ce qu'il y a quelqu'un qui parle anglais?** *(ehs keel ee ah kehl kaN kee pahrl ahN-gleh)* (Is there anyone who speaks English?)
>
> ✔ **Je veux signaler** . . . *(zhuh vuh seen-ya-lay)* (I want to report . . .)
>
>> **un accident** *(uh nak-see-dahN)* (an accident)
>>
>> **une attaque** *(ew nah-tahk)* (attack)
>>
>> **une agression** *(ew nah-grehs-yohN)* (a mugging)
>>
>> **un viol** *(aN vee-ohl)* (a rape)
>>
>> **un cambriolage** *(aN kahN-bree-oh-lazh)* (a burglary)
>>
>> **un vol** *(aN vohl)* (a theft)
>
> ✔ **Mon enfant a disparu.** *(moh nahn-fahN ah dees-pah-rew)* (My child has disappeared.)
>
> ✔ **Voilà une photo.** *(vwah-lah ewn foh-toh)* (Here is a photo.)
>
> ✔ **Quelqu'un me suit.** *(kehl kahN muh swee)* (Someone is following me.)

If things have been stolen from you, here are the French equivalents for the most likely items:

> ✔ **On m'a volé** . . . *(ohN mah voh-lay)* They stole my . . .
>
> ✔ **mon appareil photo** *(moh nah-pah-rehy foh-toh)* (my camera)
>
> ✔ **mes cartes de crédit** *(meh kahrt duh kray-dee)* (my credit cards)
>
> ✔ **mon sac** *(mohN sahk)* (my bag)
>
> ✔ **mon argent** *(moh nahr-zhahN)* (my money)
>
> ✔ **mon passeport** *(mohN pahs-pohr)* (my passport)
>
> ✔ **mon porte-monnaie** *(mohN pohrt-moh-neh)* (my wallet)
>
> ✔ **ma montre** *(mah mohNtr)* (my watch)
>
> ✔ **ma bicyclette** *(mah bee-see-kleht)* (my bicycle)
>
> ✔ **ma voiture** *(mah vwah-tewr)* (my car)

The police may then ask for more details, as in the following questions:

> ✔ **Qu'est-ce qui vous manque?** *(kehs kee voo mahNk)* (What is missing?)

> ✔ **Ça s'est passé quand?** *(sah seh pah-say kahN)* (This happened when?)

> ✔ **Où logez-vous?** *(oo loh-zhay voo)* (Where are you staying?)

> ✔ **Où étiez-vous à ce moment-là?** *(oo ay-tyay voo ah suh moh-mahN lah?)* (Where were you at that moment?)

> ✔ **Pouvez-vous décrire la personne?** *(poo-vay voo day-kreer lah pehr-sohn)* (Can you describe the person?)

> ✔ **C'était quelqu'un . . .** *(say-teh kehl-kahN)* (It was someone . . .)

>> **aux cheveux blonds/bruns/roux/gris** *(oh shuh-vuh blohN/braN/roo/gree)* (with blond/brownish/red/gray hair)

>> **un peu chauve** *(uhn puh shohv)* (balding)

>> **grand/petit/mince/gros** *(grahN/puh-tee/mahNs/groh)* (tall/short/skinny/fat)

>> **d' environ . . . ans** *(dahN-vee-rohN . . . ahN)* (of about . . . years [of age])

As a foreigner, you may feel overwhelmed and welcome some help. You can ask to do one of the following things:

> ✔ **J'ai besoin d'un avocat qui parle anglais.** *(zhay buh-zwahn daN nah–voh-kah kee pahrl ahn-gleh)* (I need a lawyer who speaks English.)

> ✔ **Je dois contacter le consulat.** *(zhuh dwah kohN-tahk-tay luh kohN-sew-lah)* (I have to contact the consulate.)

> ✔ **Je voudrais téléphoner à un/e ami/e en ville.** *(zhuh voo-dreh tay-lay-foh-nay ah aN/ewn ah-mee ahN veel)* (I would like to call a friend in town.)

FUN & GAMES

Identify the body parts (using French, of course) in the following drawing.

Head: _____   Shoulder: _____

Hair: _____   Arm: _____

Ears: _____   Chest: _____

Eyes: _____   Hand: _____

Face: _____   Knee: _____

Mouth: _____   Leg: _____

Neck: _____   Foot: _____

Part IV
The Part of Tens

The 5th Wave   By Rich Tennant

I'm not sure what he's yelling about. It's all in French. But I think he's calling you a monster.

In this part . . .

*E*very *...For Dummies* book ends with top-ten lists, and this book has some good ones. In addition to offering tips on how to learn French quickly, we provide you with French phrases you should avoid, French expressions you shouldn't hesitate to use, French holidays, and more.

Chapter 17

Ten Ways to Pick Up French Quickly

• •

Whether you had years of French in high school or in college and neglected it subsequently, or you came to love this wonderful language "later in life," you may want to get ready for a visit or get yourself psyched for it. Here are a few tips on how you can do just that.

Look stuff up in the dictionary

If you are interested in picking up a lot of everyday words fast, cut up a bunch of paper into little pieces (or use sticky pads), get out your English-French dictionary and do the following: look up the French word for everything you can touch in your house, such as the wall (**le mur**) *(luh mewr)*, the door (**la porte**) *(lah pohrt)*, the couch (**le sofa**) *(luh soh-fah)*, the refrigerator (**le réfrigérateur**) *(luh ray-free-zheh-rah-tuhr)*, a cup (**une tasse**) *(ewn tahs)*, the faucet (**le robinet**) *(luh roh-bee-neh)*, whatever. Write each word on one of those pieces of paper and tape it, stick it, or pin it to whatever it describes. You can't help but know these words fast!

Write shopping lists

Here is another thing you can do at home: Make out your shopping lists in French. Write the English equivalents after the French though, just so you won't get annoyed in the store when you can't remember what you meant. For example, write **de l'ail** *(duh lay)* (garlic) or **des pommes** *(deh pohm)* (apples).

Celebrate French day!

You can also invent "French days" at home. Try to translate the little things you do as you go along, such as, "I am going to the phone:" **Je vais au téléphone** *(zhuh veh zoh tay-lay-fohn)*. "I am looking up a number:" **Je cherche** un numéro (*zhuh shehrsh uhn new-may-roh*). "I am making coffee:" **Je fais un café** (*zhuh feh zuhn kah-fay*). "I am going to watch TV:" **Je vais regarder la télé** (*zhuh veh ruh-gahr-day lah tay-lay*).

Use language tapes

On your way to and from work, you can always listen to language tapes. Just listening to the French voice and playing it over and over again can do wonders for your retaining the words and the phrases.

Listen to French music

Buy yourself some French songs, preferably with the text printed in a companion booklet, so you can get the idea of what they are singing about. But just listening to the French helps your ear for the words tremendously.

Try a CD

If you have a computer, there are excellent French CD-ROM courses on the market. You can listen to the pronunciations, see the correct spellings, record your own voice, and the program can correct you.

Watch French movies

Another fun way to pick up expressions, accent, cultural habits, and the like is by renting or even buying a French video movie with subtitles and watching it several times. What a treat!

Read French publications

Buy French magazines or have someone bring you some back from traveling in a French-speaking country and then read the ads. Reading the ads is a guaranteed eye-opener! On international flights, airline magazines in the pouch by your seat are often bilingual with French on one side and English on the other. Take one. Airline magazines are full of interesting ads and articles.

Surf the 'Net

The Internet has many opportunities for you to find out more about French. Get your search engine going — for example Excite on Netscape — type **France** (or any other French-speaking country) into the search engine, and then select whatever interests you: culture/hobbies, economy, gastronomy, media, business, and many other areas. Browse around in English or in French and pick out words you know.

Chat

Go to a French chat room, just to listen, if you like. You may be surprised how much you can pick up by listening to informal conversations.

Chapter 18

Ten Things Never to Say

• •

*H*ave you ever had foreign visitors saying things where you just wanted to crack up laughing or hold your breath hoping no one heard? Well, this happens to the best of us linguists, but here are at least some pointers to help you avoid the worst pitfalls!

✔ Be sure never to use the familiar form of address (**tu** *[tew]* for "you" or **ton** *[tohN]*, **ta** *[tah]*, **tes** *[teh]* for "your") when speaking to anyone but children! You want to say **Vous voulez aller au cinéma?** *(voo voo-lay zah-lay oh cee-nay-mah?)* (Do you want to go to the movies?) and NOT: **Tu veux aller . . .** *(tew vuh zah-lay . . .)* because the familiar form can be taken as an uneducated approach, and some may even take it as an insult! However, you may be offered the familiar form: **Mais on peut se tutoyer!** *(meh ohN puh suh tew-twah-yeh!)* (But we can use the familiar form with each other!). This is the green light, of course, and you can't very well turn the offer down. It would be pretty insulting.

✔ When you say good-bye to someone at night, you don't want to say **Bonne nuit!** *(bohN nwee)* (Good night!) unless you mean to make a point of the fact that you are going straight to bed. Stick to **Au revoir!** *(oh ruh-vwahr)* (Good-bye!) or **Bonsoir!** *(bohN swahr)* (Good evening!).

✔ When you want to get the waiter's attention in a restaurant, don't call out: **Garçon!** *(gahr-sohN!)* (Boy!). And in airports and train stations, you want to avoid the term **Porteur!** *(pohr-tuhr!)*. The attendants absolutely hate that. It is considered downgrading and condescending. Say **monsieur** *(muhs-yuh)* (sir) instead.

✔ It is not customary in France to comment on the fact that someone is sneezing. But if you feel you must say something, make sure you **do NOT** say **à votre santé!** *(ah vohtr sahn-tay)* (to your health) because you are not toasting anyone. It would be like saying, "Cheers!" and could be taken as a ridicule — **à vos souhaits** *(ah voh soo-eh)* (to your wishes) is what you can say.

✔ When you are hot or cold and would like to do something about it, be sure *not* to say: **Je <u>suis</u> chau(e)** *(zhuh swee shoh)* (I am hot) or **je <u>suis</u> froi(e)** *(zhuh swee frwah)* (I am cold) because you are saying that you are in heat or frigid. Most likely that is not what you want people to think about you. You need to say **j'ai chaud/e** *(zheh shoh[d])* or **j'ai froid/e** *(zhay frwah[d])*, both of which use the verb to have (**avoir**).

✔ If someone asks you at dinner whether you would like another helping but, unfortunately, you are really full, you certainly don't want to translate the word "full" into French. Saying **je suis plein/e** *(zhuh swee plahn/plehn)* means that you are pregnant (and not "full" as one may think)! Instead, you can say: **j'ai fini** *(zhay fee-nee)* (I'm finished) or **j'ai assez/trop mangé** *(zhay ah-say trohp mahn-zhay)* (I ate enough/too much).

✔ Here is something to remember for the restaurant: If you want ice cubes in your drink, you usually have to say so. The trouble is, if you ask for **de la glace** *(duh lah glahs)* (ice) the waiter may ask you: **Et quel parfum?** *(eh kehl pahr-fuhM?)* (What flavor?) You want to order **des glaçons** *(deh glah-sohN)* (ice cubes).

✔ Don't ever call a policeman a **flic** *(fleek)*, no matter what you hear. It is similar to calling him a "fuzz." Use **monsieur** *(muhs-yuh)* (sir) instead.

✔ When you want change for your big bills, you should *not* say: **J'ai besoin de change** *(zhay buh-zwahN duh shahnzh)* because the listener may think you need a fresh set of clothes. You want to say instead: **j'ai besoin de monnaie** *(zhay buh-zwahN duh moh-neh)* (I need small change).

✔ You can always cause a good laugh when you start talking about: **je vais visiter mon ami Paul/ma tante** *(zhuh veh vee-zee-tay mohN nah-mee pohl/mah tahnt)*. The verb **visiter** *(vee-zee-tay)* is used for things — for sightseeing — not for people. You probably don't plan to walk around your friend or your aunt in the same way that you walk around a monument, right? You want to say **je vais voir Paul** *(zhuh veh vwahr pohl)* (I'm going to visit Paul) instead.

Chapter 19

Ten Favorite French Expressions

· ·

*O*nce you get tuned into French a little, you may suddenly hear people use these little very French expressions that seem to just sort of slip out at any given occasion. You may even have heard some of these already; now it's time to casually use them yourself.

C'est un fait accompli.

(seh taN feh tah-kohN-plee)

The literal translation is: "It's an accomplished fact." What it means (beautifully expressed actually in a few words!) is this: a thing done and therefore no longer worth opposing.

Quel faux pas!

(kehl foh pah)

The literal translation is: "What a false step!" You can use it, however, to comment on a slip-up in conduct, speech, and manners, a breach of etiquette, a blunder, or a gaffe.

Comme il faut.

(koh meel foh)

The translation of this phrase is: "As it should be," meaning the "proper" way to do something or just the way it is expected to be done.

Bon appétit!

(bohN ah-pay-tee)

This phrase literally means: "Good appetite!" However, it certainly is not commenting on anyone's good or bad appetite. It's what you wish each other when you begin to eat or when you see someone eating, much like the English "Enjoy!" except that the French say **Bon appétit!** much more freely.

Quelle horreur!

(kehl oh-ruhr)

This phrase means: "What a horror!" It is used not only for real horrors, but also to express any kind of disgust, as in these expressions: "What a terrible thought!" "How nasty!" and "I can't believe it!"

Oh là là! La catastrophe!

(oh lah lah! lah kah-tahs-trohf!)

This expression translates: "Oh gee, the catastrophy!" It's often used facetiously, when a situation seems terrible to one party, but not really to the other.

À toute à l'heure!

(ah too tah luhr)

The literal translation of this phrase is: "Until right away." You only use this expression when you really expect to see the departing person within the hour or so.

C'est la vie!

(seh lah vee)

This expression translates: "That's life!" and implies, "Oh well, what are you going to do about it?"

Comme ci, comme ça.

(kohm see kohm sah)

Literally this means: "Like this, like that" or "so-so." The phrase means not great and not terrible but in-between. Generally, you use this in answer to someone asking you how you are feeling.

C'est le ton qui fait la musique!

(seh luh tohN kee feh lah mew-zeek)

This expression literally translates: "It's the tone that makes the music." It basically means that what counts is the way you say things, not necessarily what you say.

Chapter 20

Ten Holidays to Remember

· ·

*W*hat follows are holidays that are probably not familiar to you, or at least, you may not be familiar with the ways that people in France celebrate them. There are more holidays of course, such as Christmas, New Year's Day, and Easter, but you are probably familiar with those unless you don't celebrate some of them because they aren't part of your religion.

L'Épiphanie

First Sunday after New Year's Day is **L'Épiphanie** *(lay-pee-fah-nee)* or **La Fête des Rois** *(lah feht day rwah)* (Epiphany or the Feast of the Three Kings).

The Feast of the Three Kings is a fun family/friends holiday where you eat a special cake which has a little, fun object hidden in it, usually a bean. The bean symbolizes a gift of a king. Whoever finds the bean becomes the queen or the king for the day and gets to choose his or her partner.

La Chandeleur

La Chandeleur *(lah shahn-duh-lur)* (Candlemas) takes place on February 2.

This holiday is another neat family affair where you get to eat delicious **crêpes** *(krehp)*. When the cook flips the **crêpes** in the frying pan, he or she holds a piece of gold in his or her hand — such as a gold ring — and this ritual brings good luck to everyone around.

Mardi gras

At the end of February or early March, **Mardi gras** *(mahr-dee grah)* is celebrated. It is the last day of Carnival, 40 days before Easter.

Some cities in France — Nice, for instance — and New Orleans in the United States, stage enormously beautiful parades with elaborate disguises and costumes, often ridiculing politicians and famous personalities. There are usually costume parties for young and old going on everywhere.

Le Poisson d'Avril

April 1 is **Le Poisson d'Avril** *(luh pwah-sohN dah-vreel)* (April Fools' Day).

This holiday is the day for practical jokes in word or in deed. You may see people walking around unaware of the fact that they have a paper fish stuck on their back which accounts for the name of this day: the fish **(poisson)** of April. And when you fool someone successfully, you can call him a **poisson d'avril!**

La Fête du Travail

May 1 is **La Fête du Travail** *(lah feht dew trah-vahy)* (Labor Day).

On this official holiday, people give little bouquets of lilies of the valley (**des bouquets de muguets**) *(day boo-keh duh mew-geh)* to each other. If you are lucky enough to receive 13 little white flowers on one branch, your good luck never runs out! The bouquets are sold everywhere in the streets, often alongside the parades organized by trade unions.

L'Ascension

Forty days after Easter, **L'Ascension** *(lah-sahn-syohN)* (Ascension Day) is celebrated.

This holiday is always on a Thursday and it is an official holiday, so offices, schools, and so on close for the day. Custom has it that people take Friday off, too, and go away for a long weekend. They call that **faire le pont** *(fehr luh pohn)* (to make the bridge), and you want to be aware of that weekend when you make your travel plans.

La Pentecôte

Ten days after Ascension Day, **La Pentecôte** *(lah pahnt-koht)* (Pentecost) is celebrated.

The French celebrate Pentecost weekend similar to the weekend of Ascension Day. Monday is the official holiday here and people tend to leave on Friday afternoon. Traffic gets heavy, and it can be difficult to make hotel reservations in popular areas.

Fête de la Musique

Fête de la Musique *(lah feht duh lah mew-seek)* (Music Festival) takes place on June 21.

Amateur musicians as well as professionals of all ages, as solos or as a band, play everywhere in the streets. You may hear any kind of music from classical to jazz, blues, rock, or techno. Music Festival is an absolutely wonderful day to experience.

La Prise de la Bastille

July 14 is **La Prise de la Bastille** *(lah preez duh lah bahs-teey)* (Bastille Day: the French national holiday).

Military parades take place in the streets, and people enjoy fireworks and ballroom dancing the night before, to mark the beginning of the French Revolution in 1789. The most fantastic military parade takes place on the **Champs-Élysées** *(shahN-zay-lee-say)* in front of the French president.

La Sainte Catherine

November 25 is **La Sainte Catherine** *(lah sahnt kah-tay-reen)* (St. Catherine's Day).

This day celebrates single women of 25 years of age or older. These women wear eccentric hats (to work, for example) and call themselves **Les Catherinettes** *(leh ka-tay-ree-neht)*.

Chapter 21

Ten Phrases That Make You Sound French

· ·

Chapter 19 provides you with some typically French expressions that almost everyone who speaks a little French knows and uses. The phrases in this chapter go a few steps beyond those common ones: These expressions are so very French that you may even pass for a native French speaker when you use them.

Ça m'a fait très plaisir! or C'était génial!

(sah mah feh treh pleh-zeer) or *(say-teh zhay-nyahl)*

(I really liked that!) or (That was fantastic!) Here are two ways to express your excitement and really get it across, too. You can also speak for your partner (whose French is nonexistent) by just changing the pronoun: **Ça lui a fait très plaisir!** *(sah lwee ah feh treh pleh-zeer!)* (He/She really liked that!)

Passez-moi un coup de fil!

(pah-say mwa aN koot feel)

(Give me a call.) You could say of course: **Appelez-moi!** *(ah-puh-lay mwah)* or **Téléphonez-moi!** *(tay-lay-foh-nay mwah)*, but that wouldn't sound as sophisticated!

Some possible variations are:

Passez-nous un coup de fil!

(pah-say noo aN koot feel)

(Give us a call!)

Je vais vous/lui/leur passer un coup de fil.

(zhuh veh voo/lwee/luhr pah-say aN koot feel)

(I am going to call you/him/her/them.)

On y va! or Allons-y!

(oh nee vah!) or *(ah-lohN zee!)*

(Let's go [there]!) You can also send someone off somewhere with the latter one: You can say **Allez-y!** *(ah-lay-zee)* (Go ahead!) or **Vas-y!** *(vah-zee)* for the familiar form if you want to get a little insistent about it.

Je n'en sais rien.

(zhuh nahn seh ree-ahn)

(I don't know anything about it.) In casual speech, you can also say (and this is what you hear most of the time) **J'en sais rien** *(jahn seh ree-ahn)*. Technically this phrase is grammatically incorrect, but then so is "I know nothing" instead of "I don't know anything."

Mais je rêve!

(meh zhuh rehv)

(Oh, I don't believe it!) Literally this means: "But I am dreaming!" and is an expression that has become incredibly popular in recent years, probably because it works on every level of excitement. You can use it with any personal pronoun of your choice. For example, you could say to your friend **Mais tu rêves!** *(meh tew rehv)* (You must be crazy!) if he/she comes up with some unrealistic idea, plan, or wish, or **Mais ils/elles rêvent!** *(meh eel/ehl rehv)* when you are talking about several people.

Quel amour de petit garçon!

(kehl ah-moor duh ptee gahr-sohn)

(What an adorable little boy!) Or you could just say, pointing to a little kid, a pet, or a toy: **Quel amour!** *(kehl ah-moor)* and everyone around you will be so impressed not only with your beautiful French but also with your object of admiration!

Vous n'avez pas le droit.

(voo nah-vay pah luh drwah)

(You don't have the right.) This phrase simply means: "It is forbidden," but says it ever so much more elegantly. Again, you can vary the personal pronouns, and also tenses, if you like.

Tu cherches midi à 14h.

(tew shehrsh mee-dee ah kah-tohrz uhr)

This has to be the best one of all. Try to translate this and what you come up with is: "You are looking for noon at 2 p.m." You're not sure what that is supposed to mean? Well, it is a tough one, but it's such a neat phrase and heavily used, so here it is: You are saying that so-and-so is making things more difficult than necessary, that he or she is sort of off the mark and has lost perspective: **Il/Elle cherche midi à 14h.** You can also practice saying, **Il ne faut pas chercher midi à 14h** *(eel nuh foh pah shehrsh-shay)* (You shouldn't get so obsessive about it!)

Je veux acheter une bricole

(zhuh vuh ash-tay ewn bree-kohl)

(I want to buy a little something, a doodad.) It's the word **bricole** that makes you sound so "in." It actually derives from the verb **bricoler** *(bree-koh-lay)* which means to do odd jobs.

Prenons un pot!

(pruh-nohn aN po)

(Let's take a pot)? No, that can't be it, or can it? Well, if you stretch your imagination a bit, it means: "Let's have a drink!" (Not a whole pot full maybe, but . . .)

Part V
Appendixes

The 5th Wave   By Rich Tennant

It's amazing what happens when you learn a little of their language.

In this part . . .

Last but not least, we give you the appendixes, which you will no doubt find quite useful. In addition to verb tables that show you how to conjugate regular and irregular verbs, we provide a pretty comprehensive mini-dictionary and a guide to the audio CD that's attached to the back of the book.

Appendix A

Verb Tables

· ·

French Verbs

Regular Verbs Ending with *-er* (e.g. *parler* to speak)
Past Participle: *parlé* (spoken)

	Present	Past	Future
je/j' (I)	parle	ai parlé	vais parler
tu (you, inf.)	parles	as parlé	vas parler
il/elle (he/she)	parle	a parlé	va parler
nous (we)	parlons	avons parlé	allons parler
vous (you, form.)	parlez	avez parlé	allez parler
ils/elles (they)	parlent	ont parlé	vont parler

Regular Verbs Ending with *-ir* (e.g. *finir* to finish)
Past Participle: *fini* (finished)

	Present	Past	Future
je/j' (I)	finis	ai fini	vais finir
tu (you, inf.)	finis	as fini	vas finir
il/elle (he/she)	finit	a fini	va finir
nous (we)	finissons	avons fini	allons finir
vous (you, form.)	finissez	avez fini	allez finir
ils/elles (they)	finissent	ont fini	vont finir

Regular Verbs Ending with -re (e.g. *vendre* to sell)
Past Participle: *vendu* (sold)

	Present	Past	Future
je/j' (I)	vends	ai vendu	vais vendre
tu (you, inf.)	vends	as vendu	vas vendre
il/elle (he/she)	vend	a vendu	va vendre
nous (we)	vendons	avons vendu	allons vendre
vous (you, form.)	vendez	avez vendu	allez vendre
ils/elles (they)	vendent	ont vendu	vont vendre

Verb *avoir* (to have)
Past Participle: *eu* (had)

	Present	Past	Future
je/j' (I)	ai	ai eu	vais avoir
tu (you, inf.)	as	as eu	vas avoir
il/elle (he/she)	a	a eu	va avoir
nous (we)	avons	avons eu	allons avoir
vous (you, form.)	avez	avez eu	allez avoir
ils/elles (they)	ont	ont eu	vont avoir

Verb *être* (to be)
Past Participle: *été* (been)

	Present	Past	Future
je/j' (I)	suis	ai été/e	vais être
tu (you, inf.)	es	as été/e	vas être
il/elle (he/she)	est	a été/e	va être
nous (we)	sommes	avons été	allons être
vous (you, form.)	êtes	avez été	allez être
ils/elles (they)	sont	ont été	vont être

Reflexive Verbs (e.g. *se laver* to wash oneself)
Past Participle: *lavé* (washed)

	Present	Past	Future
je (I)	me lave	me suis lavé/e	vais me laver
tu (you, inf.)	te laves	t'es lavé/e	vas te laver
il/elle (he/she)	se lave	s'est lavé/e	va se laver
nous (we)	nous lavons	nous sommes lavés/ées	allons nous laver
vous (you, form.)	vous lavez	vous êtes lavés/ées	allez vous laver
ils/elles (they)	se lavent	se sont lavés/ées	vont se laver

Irregular French Verbs

		Present	Past Participle
acheter to buy	j'	achète	
	tu	achètes	
	il/elle	achètes	acheté
	nous	achetons	(w/avoir)
	vous	achetez	
	ils/elles	achètent	
aller to go	je	vais	
	tu	vas	
	il/elle	va	allé/e/s
	nous	allons	(w/être)
	vous	allez	
	ils/elles	vont	
appeler to call	j'	appelle	
	tu	appelles	
	il/elle	appelle	appelé
	nous	appelons	(w/avoir)
	vous	appelez	
	ils/elles	appellent	
boire to drink	je	bois	
	tu	bois	
	il/elle	boit	bu
	nous	buvons	(w/avoir)
	vous	buvez	
	ils/elles	boivent	
commencer to start, begin	je	commence	
	tu	commences	
	il/elle	commence	commencé
	nous	commençons	(w/avoir)
	vous	commencez	
	ils/elles	commencent	

		Present	**Past Participle**
comprendre to understand	*je*	comprends	
	tu	comprends	
	il/elle	comprend	compris
	nous	comprenons	(w/avoir)
	vous	comprenez	
	ils/elles	comprennent	

conduir to drive	*je*	conduis	
	tu	conduis	
	il/elle	conduit	conduit
	nous	conduisons	(w/avoir)
	vous	conduisez	
	ils/elles	conduisent	

connaître to know	*je*	connais	
	tu	connais	
	il/elle	connaît	connu
	nous	connaissons	(w/avoir)
	vous	connaissez	
	ils/elles	connaissent	

devoir to have to	*je*	dois	
	tu	dois	
	il/elle	doit	dû
	nous	devons	(w/avoir)
	vous	devez	
	ils/elles	doivent	

dire to say	*je*	dis	
	tu	dis	
	il/elle	dit	dit
	nous	disons	(w/avoir)
	vous	dites	
	ils/elles	disent	

		Present	Past Participle
écrire to write	j'	écris	
	tu	écris	
	il/elle	écrit	écrit
	nous	écrivons	(w/avoir)
	vous	écrivez	
	ils/elles	écrivent	

entendre to hear	j'	entends	
	tu	entends	
	il/elle	entend	entendu
	nous	entendons	(w/avoir)
	vous	entendez	
	ils/elles	entendent	

envoyer to send	j'	envoie	
	tu	envoies	
	il/elle	envoie	envoyé
	nous	envoyons	(w/avoir)
	vous	envoyez	
	ils/elles	envoient	

espérer to hope	j'	espère	
	tu	espères	
	il/elle	espère	espéré
	nous	espérons	(w/avoir)
	vous	espérez	
	ils/elles	espèrent	

faire to do, make	je	fais	
	tu	fais	
	il/elle	fait	fait
	nous	faisons	(w/avoir)
	vous	faites	
	ils/elles	font	

		Present	Past Participle
lire	*je*	lis	
to read	*tu*	lis	
	il/elle	lit	lu
	nous	lisons	(w/avoir)
	vous	lisez	
	ils/elles	lisent	

manger	*je*	mange	
to eat	*tu*	manges	
	il/elle	mange	mangé
	nous	mangeons	(w/avoir)
	vous	mangez	
	ils/elles	mangent	

mettre	*je*	mets	
to put	*tu*	mets	
	il/elle	met	mis
	nous	mettons	(w/avoir)
	vous	mettez	
	ils/elles	mettent	

offrir	*j'*	offre	
to offer	*tu*	offres	
	il/elle	offre	offert
	nous	offrons	(w/avoir)
	vous	offrez	
	ils/elles	offrent	

partir	*je*	pars	
to leave	*tu*	pars	
	il/elle	part	parti/e/s
	nous	partons	(w/être)
	vous	partez	
	ils/elles	partent	

		Past	**Past Participle**
payer to pay	*je*	paie	
	tu	paies	
	il/elle	paie	payé
	nous	payons	(w/avoir)
	vous	payez	
	ils/elles	paient	
pouvoir can	*je*	peux	
	tu	peux	
	il/elle	peut	pu
	nous	pouvons	(w/avoir)
	vous	pouvez	
	ils/elles	peuvent	
prendre to take	*je*	prends	
	tu	prends	
	il/elle	prend	pris
	nous	prenons	(w/avoir)
	vous	prenez	
	ils/elles	prennent	
recevoir to get	*je*	reçois	
	tu	reçois	
	il/elle	reçoit	reçu
	nous	recevons	(w/avoir)
	vous	recevez	
	ils/elles	reçoivent	
rendre to give back	*je*	rends	
	tu	rends	
	il/elle	rend	rendu
	nous	rendons	(w/avoir)
	vous	rendez	
	ils/elles	rendent	

		Present	Past Participle
rire	*je*	ris	
to laugh	*tu*	ris	
	il/elle	rit	ri
	nous	rions	(w/avoir)
	vous	riez	
	ils/elles	rient	

		Present	Past Participle
savoir	*je*	sais	
to be able to	*tu*	sais	
	il/elle	sait	su
	nous	savons	(w/avoir)
	vous	savez	
	ils/elles	savent	

		Present	Past Participle
servir	*je*	sers	
to serve	*tu*	sers	
	il/elle	sert	servi
	nous	servons	(w/avoir)
	vous	servez	
	ils/elles	servent	

		Present	Past Participle
sortir	*je*	sors	
to go out	*tu*	sors	
	il/elle	sort	sorti/e/s
	nous	sortons	(w/être)
	vous	sortez	
	ils/elles	sortent	

		Present	Past Participle
tenir	*je*	tiens	
to hold	*tu*	tiens	
	il/elle	tient	tenu
	nous	tenons	(w/avoir)
	vous	tenez	
	ils/elles	tiennent	

		Present	Past Participle
venir	*je*	viens	
to come	*tu*	viens	
	il/elle	vient	venu/e/s
	nous	venons	(w/être)
	vous	venez	
	ils/elles	viennent	
vivre	*je*	vis	
to live	*tu*	vis	
	il/elle	vit	vécu
	nous	vivons	(w/avoir)
	vous	vivez	
	ils/elles	vivent	
voir	*je*	vois	
to see	*tu*	vois	
	il/elle	voit	vu
	nous	voyons	(w/avoir)
	vous	voyez	
	ils/elles	voient	
vouloir	*je*	veux	
to want	*tu*	veux	
	il/elle	veut	voulu
	nous	voulons	(w/avoir)
	vous	voulez	
	ils/elles	veulent	

French-English Mini Dictionary

A

à bientôt/*ah-byan-to*/see you soon
à côté de/*ah ko-tay duh*/next to
à demain/*ah duh-man*/see you tomorrow
à droite/*ah drwaht*/on the right
à gauche/*ah gosh*/on the left
à l'heure/*ah luh*/on time
absolument/*ahb-so-lew-mahN*/absolutely
accepter/*ah-ksehp-tay*/to accept
acheter/*ah-shuh-tay*/to buy
addition/f/*ah-dee-syohn*/check
adresse/f/*ah-drehss*/address
adresse électronique/f/*ah-dreh-say-lehk-tro-neek*/e-mail address
affaires/f/*zah-fehr*/business
agneau/m/*an-yo*/lamb
aider/*eh-day*/to help
aimer/*ay-may*/to like; to love
aller/*ah-lay*/to go
aller-retour/m/*ah-lay ruh-toor*/round trip
aller-simple/m/*ah-lay sahnpl*/one-way (ticket)
ami/amie/m,f/*ah-mee*/friend
août/m/*oot*/August
appeler/*ah-pehl-lay*/to call
argent/m/*ahr-zhahn*/money
arrêt/m/*ah-reh*/stop

arriver/*ah-ree-vay*/to arrive
assiette/f/*ah-syeht*/plate
attendre/*ah-tehn-druh*/to wait
au fond/*o fohN*/in the back
au revoir/*ohr-vwahr*/good bye
aubaine/*o-behn*/sales [Quebec]
aujourd'hui/*o-zhoor-dwee*/today
aussi/*o-see*/also
avocat/m/*ah-vo-kah*/lawyer
avoir/*ah-vwahr*/to have
avril/m/*ah-vreel*/April

B

banane/f/*banaN*/banana
basket/m/*bahs-keht*/basketball
baskets/f/*bahs-keht*/sneakers
beau/*bo*/nice, beautiful
beurre/m/*buhr*/butter
bicyclette/f/*bee-see-kleht*/bicycle
bien sûr/*byan sewr*/of course
bière/f/*byehr*/beer
billet/m/*bee-yeh*/ticket
bizarre/*beez-ahr*/weird, bizarre
blanc/*blahn*/white
blazer/m/*blah-zehr*/blazer
bleu/bleue/*bluh*/blue
boeuf/m/*buhf*/beef
boire/*bwar*/to drink

bon/*bohN*/good
bonjour/*bohN-zhoor*/good day
bonne nuit/*bohN ne-wee*/good night
bonsoir/*bohn-swahr*/good night
bottes/f/ *boht*/boots
boucherie/f/*boo-shree*/butcher shop
boulangerie/f/*boo-lahn-zhree*/bakery
bras/m/*brah*/arm
bruyant/*bree-ahn*/noisy
bureau/m/*bew-ro*/office

C

ça va /*sah vah*/Okay
café/m/*kah-fay*/coffee
caisse/f/*kehs*/the cash-register
campagne/f/*cahN-pahn-yuh*/countryside
carotte/f/*kah-roht*/carrot
carte de crédit/f/*kahr-tuh duh cray-dee*/credit card
celui-ci [m]/**celle-ci** [f]/*suh-lwee-see/sehl-see*/this one
celui-là [m] /**celle-là** [f]/*suh-lwee-lah/sehl-lah*/that one
champignon/m/*sham pin yohN*/mushroom
chapeau /m/*shap-oh*/hat
charcuterie/f/*shahr-kew-tree*/butcher shop that specializes in pork and prepared foods
charmant/**charmante**/m/f/*shahr-mahN*/charming
chaud/*sho*/warm/hot
chemise/f/*ewn shuh-meez*/shirt
chemisier/m/*shuh-mee-zyay*/blouse
cher/*shehr*/expensive
choisir/*shwah-zeer*/to choose
cinq/*sayNk*/five

clair/*klehr*/light-colored
code postal/m/*cohd pohs-tahl*/zip code
coffre/m/*kohfr*/trunk
collègue/m/*koh-lehg*/co-worker
comment/*kohmahN*/how
compagnie/f/*kohn-pah-nyee*/company
complet/f/*kohN-pleh*/suit [France]
conduire/*kohn-dweer*/to drive
confiture/f/*kohn-fee-tewr*/jam
costume de bains/m/*kohs-tewm duh ban*/bathing suit [Québec]
côtes/f/*koht*/ribs
cou/m/*koo*/neck
couleur/f/*koo-luhr*/color
couteau/m/*koo-to*/knife
cravate/f/*krah-vaht*/tie
crème/m/*krehm*/cream
crèmerie/f/*kraym-ree*/dairy product and cheese store
crudités/f/*krew-dee-tay*/mixed greens
cuillère/f/*kwee-yehr*/spoon or teaspoon

D

d'accord/*dah-kohr*/all right; okay
danser/*dahn-say*/to dance
décembre/m/*day-sahNbr*/December
dehors/*duh-ohr*/outside
déjeuner/m/*day-zhuh-nay*/to lunch
dentiste/m/*dahN-teest*/dentist
dessert/m/*deh-sehr*/dessert
deux/*duh*/two
devoir /*duh-vwahr*/to have to
dix/*dees*/ten
dix-huit/*dees-wheet*/eighteen
dix-neuf/*dees-nuhf*/nineteen
dix-sept/*dees-seht*/seventeen

docteur/m/*dohk-tuhr*/doctor
doigt/m/*dwah*/finger
donner/*do-nay*/to give
dormir/*dor-meer*/to sleep
doux/*doo*/mild
douze/*dooz*/twelve

E

eau/f/*lo*/water
échecs/mpl/*ayshehk*/chess
elle/f/*ehl*/she
elles/f/*ehl*/they
employé/m/*ahN-plwa-yay*/employee
en retard/*ahn ruh-tahr*/late
enchanté/*ahN-shahN-tay*/delighted
enfant/m,f/*ahN-fahN*/child
ennuyeu/*ehn-wee-uh*/boring
entrées/f/*ahn-tray*/appetizers
épaule/f/*ay-pohl*/shoulder
épicerie/f/*ay-pees-ree*/grocery-store [general store]
être/*ehtr*/to be
étroit/*ay-trwah*/narrow

F

facile/*fah-seel*/easy
faim/*faN*/hungry
fatigué/*fah-tee-gay*/tired
femme/f/*fahm*/wife
fenêtre/f/*fuh-nehtr*/window
fêtes/f/*feht*/holidays
février/m/*fay-vree-ay*/February
figure/f/*fee-gewr*/face
fille/f/*fee-y*/daughter or girl
fils/m/*fees*/son

fin/f/*fahN*/end
finir/*fee-neer*/to finish
fleur/f/*fluhr*/flower
foncé/*fohN-say*/dark
football Américain/m/*fewtbahl ah-may-ree-kehn*/American football
football/soccer-(Canada)/m/*fewt bahl/ soh-kehr*/soccer
fourchette/f/*ewn foor-sheht*/fork
fraise/f/*frehz*/strawberry
frère/m/*frerh*/brother
froid/*frwah*/cold
fromage/m/*fro-mazh*/cheese
fruits/m/*lay frwee*/fruit

G

gagner/*gahn-yay*/to win
garçon/m/*gahr-sohN*/boy
gare/f/*gah*/train station
gâteau au chocolat/m/*gah-to o sho-ko-lah*/chocolate cake
genou/m/*zhuh-noo*/knee
glace/f/*glahs*/ice cream
grand/*grahNd*/big, tall, large
grand magasin/m/*grahN mah-gah-zanN*/department store
grippe/f/*greep*/flu
guitare/f/*gee-tahr*/guitar

H

habit/m/*ah-bee*/suit [Québec]
habiter/*ah-bee-tay*/to live
haricots verts/m/*ah-ree-ko vehr*/green beans
huit/*wheet*/eight

I

il/m/*eel*/he
il y a/*ee-lee-yah*/there is
ils/m/*eel*/they
imperméable/m/*an-pehr-may-ahbl*/raincoat
infirmier/m/*aN-feer-myay*/nurse
ingénieur/m/*aN-zhay-nyuhr*/engineer

J

janvier/m/*zhan-vyay*/January
jardin/m/*zhahr-daN*/yard
jaune /*zhon*/yellow
je/*zhuh*/I
jean/m/*dzheen*/jeans
joli/*zho-lee*/pretty
jouer/*zhoo-ay*/to play
jour/m/*zhoor*/day
juillet/m/*zhwee-yeh*/July
juin /m/*zhwahN*/June
jupe/f/*zhewp*/skirt
jusqu'à/*zhews-kah*/until

L

là-bas/*lah-bah*/over there
laine/f/*lehn*/wool
laitue/f/*leh-tooeh*/lettuce
large/*lahrzh*/large
légumes/m/*lay-gewm*/vegetables
lendemain/m/*lahN-duh-mahN*/next day
livre/f/*leevr*/pound = 500 g, about 1.1lb.
lui/m/*lew-ee*/him

M

madame/f/*mah-dahm*/madam, missus
magasin/m/*mah-gah-zan*/store
mai/m/*meh*/May
main/f/*mahn*/hand
maintenant/*man-tuh-nahN*/now
mais/*meh*/but
maison/f/*meh-zohN*/house
maladie/f/*mah-lah-dee*/illness
manger/*mahn-zhay*/to eat
manquer/*mahn-kay*/to miss
manteau/m/*mahN-to*/coat
marchand/m/*mahr-shan*/vendor
margarine/f/*mahr-gah-reen*/margarine
mari/m/*mah-ree*/husband
marron/*mah-rohN*/brown
mars/m/*mahrs*/March
mauvais/*mo-veh*/bad
médecin/m/*mayd-saN*/physician
même/*mehm*/even
mer/f/*mehr*/ocean
merci/*mehr-see*/thank you
mère/f/*mehr*/mother
mettre/*meh-truh*/to put
moderne/*moh-dehrn*/modern
moi/*mwa*/me
monsieur/m/*muh-syuh*/mister
montagne/f/*mohn-tahn-yuh*/mountain
montre/f/*mohntr*/watch
montrer/*mohN-tray*/to show
moyen/*mwa-yan*/average

N

natation/f/*nah-tah-see-ohN*/swimming

neige/m/*nehzh*/snow

neuf/*nuhf*/nine

nez/m/*nay*/nose

noir/noire/*nwahr*/black

nom/m/*nohN*/last name

nous/*noo*/we

novembre/m/*noh-vahnbr*/November

numéro de téléphone/m/*new-may-ro duh tay-lay-fohn*/phone number

O

octobre/m/*ok-tohbr*/October

œil/m/*uhy*/eye

oignon/m/*oyhn-ohN*/onion

onze/*ohNz*/eleven

orange/f/*or ahnzh*/orange

oreille/f/*oh-rehy*/ear

où/*oo*/where

P

pain /m/*pan*/bread

pantalon/m/*pahN-tah-lohN*/slacks

parfait/*pahr-feh*/perfect

parler/*pahr-lay*/to speak/to talk

partir/*pahr-teer*/to leave

pas du tout/*pah dew too*/not at all

passeport/m/*pahs-pohr*/passport

pâtisserie/f/*pah-tees-ree*/pastry shop

pays/m/*peh-ee*/country

pêche/f/*pehsh*/peach

penser/*pahN-say*/to think

père/m/*pehr*/father

personnes/fpl/*pehr-sohn*/people

petit/*puh-teet*/small, short

petit déjeuner/m/*puh-tee day-zhuh-nay*/breakfast

petite-fille/f/*puh-teet feey*/granddaughter

petit-fils/m/*puh-tee fees*/grandson

petits pois/m/*puh-tee pwa*/peas

petits-enfants/mpl/*puh-tee-zahN-fahN*/grandchildren

photo/f/*fo-to*/picture

piano/m/*pee-ahn-oh*/piano

pied/m/*pyeh*/foot

plage/f/*plahzh*/beach

pointure/f/*pwan-tewr*/shoe size

poire/f/*pwar*/pear

poisson/m/*pwa-sohn*/fish

poitrine/f/*pwah-treen*/chest

poivre/m/*pwavr*/pepper

police/f/*poh-lees*/police

pomme/f/*pohm*/apple

pommes de terre/f/*pohm duh tehr*/potatoes

porc/m/*pohr*/pork

porte/f/*pohrt*/door

porte-monnaie/m/*pohrt-moh-neh*/wallet

porter/*pohr-tay*/to wear

poulet/m/*poo-leh*/chicken

pourboire/m/*poor-bwar*/tip

pourquoi/*poor-kwa*/why

pouvoir/*poo-vwar*/can or may or to be able to

préférer/*pray-fay-ray*/to prefer

prendre/*prahndr*/to take

prénom/m/*pray-nohN*/first name

présenter/*pray-zahN-tay*/to introduce

professeur /m/*pro-feh-suhr*/high school teacher or college professor

puis/*pew-ee*/then

pull/m/*pewl*/sweater

Q

qu'est-ce que/*kehs-kuh*/what

quand/*kahN*/when

quatorze/*kaht-ohrz*/fourteen

quatre/*kahtruh*/four

quelle/*kehl*/which

quelque chose/*kehl-kuh shoz*/something

qui/*kee*/who

quinze/*kahNz*/fifteen

R

regarder/*reh-gahr-day*/to watch

rendre/*rahndr*/to return (something)

repas/m/*ruh-pah*/meal

répondre/*ray-pohN-druh*/to answer

rester/*rehs-tay*/to stay

retraité/m,f/*ruh-treh-tay*/retired person

riz/f/*ree*/rice

robe/f/*rohb*/dress

rouge/*roozh*/red

rue/f/*rew*/street

S

sac/m/*sahk*/bag

salade verte/f/*sah-lahd vehrt*/green salad, salad with lettuce only

salut/*sah-lew*/hi

secrétaire/m/*suh-cray-tehr*/secretary

seize/*sehz*/sixteen

séjour/m/*say-zhoor*/stay

sel /m/*sehl*/salt

semaine/f/*suh-mehn*/week

sept/*seht*/seven

septembre/m/*sehp-tahNbr*/September

serveur, serveuse/m,f/*sehr-vuhr*/ waiter/waitress

serviette/f/*sehr-vyeht*/napkin

seulement/*suhl-mahN*/only

siège/m/*syehzh*/seat

six/*sees*/six

slip/m/*sleep*/underpants

soeur/f/*suhr*/sister

soif /*swaf*/thirsty

soldes/*sohld*/sales [France]

soleil/m/*soh-lehy*/sun

sortir/*sor-teer*/to exit

soucoupe/f/*soo-koop*/saucer

sucre/m/*sewkr*/sugar

supermarché/m/*sew-pehr-mahr-shay*/ supermarket

sur/*sewr*/on; on top of

sweat/m/*sweet*/sweat shirt

T

tant pis/*tahN pee*/too bad

tarte aux pommes/f/*tahr-to-pohm*/apple pie

tasse/f/*tahs*/cup

téléphoner/*tay-lay-foh-nay*/to telephone or call

tennis/m/*tehn-ee*/tennis

thé/m/*tay*/tea

toi/*twa*/you

tomate/f/*to-maht*/tomato

toujours/*too-zhoor*/always

tous/*toos*/all

train/m/*trahn*/train

travailler/*trah-va-yay*/to work

treize/*trehz*/thirteen

trois/*twah*/three

trop/*tro*/too much

tu/*tew*/you, informal

U

un/une/*uhN/yn*/one

V

valise/f/*vah-leez*/suitcase

veau/m/*vo*/veal

vendre/*vahndr*/to sell

venir/*vuh-neer*/to come

verre/m/*vehr*/glass

vert/verte/m,f/*vehr/vehrt*/green

veste/f/*vehst*/jacket (for men and women)

veston/m/*vehs-tohN*/man's suit jacket

viande/f/*vyahnd*/meat

ville/f/*veel*/city/town

vin/m/*van*/wine

vingt/*vahN*/twenty

vingt-cinq/*vahN sayNk*/twenty-five

vingt-deux/*vahNduh*/twenty-two

vingt-et-un/*vahNt-ay-uhN*/twenty-one

vingt-huit/*vahN wheet*/twenty-eight

vingt-neuf/*vihN nuhf*/twenty-nine

vingt-quatre/*vahN kahtruh*/twenty-four

vingt-sept/*vahN seht*/twenty-seven

vingt-six/*vahN sees*/twenty-six

vingt-trois/*vaNh-twah*/twenty-three

violon/m/*vee-oh-lohn*/violin

voir/*vwahr*/to see

voiture/f/*vwah-tewr*/car

vol/m/*vohl*/flight

vouloir/*voo-lwahr*/to want

vous/*voo*/you, formal

voyage d'affaires/m/*vwa-yahzh dah-fehr*/business trip

voyager/*vwah-yazhay*/to travel

English-French
Mini Dictionary

A

absolutely/**absolument**/*ahb-so-lew-mahN*

accept/**accepter**/*ah-ksehp-tay*

address/**adresse**/f/*ah-drehss*

all/**tous**/*toos*

all right; okay/**d'accord**/*dah-kohr*

also/**aussi**/*o-see*

always/**toujours**/*too-zhoor*

American football/**football américain**/m/*fewtbahl ah-may-ree-kehn*

answer/**répondre**/*ray-pohN-druh*

appetizers/**entrées**/f/*ahn-tray*

apple/**pomme**/f/*pohm*

apple pie/**tarte aux pommes**/f/*tahr-to-pohm*

April/**avril**/m/*ah-vreel*

arm/**bras**/m/*brah*

arrive/**arriver**/*ah-ree-vay*

August/**août**/m/*oot*

average/**moyen**/*mwa-yan*

B

bad/**mauvais**/*mo-veh*

bag/**sac**/m/*sahk*

bakery/**boulangerie**/f/*boo-lahn-zhree*

banana/**banane**/f/*banaN*

basketball/**basket**//m/*bahs-keht*

bathing suit [Québec]/**costume de bains**/m/*kohs-tewm duh ban*

be/**être**/*ehtr*

be able to/**pouvoir**/*poov-wahr*

beach/**plage**/f/*plahzh*

beef/**boeuf**/m/*buhf*

beer/**bière**/f/*byehr*

bicycle/**bicyclette**/f/*bee-see-kleht*

big, tall, large/**grand**/*grahNd*

black/**noir/noire**/*nwahr*

blazer/**blazer**/m/*blah-zehr*

blouse/**chemisier**/m/*shuh-mee-zyay*

blue/**bleu/bleue**/*bluh*

boots/**bottes**/f/ *boht*

boring/**ennuyeu**/*ehn-wee-uh*

boy/**garçon**/m/*gahr-sohN*

bread/**pain** /m/*pan*

breakfast/**petit déjeuner**/m/*puh-tee day-zhuh-nay*

brother/**frère**/m/*frerh*

brown/**marron**/*mah-rohN*

business/**affaires**/f/*zah-fehr*

business trip/**voyage d'affaires**/m/*vwa-yahzh dah-fehr*

but/**mais**/*meh*

butcher shop/**boucherie**/f/*boo-shree*

butcher shop that specializes in pork and prepared foods/**charcuterie**/f/*shahr-kew-tree*

butter/**beurre**/m/*buhr*

buy/**acheter**/*ah-shuh-tay*

C

call/**appeler**/*ah-pehl-lay*

can or may/**pouvoir**/*poo-vwar*

car/**voiture**/f/*vwah-tewr*

carrot/**carotte**/f/*kah-roht*

charming/**charmant**/**charmante**/m/f/*shahr-mahN*

check/**addition**/f/*ah-dee-syohn*

cheese/**fromage**/m/*fro-mazh*

chess/**échecs**/mpl/*ayshehk*

chest/**poitrine**/f/*pwah-treen*

chicken/**poulet**/m/*poo-leh*

child/**enfant**/m,f/*ahN-fahN*

chocolate cake/**gâteau au chocolat**/m/*gah-to o sho-ko-lah*

choose/**choisir**/*shwah-zeer*

city/**ville**/f/*veel*

coat/**manteau**/m/*mahN-to*

coffee/**café**/m/*kah-fay*

cold/**froid**/*frwah*

color/**couleur**/f/*koo-luhr*

come/**venir**/*vuh-neer*

company/**compagnie**/f/*kohn-pah-nyee*

confectioner's shop/**pâtisserie**/f/*pah-tees-ree*

countryside/**campagne**/f/*cahN-pahn-yuh*

country/**pays**/m/*peh-ee*

co-worker/**collègue**/m/*koh-lehg*

cream/**crème**/m/*krehm*

credit card/**carte de crédit**/f/*kahr-tuh duh cray-dee*

cup/**tasse**/f/*tahs*

D

dairy product and cheese store/**crèmerie**/f/*kraym-ree*

dance/**danser**/*dahn-say*

dark/**foncé**/*fohN-say*

daughter/**fille**/f/*fee-y*

day/**jour**/m/*zhoor*

December/**décembre**/m/*day-sahNbr*

delighted/**enchanté**/*ahN-shahN-tay*

dentist/**dentiste**/m/*dahN-teest*

department store/**grand magasin**/m/*grahN mah-gah-zanN*

dessert/**dessert**/m/*deh-sehr*

doctor/**docteur**/m/*dohk-tuhr*

door/**porte**/f/*pohrt*

dress/**robe**/f/*rohb*

drink/**boire**/*bwar*

drive/**conduire**/*kohn-dweer*

E

ear/**oreille**/f/*oh-rehy*

easy/**facile**/*fah-seel*

eat/**manger**/*mahn-zhay*

eight/**huit**/*wheet*

eighteen/**dix-huit**/*dees-wheet*

eleven/**onze**/*ohNz*

e-mail address/**adresse électronique**/f/*ah-dreh-say-lehk-tro-neek*

employee/**employé**/m/*ahN-plwa-yay*

end/**fin**/*fahN*

engineer/**ingénieur**/m/*aN-zhay-nyuhr*

even/**même**/*mehm*

exit/**sortir**/*sor-teer*

expensive/**cher**/*shehr*

eye/**œil**/m/*uhy*

F

face/**figure**/f/*fee-gewr*
father/**père**/m/*pehr*
February/**février**/m/*fay-vree-ay*
fifteen/**quinze**/*kahNz*
finger/**doigt**/m/*dwah*
finish/**finir**/*fee-neer*
first name/**prénom**/m/*pray-nohN*
fish/**poisson**/m/*pwa-sohn*
five/**cinq**/*sayNk*
flight/**vol**/m/*vohl*
flower/**fleur**/f/*fluhr*
flu/**grippe**/f/*greep*
foot/**pied**/m/*pyeh*
fork/**fourchette**/f/*ewn foor-sheht*
four/**quatre**/*kahtruh*
fourteen/**quatorze**/*kaht-ohrz*
friend/**ami/amie**/m,f/*ah-mee*
fruit/**fruits**/m/*lay frwee*

G

girl/**fille**/f/*feey*
give/**donner**/*do-nay*
glass/**verre**/m/*vehr*
go/**aller**/*ah-lay*
good/**bon**/*bohN*
good bye/**au revoir**/*ohr-vwahr*
good day/**bonjour**/*bohN-zhoor*
good night/**bonne nuit**/*bohN ne-wee*
good night/**bonsoir**/*bohn-swahr*
grandchildren/**petits-enfants**/*puh-tee-zahN-fahN*
granddaughter/**petite-fille**/f/*puh-teet feey*

grandson/**petit-fils**/m/*puh-tee fees*
green/**vert/verte**/*vehr/vehrt*
green beans/**haricots verts**/m/*ah-ree-ko vehr*
green salad, salad with lettuce only/**salade verte**/f/*sah-lahd vehrt*
grocery-store [general store]/**épicerie**/f/*ay-pees-ree*
guitar/**guitare**/f/*gee-tahr*

H

hand/**main**/f/*mahn*
hat/**chapeau**/m/*shap-oh*
have/**avoir**/*ah-vwahr*
he/**il**/m/*eel*
him/**lui**/m/*lew-ee*
help/**aider**/*eh-day*
hi/**salut**/*sah-lew*
high school teacher or college professor/**professeur**/m/*pro-feh-suhr*
holidays/**fêtes**/f/*feht*
house/**maison**/f/*meh-zohN*
how/**comment**/*kohmahN*
husband/**mari**/m/*mah-ree*
hungry/**faim**/*faN*

I

I/**je**/*zhuh*
ice cream/**glace**/f/*glahs*
illness/**maladie**/f/*mah-lah-dee*
in the back/**au fond**/*o fohN*
introduce/**présenter**/*pray-zahN-tay*

J

jacket (for men and women)/**veste**/f/*vehst*
jam/**confiture**/f/*kohn-fee-tewr*
January/**janvier**/m/*zhan-vyay*
jeans/**jean**/m/*dzheen*
July/**juillet**/m/*zhwee-yeh*
June/**juin** /m/*zhwahN*

K

knee/**genou**/m/*zhuh-noo*
knife/**couteau**/m/*koo-to*

L

lamb/**agneau**/m/*an-yo*
large/**large**/*lahrzh*
last name/**nom**/m/*nohN*
late/**en retard**/*ahn ruh-tahr*
lawyer/**avocat**/m/*ah-vo-kah*
leave/**partir**/*pahr-teer*
lettuce/**laitue**/f/*leh-tooeh*
light-colored/**clair**/*klehr*
like; love/**aimer**/*ay-may*
live/**habiter**/*ah-bee-tay*
lunch/**déjeuner**/m/*day-zhuh-nay*

M

madam, missus/**madame**/f/*mah-dahm*
man's suit jacket/**veston**/m/*vehs-tohN*
March/**mars**/m/*mahrs*
margarine/**margarine**/f/*mahr-gah-reen*
May/**mai**/m/*meh*

me/**moi**/*mwa*
meal/**repas**/m/*ruh-pah*
meat/**viande**/f/*vyahnd*
mild/**doux**/*doo*
miss/**manquer**/*mahn-kay*
mister/**monsieur**/m/*muh-syuh*
mixed greens/**crudités**/f/*krew-dee-tay*
modern/**moderne**/*moh-dehrn*
money/**argent**/m/*ahr-zhahn*
mother/**mère**/f/*mehr*
mountain/**montagne**/f/*mohn-tahn-yuh*
mushroom/**champignon**/m/*sham pin yohN*
must/**devoir** /*duh-vwahr*

N

napkin/**serviette**/f/*sehr-vyeht*
narrow/**étroit**/*ay-trwah*
neck/**cou**/m/*koo*
next day/**lendemain**/m/*lahN-duh-mahN*
next to/**à côté de**/*ah ko-tay duh*
nice, beautiful/**beau**/*bo*
nine/**neuf**/*nuhf*
nineteen/**dix-neuf**/*dees-nuhf*
noisy/**bruyant**/*bree-ahn*
nose/**nez**/m/*nay*
not at all/**pas du tout**/*pah dew too*
November/**novembre**/m/*noh-vahnbr*
now/**maintenant**/*man-tuh-nahN*
nurse/**infirmier**/m/*aN-feer-myay*

O

ocean/**mer**/f/*mehr*
October/**octobre**/m/*ok-tohbr*
of course/**bien sûr**/*byan sewr*

office/**bureau**/m/*bew-ro*

Okay/**ça va** /*sah vah*

on the left/**à gauche**/*ah gosh*

on the right/**à droite**/*ah drwaht*

on time/**à l'heure**/*ah luh*

on; on top of/**sur**/*sewr*

one/**un/une**/*uhN*/yn

one-way (ticket)/**aller-simple**/m/*ah-lay sahnpl*

onion/**oignon**/m/*oyhn-ohN*

only/**seulement**/*suhl-mahN*

orange/**orange**/f/*or ahnzh*

outside/**dehors**/*duh-ohr*

over there/**là-bas**/*lah-bah*

P

passport/**passeport**/m/*pahs-pohr*

peach/**pêche**/f/*pehsh*

pear/**poire**/f/*pwar*

peas/**petits pois**/m/*puh-tee pwa*

people/**personnes**/fpl/*pehr-sohn*

pepper/**poivre**/m/*pwavr*

perfect/**parfait**/*pahr-feh*

phone number/**numéro de téléphone**/m/*new-may-ro duh tay-lay-fohn*

physician/**médecin**/m/*mayd-saN*

piano/**piano**/m/*pee-ahn-oh*

picture/**photo**/f/*fo-to*

plate/**assiette**/f/*ah-syeht*

play/**jouer**/*zhoo-ay*

police/**police**/f/*poh-lees*

pork/**porc**/m/*pohr*

potatoes/**pommes de terre**/f/*pohm duh tehr*

pound = 500 g, about 1.1lb./**livre**/f/*leevr*

prefer/**préférer**/*pray-fay-ray*

pretty/**joli**/*zho-lee*

put/**mettre**/*meh-truh*

R

raincoat/**imperméable**/m/*an-pehr-may-ahbl*

red/**rouge**/*roozh*

retired person/**retraité**/m,f/*ruh-treh-tay*

return (something)/**rendre**/*rahndr*

ribs/**côtes**/f/*koht*

rice/**riz**/f/*ree*

round trip/**aller-retour**/m/*ah-lay ruh-toor*

S

sales [France]/**soldes**/*sohld*

sales [Quebec]/**aubaine**/*o-behn*

salt/**sel** /m/*sehl*

saucer/**soucoupe**/f/*soo-koop*

seat/**siège**/m/*syehzh*

secretary/**secrétaire**/m/*suh-cray-tehr*

see/**voir**/*vwahr*

see you soon/**à bientôt**/*ah-byan-to*

see you tomorrow/**à demain**/*ah duh-man*

sell/**vendre**/*vahndr*

September/**septembre**/m/*sehp-tahNbr*

seven/**sept**/*seht*

seventeen/**dix-sept**/*dees-seht*

she/**elle**/f/*ehl*

shirt/**chemise**/f/*ewn shuh-meez*

shoe size/**pointure**/f/*pwan-tewr*

shoulder/**épaule**/f/*ay-pohl*

show/**montrer**/*mohN-tray*

sister/**soeur**/f/*suhr*

six/**six**/*sees*

sixteen/**seize**/*sehz*

skirt/**jupe**/f/*zhewp*

slacks/**pantalon**/m/*pahN-tah-lohN*

sleep/**dormir**/*dor-meer*

small, short/**petit**/*puh-teet*

sneakers/**baskets**/f/*bahs-keht*

snow/**neige**/m/*nehzh*

soccer/**football**/**soccer-(Canada)**/m/*fewt bahl/soh-kehr*

something/**quelque chose**/*kehl-kuh shoz*

son/**fils**/m/*fees*

speak/talk/**parler**/*pahr-lay*

spoon/**cuillère**/f/*kwee-yehr*

stay/**séjour**/m/*say-zhoor*

stay/**rester**/*rehs-tay*

stop/**arrêt**/m/*ah-reh*

store/**magasin**/m/*mah-gah-zan*

strawberry/**fraise**/f/*frehz*

street/**rue**/f/*rew*

sugar/**sucre**/m/*sewkr*

suit [France]/**complet**/f/*kohN-pleh*

suit [Québec]/**habit**/m/*ah-bee*

suitcase/**valise**/f/*vah-leez*

sun/**soleil**/m/*soh-lehy*

supermarkets/**supermarché**/m/*sew-pehr-mahr-shay*

sweat shirt/**sweat**/m/*sweet*

sweater/**pull**/m/*pewl*

swimming/**natation**/f/*nah-tah-see-ohN*

T

take/**prendre**/*prahndr*

tea/**thé**/m/*tay*

teaspoon/**cuillère**/f/*kwee-yehr*

telephone or call/**téléphoner**/*tay-lay-foh-nay*

ten/**dix**/*dees*

tennis/**tennis**/m/*tehn-ee*

thank you/**merci**/*mehr-see*

that one/**celui-là** [m]/**celle-là** [f]/*suh-lwee-lah/sehl-lah*

the cash-register/**caisse**/f/*kehs*

then/**puis**/*pew-ee*

there is/**il y a**/*ee-lee-yah*

they/**elles**/f/*ehl*

they/**ils**/m/*eel*

think/**penser**/*pahN-say*

thirsty/**soif**/*swaf*

thirteen/**treize**/*trehz*

this one/**celui-ci** [m]/**celle-ci** [f]/*suh-lwee-see/sehl-see*

three/**trois**/*twah*

ticket/**billet**/m/*bee-yeh*

tie/**cravate**/f/*krah-vaht*

tip/**pourboire**/m/*poor-bwar*

tired/**fatigué**/*fah-tee-gay*

today/**aujourd'hui**/*o-zhoor-dwee*

tomato/**tomate**/f/*to-maht*

too bad/**tant pis**/*tahN pee*

too much/**trop**/*tro*

town/**villle**/f/*veel*

train/**train**/m/*trahn*

train station/**gare**/f/*gah*

travel/**voyager**/*vwah-yazhay*

trunk/**coffre**/m/*kohfr*

twelve/**douze**/*dooz*

twenty/**vingt**/*vahN*

twenty-eight/**vingt-huit**/*vahN wheet*

twenty-five/**vingt-cinq**/*vahN sayNk*

twenty-four/**vingt-quatre**/*vahN kahtruh*

twenty-nine/**vingt-neuf**/*vihN nuhf*

twenty-one/**vingt-et-un**/*vahNt-ay-uhN*

twenty-seven/**vingt-sept**/*vahN seht*
twenty-six/**vingt-six**/*vahN sees*
twenty-three/**vingt-trois**/*vaNh-twah*
twenty-two/**vingt-deux**/*vahNduh*
two/**deux**/*duh*

U

underpants/**slip**/m/*sleep*
until/**jusqu'à**/*zhews-kah*

V

veal/**veau**/m/*vo*
vegetables/**légumes**/m/*lay-gewm*
vendor/**marchand**/m/*mahr-shan*
violin/**violon**/m/*vee-oh-lohn*

W

wait/**attendre**/*ah-tehn-druh*
waiter/waitress/**serveur, serveuse**/m,f/*sehr-vuhr*
wallet/**porte-monnaie**/m/*pohrt-moh-neh*
want/**vouloir**/*voo-lwahr*
warm/hot/**chaud**/*sho*
watch/**regarder**/*reh-gahr-day*
watch/**montre**/f/*mohntr*
water/**eau**/f/*lo*
we/**nous**/*noo*
wear/**porter**/*pohr-tay*
week/**semaine**/f/*suh-mehn*
weird, bizarre/**bizarre**/*beez-ahr*
what/**qu'est-ce que**/*kehs-kuh*
when/**quand**/*kahN*
where/**où**/*oo*

which/**quelle**/*kehl*
white/**blanc**/*blahn*
who/**qui**/*kee*
why/**pourquoi**/*poor-kwa*
wide/**large**/*larzh*
wife/**femme**/f/*fahm*
win/**gagner**/*gahn-yay*
window/**fenêtre**/f/*fuh-nehtr*
wine/**vin**/m/*van*
wool/**laine**/f/*lehn*
work/**travailler**/*trah-va-yay*

Y

yard/**jardin**/m/*zhahr-daN*
yellow/**jaune**/*zhon*
you/**toi**/*twa*
you, formal/**vous**/*voo*
you, informal/**tu**/*tew*

Z

zip code/**code postal**/m/*cohd pohs-tahl*

Appendix C

About the CD

• •

*F*ollowing is a list of the tracks that appear on this book's audio CD, which you can find inside the back cover. Note that this is an audio-only CD, so just pop it into your stereo (or whatever you use to listen to regular music CDs).

Track 1: Introduction and Pronunciation Guide: How to pronounce all of the sounds in the French alphabet

Track 2: Chapter 3: Greetings and Introductions: Saying "hello" and "how are you"

Track 3: Chapter 3: Greetings and Introductions: Introducing yourself

Track 4: Chapter 3: Greetings and Introductions: More introductions and pleasantries

Track 5: Chapter 4: Making Small Talk: A little small talk while on a plane.

Track 6: Chapter 4: Making Small Talk: Talking about one's family

Track 7: Chapter 4: Making Small Talk: Chatting about the weather

Track 8: Chapter 5: Dining Out: Deciding what to drink

Track 9: Chapter 5: Dining Out: A waiter taking food orders

Track 10: Chapter 5: Dining Out: Deciding on dessert

Track 11: Chapter 6: Shopping Made Easy: Getting help from a salesperson

Track 12: Chapter 6: Shopping Made Easy: Do the clothes fit?

Track 13: Chapter 6: Shopping Made Easy: Shopping for a sports coat

Track 14: Chapter 6: Shopping Made Easy: Making the sale

Track 15: Chapter 7: Going Out on the Town: Rushing to make it to a concert

Index

Notes

Notes

Notes

Notes

Berlitz ®   *The world's most trusted name in foreign language learning.*

Get one

Free

lesson

Redeemable at any
Berlitz Language Center in
The United States and Canada

Take a language lesson on us!

Millions of people have learned to speak a new language with Berlitz. Why not you?

No matter where you're going or where you're from, odds are Berlitz is already there. We are the global leader in language services with over 70 locations in the United States and Canada. And right now, you can get a free trial language lesson at any one of them and in any language! Experience the unique Berlitz Method® and start speaking a new language confidently from your very first class. Berlitz has over 120 years of proven success, so no matter what your language needs, you can be sure you're getting the best value for your money.

To schedule your free lesson, call Berlitz toll free at 1-800-457-7958 (outside the U.S. call 609-514-9650) for the Language Center nearest you. Or check your telephone book or visit our Web site at www.berlitz.com.

To confirm availability of a teacher for the language of your choice, you must call 24 hours in advance. No purchase is necessary.

✱ cut out and bring coupon to your nearest Berlitz Language Center in the U.S. and Canada

Learn French the Berlitz® Way!

There's no better way to understand more about other cultures and people than by trying to speak their language. Whether you want to speak a few essential phrases during your next business trip or vacation or you want to achieve real fluency, Berlitz can help you reach your goals. Here are some time-honored Berlitz tips to help get you on your way:

- Immerse yourself in the language. Read French on the Internet, in newspapers, and in fashion magazines — you'll be surprised at how much you can understand already. Watch French news programs on cable TV, rent French language films, or consider hosting a French-speaking exchange student for the summer. And check out your nearest Berlitz language center for information about special courses and cultural nights.
- Take home a self-study language course and set aside time to work with the material a couple of times a week. Berlitz courses are available in book, cassette, audio CD, and CD-ROM formats.
- Set your own pace, but try to put aside a regular block of time at least twice a week to work with your new language. It's more important to set a steady pace than an intensive one. Several 30-minute sessions during the week are better than one longer session a couple of times per month.
- Speak out loud. Don't just read to yourself or listen to a self-study program. Learning a language is as much a physical workout as it is an intellectual one. You have to train your vocal chords to do things they aren't used to doing. Remember: You only learn to speak by speaking!
- Talk to French people! And don't be afraid to make mistakes. You'll notice that most people appreciate an attempt to speak their language.
- Try speaking English with a French accent. Then, when you start speaking French, your brain will already be in the mood.
- Keep an open mind. Don't expect your new language to work the same as your own, and don't look for a neat set of rules. Accept the differences.
- Enjoy yourself! Learning a foreign language can help you see the world and yourself from an entirely different perspective.

About Berlitz®

The name "Berlitz" has meant excellence in language services for over 120 years. Today, at over 400 locations and in 50 countries worldwide, Berlitz offers a full range of language and language-related services, including instruction, cross-cultural training, document translation, software localization, and interpretation services. Berlitz also offers a wide array of publishing products such as self-study language courses, phrase books, travel guides, and dictionaries.

Berlitz has programs to meet everyone's needs: The world-famous **Berlitz Method®** is the core of all Berlitz language instruction. From the time of its introduction in 1878, millions have used this method to learn a new language. Join any one of the classes available throughout the world, and immerse yourself in a new language and culture with the help of a Berlitz trained native instructor.

For those who may not have time for live instruction, **self-study language courses** may be the answer. In addition to several outstanding courses, Berlitz publishes **Bilingual Dictionaries**, **Workbooks**, and **Handbooks**.

Put the world in your pocket . . . with **Berlitz Pocket Guides** and **Phrase Books**, the renowned series that together are the ideal travel companions that will make the most of every trip. These portable full-color pocket guides are packed with information on history, language, must-see sights, shopping, and restaurant information; the Phrase Books help you communicate with ease and confidence.

Berlitz Kids™ has a complete range of fun products such as the **Kids Language Packs**, **1,000 Words**, and **Picture Dictionaries**. Parents and teachers will find **Help Your Child with a Foreign Language** especially informative and enlightening.

Berlitz Cross-Cultural™ programs are designed to bridge cultural gaps for international travelers and business transferees and their families. From vital information about daily life to social and business do's and don'ts, these programs can prepare you for life in any part of the world.

For more information, please consult your local telephone directory for the Language Center nearest you. Or visit the Berlitz Web site at www.berlitz.com, where you can enroll or shop directly online.

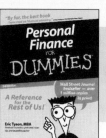

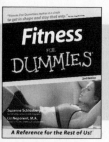
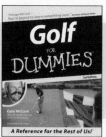
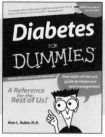

FOR DUMMIES®

A world of resources to help you grow

HOME, GARDEN & HOBBIES

0-7645-5295-3

0-7645-5130-2

0-7645-5106-X

FOOD & WINE

0-7645-5250-3

0-7645-5390-9

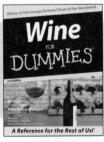

0-7645-5114-0

TRAVEL

0-7645-5453-0

0-7645-5438-7

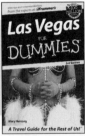

0-7645-5448-4

FOR DUMMIES®

Plain-English solutions for everyday challenges

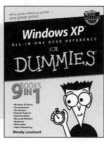
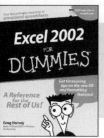

FOR DUMMIES®

Helping you expand your horizons and realize your potential

INTERNET

The Internet FOR DUMMIES
John R. Levine
Carol Baroudi
Margaret Levine Young

0-7645-0894-6

The Internet ALL-IN-ONE DESK REFERENCE FOR DUMMIES

0-7645-1659-0

eBay FOR DUMMIES
Marsha Collier
Roland Woerner
Stephanie Becker

0-7645-1642-6

DIGITAL MEDIA

Digital Photography FOR DUMMIES
Julie Adair King

0-7645-1664-7

Photoshop Elements 2 FOR DUMMIES
Deke McClelland
Galen Fott

0-7645-1675-2

Digital Video FOR DUMMIES
Martin Doucette

0-7645-0806-7

GRAPHICS

PowerPoint 2002 FOR DUMMIES
Doug Lowe

0-7645-0817-2

Photoshop 7 FOR DUMMIES
Deke McClelland
Barbara Obermeier

0-7645-1651-5

Macromedia Flash MX FOR DUMMIES
Gurdy Leete
Ellen Finkelstein

0-7645-0895-4

Available wherever books are sold. Go to www.dummies.com or call 1-877-762-2974 to order direct.

FOR DUMMIES®

The advice and explanations you need to succeed

SELF-HELP, SPIRITUALITY & RELIGION

0-7645-5302-X

0-7645-5418-2

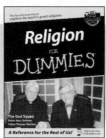

0-7645-5264-3

Also available:

The Bible For Dummies
(0-7645-5296-1)

Buddhism For Dummies
(0-7645-5359-3)

Christian Prayer For Dummies
(0-7645-5500-6)

Dating For Dummies
(0-7645-5072-1)

Judaism For Dummies
(0-7645-5299-6)

Potty Training For Dummies
(0-7645-5417-4)

Pregnancy For Dummies
(0-7645-5074-8)

Rekindling Romance For Dummies
(0-7645-5303-8)

Spirituality For Dummies
(0-7645-5298-8)

Weddings For Dummies
(0-7645-5055-1)

PETS

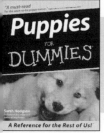

0-7645-5255-4

0-7645-5286-4

0-7645-5275-9

Also available:

Labrador Retrievers For Dummies
(0-7645-5281-3)

Aquariums For Dummies
(0-7645-5156-6)

Birds For Dummies
(0-7645-5139-6)

Dogs For Dummies
(0-7645-5274-0)

Ferrets For Dummies
(0-7645-5259-7)

German Shepherds For Dummies
(0-7645-5280-5)

Golden Retrievers For Dummies
(0-7645-5267-8)

Horses For Dummies
(0-7645-5138-8)

Jack Russell Terriers For Dummies
(0-7645-5268-6)

Puppies Raising & Training Diary For Dummies
(0-7645-0876-8)

EDUCATION & TEST PREPARATION

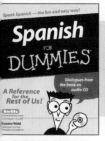

0-7645-5194-9

0-7645-5325-9

0-7645-5210-4

Also available:

Chemistry For Dummies
(0-7645-5430-1)

English Grammar For Dummies
(0-7645-5322-4)

French For Dummies
(0-7645-5193-0)

The GMAT For Dummies
(0-7645-5251-1)

Inglés Para Dummies
(0-7645-5427-1)

Italian For Dummies
(0-7645-5196-5)

Research Papers For Dummies
(0-7645-5426-3)

The SAT I For Dummies
(0-7645-5472-7)

U.S. History For Dummies
(0-7645-5249-X)

World History For Dummies
(0-7645-5242-2)

Available wherever books are sold. Go to www.dummies.com or call 1-877-762-2974 to order direct.

FOR DUMMIES®

We take the mystery out of complicated subjects

WEB DEVELOPMENT

0-7645-1643-4

0-7645-0723-0

0-7645-1630-2

Also available:

ASP.NET For Dummies
(0-7645-0866-0)

Building a Web Site For
Dummies
(0-7645-0720-6)

ColdFusion "MX" for Dummies
(0-7645-1672-8)

Creating Web Pages
All-in-One Desk Reference
For Dummies
(0-7645-1542-X)

FrontPage 2002 For Dumr
(0-7645-0821-0)

HTML 4 For Dummies Qui
Reference
(0-7645-0721-4)

Macromedia Studio "MX"
All-in-One Desk Reference
For Dummies
(0-7645-1799-6)

Web Design For Dummies
(0-7645-0823-7)

PROGRAMMING & DATABASES

0-7645-0746-X

0-7645-1657-4

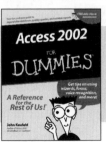

0-7645-0818-0

Also available:

Beginning Programming For
Dummies
(0-7645-0835-0)

Crystal Reports "X"
For Dummies
(0-7645-1641-8)

Java & XML For Dummies
(0-7645-1658-2)

Java 2 For Dummies
(0-7645-0765-6)

JavaScript For Dummies
(0-7645-0633-1)

Oracle9i For Dummies
(0-7645-0880-6)

Perl For Dummies
(0-7645-0776-1)

PHP and MySQL For
Dummies
(0-7645-1650-7)

SQL For Dummies
(0-7645-0737-0)

VisualBasic .NET For
Dummies
(0-7645-0867-9)

Visual Studio .NET All-in-C
Desk Reference For Dumr
(0-7645-1626-4)

LINUX, NETWORKING & CERTIFICATION

0-7645-1545-4

0-7645-0772-9

0-7645-0812-1

Also available:

CCNP All-in-One Certification
For Dummies
(0-7645-1648-5)

Cisco Networking For
Dummies
(0-7645-1668-X)

CISSP For Dummies
(0-7645-1670-1)

CIW Foundations For
Dummies with CD-ROM
(0-7645-1635-3)

Firewalls For Dummies
(0-7645-0884-9)

Home Networking For
Dummies
(0-7645-0857-1)

Red Hat Linux All-in-One
Desk Reference For Dumr
(0-7645-2442-9)

TCP/IP For Dummies
(0-7645-1760-0)

UNIX For Dummies
(0-7645-0419-3)